SQL for Data Analytics

Perform fast and efficient data analysis with the power of SQL

Upom Malik

Matt Goldwasser

Benjamin Johnston

SQL for Data Analytics

Authors: Upom Malik, Matt Goldwasser, and Benjamin Johnston

Technical Reviewer: Halil Burak Cetinkaya

Managing Editor: Aditya Shah

Acquisitions Editor: Aditya Date

Production Editor: Shantanu Zagade

Editorial Board: Shubhopriya Banerjee, Mayank Bhardwaj, Ewan Buckingham, Mahesh Dhyani, Taabish Khan, Manasa Kumar, Alex Mazonowicz, Pramod Menon, Bridget Neale, Dominic Pereira, Shiny Poojary, Erol Staveley, Ankita Thakur, Nitesh Thakur, and Jonathan Wray

First Published: August 2019

Production Reference: 2160221

ISBN: 978-1-78980-735-6

Published by Packt Publishing Ltd.

Livery Place, 35 Livery Street

Birmingham B3 2PB, UK

Table of Contents

Chapter 6: Importing and Exporting Data   143

Chapter 9: Using SQL to Uncover the Truth – a Case Study 275

Appendix 313

Index 361

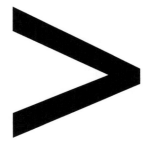

Preface

About

This section briefly introduces the authors, the coverage of this book, the technical skills you'll need to get started, and the hardware and software requirements required to complete all of the included activities and exercises.

About the Book

Understanding and finding patterns in data has become one of the most important ways to improve business decisions. If you know the basics of SQL, but don't know how to use it to gain business insights from data, this book is for you.

SQL for Data Analytics covers everything you need to progress from simply knowing basic SQL to telling stories and identifying trends in data. You'll be able to start exploring your data by identifying patterns and unlocking deeper insights. You'll also gain experience working with different types of data in SQL, including time series, geospatial, and text data. Finally, you'll learn how to become productive with SQL with the help of profiling and automation to gain insights faster.

By the end of the book, you'll able to use SQL in everyday business scenarios efficiently and look at data with the critical eye of an analytics professional.

About the Authors

Upom Malik is a data scientist who has worked in the technology industry for over 6 years. He has a master's degree in chemical engineering from Cornell University and a bachelor's degree in biochemistry from Duke University. He uses SQL and other tools to solve interesting challenges in finance, energy, and consumer technologies. While working on analytical problems, he has lived out of a suitcase and spent the last year as a digital nomad. Outside of work, he likes to read, hike the trails of the Northeastern United States, and savor ramen bowls from around the world.

Matt Goldwasser is a lead data scientist at T. Rowe Price. He enjoys demystifying data science for business stakeholders and deploying production machine learning solutions. Matt has been using SQL to perform data analytics in the financial industry for the last 8 years. He has a bachelor's degree in mechanical and aerospace engineering from Cornell University. In his spare time, he enjoys teaching his infant son data science.

Benjamin Johnston is a senior data scientist for one of the world's leading data-driven medtech companies and is involved in the development of innovative digital solutions throughout the entire product development pathway, from problem definition to solution research and development, through to final deployment. He is currently completing his PhD in machine learning, specializing in image processing and deep convolutional neural networks. He has more than 10 years' experience in medical device design and development, working in a variety of technical roles, and holds first-class honors bachelor's degrees in both engineering and medical science from the University of Sydney, Australia.

Learning Objectives

By the end of this book, you will be able to:

- Use SQL to summarize and identify patterns in data
- Apply special SQL clauses and functions to generate descriptive statistics
- Use SQL queries and subqueries to prepare data for analysis
- Perform advanced statistical calculations using the window function
- Analyze special data types in SQL, including geospatial data and time data
- Import and export data using a text file and PostgreSQL
- Debug queries that won't run
- Optimize queries to improve their performance for faster results

Audience

If you're a database engineer looking to transition into analytics, or a backend engineer who wants to develop a deeper understanding of production data, you will find this book useful. This book is also ideal for data scientists or business analysts who want to improve their data analytics skills using SQL. Knowledge of basic SQL and database concepts will aid in understanding the concepts covered in this book.

Approach

SQL for Data Analysis perfectly balances theory and practical exercises and provides a hands-on approach to analyzing data. It focuses on providing practical instruction for both SQL and statistical analysis so that you can better understand your data. The book takes away the crumbs and focuses on being practical. It contains multiple activities that use real-life business scenarios for you to practice and apply your new skills in a highly relevant context.

Hardware Requirements

For the optimal experience, we recommend the following hardware configuration:

- Processor: Intel Core i5 or equivalent
- Memory: 4 GB of RAM
- Storage: 5 GB of available space

Software Requirements

We also recommend that you have the following software installed in advance:

- OS: Windows 7 SP1 64-bit, Windows 8.1 64-bit, Windows 10 64-bit, Linux (Ubuntu 16.04 or later, Debian, Red Hat, or Suse), or the latest version of macOS

- PostgreSQL 10.9 (https://www.postgresql.org/download/)

- Anaconda Python 3.7 (https://www.anaconda.com/distribution/#download-section)

- Git 2 or later

Conventions

Code words in text, database table names, folder names, filenames, file extensions, pathnames, dummy URLs, user input, and Twitter handles are shown as follows:

"It is worth noting here that the formatting can look a little messy for the **\copy** command, because it does not allow for commands with new lines. A simple way around this is to create a view containing your data before the **\copy** command and then drop the view after your **\copy** command has finished."

A block of code is set as follows:

```
CREATE TEMP VIEW customers_sample AS (
    SELECT *
    FROM customers
    LIMIT 5
);
\copy customers_sample TO 'my_file.csv' WITH CSV HEADER
DROP VIEW customers_sample;
```

Installation and Setup

Each great journey begins with a humble step, and our upcoming adventure in the land of data wrangling is no exception. Before we can do awesome things with data, we need to be prepared with the most productive environment. In this short section, we shall see how to do that.

Installing PostgreSQL 10.9

Installing on Windows:

Download the PostgreSQL version 10 installer via https://www.postgresql.org/download/windows/ and follow the prompts.

Installing on Linux:

You can install PostgreSQL on Ubuntu or Debian Linux via the command line using:

```
sudo apt-get install postgresl-11
```

Installing on macOS:

Download the PostgreSQL version 10 installer via https://www.postgresql.org/download/macosx/ and follow the prompts.

Installing Python

Installing Python on Windows:

1. Find your desired version of Python on the official installation page at https://www.anaconda.com/distribution/#windows.

2. Ensure you select Python 3.7 from the download page.

3. Ensure that you install the correct architecture for your computer system; that is, either 32-bit or 64-bit. You can find out this information in the **System Properties** window of your OS.

4. After you download the installer, simply double-click on the file and follow the user-friendly prompts on-screen.

Installing Python on Linux:

To install Python on Linux, you have a couple of good options:

1. Open Command Prompt and verify that p\Python 3 is not already installed by running python3 --version.

2. To install Python 3, run this:

```
sudo apt-get update
sudo apt-get install python3.7
```

3. If you encounter problems, there are numerous sources online that can help you troubleshoot the issue.

4. Install Anaconda Linux by downloading the installer from https://www.anaconda.com/distribution/#linux and following the instructions.

Installing Python on macOS:

Similar to Linux, you have a couple of methods for installing Python on a Mac. To install Python on macOS X, do the following:

1. Open the Terminal for Mac by pressing CMD + *Spacebar*, type `terminal` in the open search box, and hit *Enter*.

2. Install Xcode through the command line by running `xcode-select --install`.

3. The easiest way to install Python 3 is using Homebrew, which is installed through the command line by running `ruby -e "$(curl -fsSL https://raw.githubusercontent.com/Homebrew/install/master/install)"`.

4. Add Homebrew to your `$PATH` environment variable. Open your profile in the command line by running `sudo nano ~/.profile` and inserting `export PATH="/usr/local/opt/python/libexec/bin:$PATH"` at the bottom.

5. The final step is to install Python. In the command line, run `brew install python`.

6. Again, you can also install Python via the Anaconda installer available from https://www.anaconda.com/distribution/#macos.

Installing Git

Installing Git on Windows or macOS X:

Git for Windows/Mac can be downloaded and installed via https://git-scm.com/. However, for an improved user experience, it is recommended that you install Git through an advanced client such as GitKraken (https://www.gitkraken.com/).

Installing Git on Linux:

Git can be easily installed via the command line:

```
sudo apt-get install git
```

If you prefer a graphical user interface, GitKraken (https://www.gitkraken.com/) is also available for Linux.

Loading the Sample Databases

The vast majority of exercises in this book use a sample database, `sqlda`, which contains fabricated data for a fictional electric vehicle company called ZoomZoom. To load the sample datasets, please follow the instructions at: https://github.com/TrainingByPackt/SQL-for-Data-Analytics/blob/master/Datasets/Loading_the_sample_datasets_instructions.pdf.

Running SQL Files

Commands and statements can be executed via a ***.sql** file from the command line using the command:

```
psql < commands.sql
```

Alternatively, they can be executed via the SQL interpreter:

```
database=#
```

Additional Resources

The code bundle for this book is also hosted on GitHub at https://github.com/TrainingByPackt/SQL-for-Data-Analytics. We also have other code bundles from our rich catalog of books and videos available at https://github.com/PacktPublishing/. Check them out!

You can download the graphic bundle for the book from here: https://github.com/TrainingByPackt/SQL-for-Data-Analytics/blob/master/Graphic%20Bundle/Graphic%20Bundle_ColorImages.pdf.

1

Understanding and Describing Data

Learning Objectives

By the end of this chapter, you will be able to:

- Explain data and its types
- Classify data based on its characteristics
- Calculate basic univariate statistics about data
- Identify outliers
- Use bivariate analysis to understand the relationship between two variables

In this chapter, we will cover the basics of data analytics and statistics. You will also learn how to identify outliers and gain an understanding of the relationship between variables.

Introduction

Data has fundamentally transformed the 21st century. Thanks to easy access to computers, companies and organizations have been able to change the way they work with larger and more complex datasets. Using data, insights that would have been virtually impossible to find 50 years ago can now be found with just a few lines of computer code. In this chapter, we will discuss what data is and how data analysis can be used to unlock insights and recognize patterns.

The World of Data

Let's start with the first question: what is data? **Data** (the plural of the word datum) can be thought of as recorded measurements of something in the real world. For example, a list of heights is data – that is, height is a measure of the distance between a person's head and their feet. We usually call that something the data is describing a **unit of observation**. In the case of these heights, a person is the unit of observation.

As you can imagine, there is a lot of data that we can gather to describe a person – including their age, weight, whether they are a smoker, and more. One or more of these measurements used to describe one specific unit of observation is called a **data point**, and each measurement in a data point is called a **variable** (this is also often referred to as a **feature**). When you have several data points together, you have a **dataset**.

Types of Data

Data can also be broken down into two main categories: **quantitative** and **qualitative**:

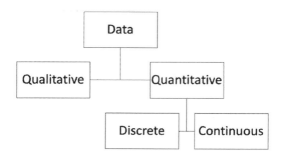

Figure 1.1: The classification of types of data

Quantitative data is a measurement that can be described as a number; qualitative data is data that is described by non-numerical values, such as text. Your height is data that would be described as quantitative. However, describing yourself as either a "smoker" or a "non-smoker" would be considered qualitative data.

Quantitative data can be further classified into two subcategories: **discrete** and **continuous**. Discrete quantitative values are values that can take on a fixed level of precision – usually integers. For example, the number of surgeries you have had in your life is a discrete value – you can have 0, 1, or more surgeries, but you cannot have 1.5 surgeries. A continuous variable is a value that, in theory, could be divided with an arbitrary amount of precision. For example, your body mass could be described with arbitrary precision to be 55, 55.3, 55.32, and so on. In practice, of course, measuring instruments limit our precision. However, if a value could be described with higher precision, then it is generally considered continuous.

> **Note**
>
> Qualitative data can generally be converted into quantitative data, and quantitative data can also be converted into qualitative data. This is explained later in the chapter using an example.

Let's think about this using the example of being a "smoker" versus a "non-smoker". While you can describe yourself to be in the category of "smoker" or "non-smoker", you could also reimagine these categories as answers to the statement "you smoke regularly", and then use the Boolean values of 0 and 1 to represent "true" and "false," respectively.

Similarly, in the opposite direction, quantitative data, such as height, can be converted into qualitative data. For example, instead of thinking of an adult's height as a number in inches or centimeters (cm), you can classify them into groups, with people greater than 72 inches (that is, 183 cm) in the category "tall," people between 63 inches and 72 inches (that is, between 160 and 183 cm) as "medium," and people shorter than 63 inches (that is, 152 cm) as "short."

Data Analytics and Statistics

Raw data, by itself, is simply a group of values. However, it is not very interesting in this form. It is only when we start to find patterns in the data and begin to interpret them that we can start to do interesting things such as make predictions about the future and identify unexpected changes. These patterns in the data are referred to as **information**. Eventually, a large organized collection of persistent and extensive information and experience that can be used to describe and predict phenomena in the real world is called **knowledge**. **Data analysis** is the process by which we convert data into information and, thereafter, knowledge. When data analysis is combined with making predictions, we then have **data analytics**.

There are a lot of tools that are available to make sense of data. One of the most powerful tools in the toolbox of data analysis is using mathematics on datasets. One of these mathematical tools is **statistics**.

Types of Statistics

Statistics can be further divided into two subcategories: **descriptive statistics** and **inferential statistics**.

Descriptive statistics are used to describe data. Descriptive statistics on a single variable in a dataset are referred to as **univariate** analysis, while descriptive statistics that look at two or more variables at the same time are referred to as **multivariate** analysis.

In contrast, inferential statistics think of datasets as a **sample**, or a small portion of measurements from a larger group called a **population**. For example, a survey of 10,000 voters in a national election is a sample of the entire population of voters in a country. Inferential statistics are used to try to infer the properties of a population, based on the properties of a sample.

> Note
>
> In this book, we will primarily be focusing on descriptive statistics. For more information on inferential statistics, please refer to a statistics textbook, such as Statistics, by David Freedman, Robert Pisani, and Roger Purves.

Example:

Imagine that you are a health policy analyst and are given the following dataset with information about patients:

Year of Birth	Country of Birth	Height (cm)	Eye Color	Number of Doctor Visits in the Year 2018
1977	Egypt	182	Blue	1
1988	China	196	Hazel	2
1986	USA	180	Brown	2
1990	USA	166	Brown	1
1975	India	181	Green	3
1951	Germany	184	Brown	1
2000	Australia	174	Gray	5
1995	India	183	Brown	1
1992	China	187	Brown	2
1987	USA	169	Blue	2

Figure 1.2: Healthcare data

When given a dataset, it's often helpful to classify the underlying data. In this case, the unit of observation for the dataset is an individual patient, because each row represents an individual observation, which is a unique patient. There are 10 data points, each with 5 variables. Three of the columns, **Year of Birth**, **Height**, and **Number of Doctor Visits**, are quantitative because they are represented by numbers. Two of the columns, **Eye Color** and **Country of Birth**, are qualitative.

Activity 1: Classifying a New Dataset

In this activity, we will classify the data in a dataset. You are about to start a job in a new city at an up-and-coming start-up. You're excited to start your new job, but you've decided to sell all your belongings before you head off. This includes your car. You're not sure at what price to sell it for, so you decide to collect some data. You ask some friends and family who recently sold their cars what the make of the car was, and how much they sold the cars for. Based on this information, you now have a dataset.

The data is as follows:

Date	Make	Sales Amount (Thousands of $)
2/1/18	Ford	12
2/2/18	Honda	15
2/2/18	Mazda	19
2/3/18	Ford	20
2/4/18	Toyota	10
2/4/18	Toyota	10
2/4/18	Mercedes	30
2/5/18	Ford	11
2/6/18	Chevy	12.5
2/6/18	Chevy	19

Figure 1.3: Used car sales data

Steps to follow:

1. Determine the unit of observation.
2. Classify the three columns as either quantitative or qualitative.
3. Convert the **Make** column into quantitative data columns.

> **Note**
>
> The solution for this activity can be found on page 314.

Methods of Descriptive Statistics

As previously mentioned, descriptive statistics is one of the ways in which we can analyze data in order to understand it. Both univariate and multivariate analysis can give us an insight into what might be going on with a phenomenon. In this section, we will take a closer look at the basic mathematical techniques that we can use to better understand and describe a dataset.

Univariate Analysis

As previously mentioned, one of the main branches of statistics is univariate analysis. These methods are used to understand a single variable in a dataset. In this section, we will look at some of the most common univariate analysis techniques.

Data Frequency Distribution

The distribution of data is simply a count of the number of values that are in a dataset. For example, let's say that we have a dataset of 1,000 medical records, and one of the variables in the dataset is eye color. If we look at the dataset and find that 700 people have brown eyes, 200 people have green eyes, and 100 people have blue eyes, then we have just described the distribution of the dataset. Specifically, we have described the **absolute frequency distribution**. If we were to describe the counts not by the actual number of occurrences in the dataset, but as the proportion of the total number of data points, then we are describing its **relative frequency distribution**. In the preceding eye color example, the relative frequency distribution would be 70% brown eyes, 20% green eyes, and 10% blue eyes.

It's easy to calculate a distribution when the variable can take on a small number of fixed values such as eye color. But what about a quantitative variable that can take on many different values, such as height? The general way to calculate distributions for these types of variables is to make interval "buckets" that these values can be assigned to and then calculate distributions using these buckets. For example, height can be broken down into 5-cm interval buckets to make the following absolute distribution (please refer to *Figure 1.6*). We can then divide each row in the table by the total number of data points (that is, 10,000) and get the relative distribution.

Another useful thing to do with distributions is to graph them. We will now create a **histogram**, which is a graphical representation of the continuous distribution using interval buckets.

Exercise 1: Creating a Histogram

In this exercise, we will use Microsoft Excel to create a histogram. Imagine, as a healthcare policy analyst, that you want to see the distribution of heights to note any patterns. To accomplish this task, we need to create a histogram.

> **Note**
>
> We can use spreadsheet software such as Excel, Python, or R to create histograms. For convenience, we will use Excel. Also, all the datasets used in this chapter, can be found on GitHub: https://github.com/TrainingByPackt/SQL-for-Data-Analytics/tree/master/Datasets.

Perform the following steps:

1. Open Microsoft Excel to a blank workbook:

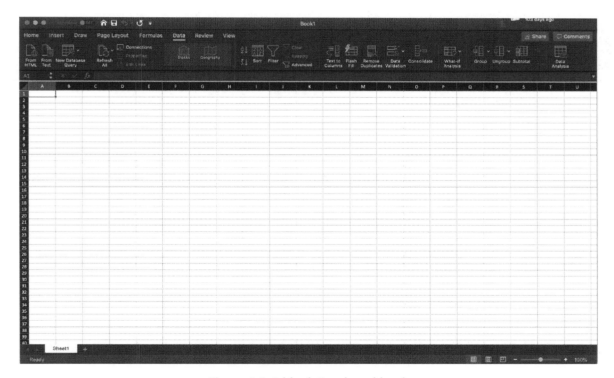

Figure 1.4: A blank Excel workbook

2. Go to the **Data** tab and click on **From Text**.

3. You can find the **heights.csv** dataset file in the **Datasets** folder of the GitHub repository. After navigating to it, click on **OK**.

4. Choose the **Delimited** option in the **Text Import Wizard** dialog box, and make sure that you start the import at row **1**. Now, click on **Next**:

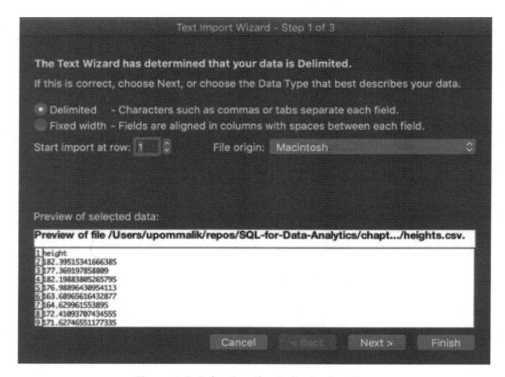

Figure 1.5: Selecting the Delimited option

5. Select the delimiter for your file. As this file is only one column, it has no delimiters, although CSVs traditionally use commas as delimiters (in future, use whatever is appropriate for your dataset). Now, click on **Next**.

6. Select **General** for the **Column Data Format**. Now, click on **Finish**.

7. For the dialog box asking **Where you want to put the data?**, select **Existing Sheet**, and leave what is in the textbox next to it as is. Now, click on **OK**.

8. In column **C**, write the numbers **140**, **145**, and **150** in increments of 5 all the way to **220** in cells **C2** to **C18**, as seen in *Figure 1.6*:

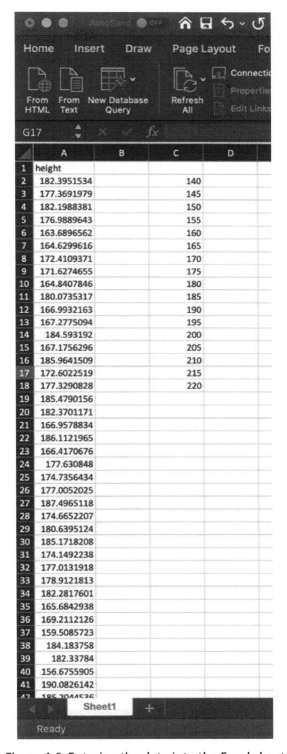

Figure 1.6: Entering the data into the Excel sheet

9. Under the **Data** tab, click on **Data Analysis** (if you don't see the **Data Analysis** tab, follow these instructions to install it: https://support.office.com/en-us/article/load-the-analysis-toolpak-in-excel-6a63e598-cd6d-42e3-9317-6b40ba1a66b4).

10. From the selection box that pops up, select **Histogram**. Now, click on **OK**.

11. For **Input Range**, click on the selection button in the far-right side of the textbox. You should be returned to the **Sheet1** worksheet, along with a blank box with a button that has a red arrow in it. Drag and highlight all the data in **Sheet1** from **A2** to **A10001**. Now, click on the arrow with the red button.

12. For **Bin Range**, click on the selection button in the far-right side of the textbox. You should be returned to the **Sheet1** worksheet, along with a blank box with a button that has a red arrow in it. Drag and highlight all the data in **Sheet1** from **C2** to **C18**. Now, click on the arrow with the red button.

13. Under **Output Options**, select **New Worksheet Ply**, and make sure **Chart Output** is marked, as seen in *Figure* 1.7. Now, click on **OK**:

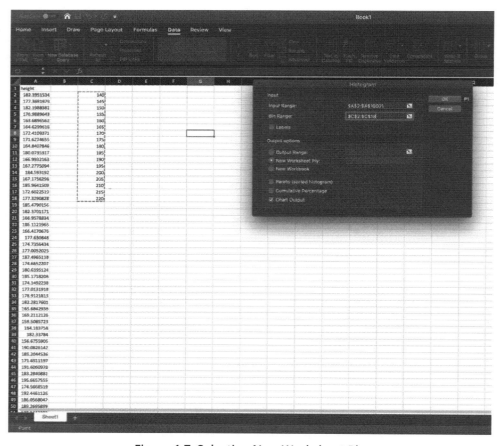

Figure 1.7: Selecting New Worksheet Ply

14. Click on **Sheet2**. Find the graph and double-click on the title where it says **Histogram**. Type the word **Heights**. You should produce a graph that is similar to the one in the following diagram:

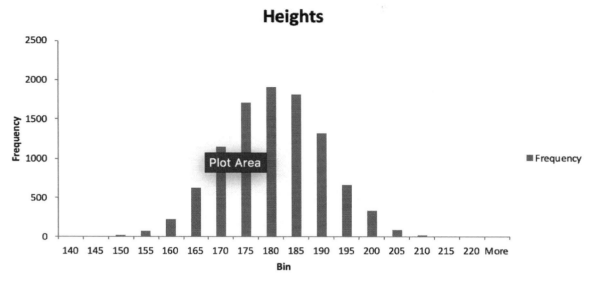

Figure 1.8: Height distribution for adult males

Looking at the shape of the distribution can help you to find interesting patterns. Notice here the symmetric bell-shaped curl of this distribution. This distribution is often found in many datasets and is known as the *normal distribution*. This book won't go into too much detail about this distribution but keep an eye out for it in your data analysis – it shows up quite often.

Quantiles

One way to quantify data distribution numerically is to use quantiles. N-quantiles are a set of n-1 points used to divide a variable into n groups. These points are often called **cut points**. For example, a 4-quantile (also referred to as quartiles) is a group of three points that divide a variable into four, approximately equal groups of numbers. There are several common names for quantiles that are used interchangeably, and these are as follows:

N	Common Name
3	Terciles
4	Quartiles
5	Quintiles
10	Deciles
20	Ventiles
100	Percentiles

Figure 1.9: Common names for n-quantiles

The procedure for calculating quantiles actually varies from place to place. We will use the following procedure to calculate the n-quantiles for d data points for a single variable:

1. Order the data points from lowest to highest.

2. Determine the number n of n-quantiles you want to calculate and the number of cut points, n-1.

3. Determine what number k cut point you want to calculate, that is, a number from 1 to n-1. If you are starting the calculation, set k equal to 1.

4. Find the index, i, for the k-th cut point using the following equation:

$$i = \left\lceil \frac{k}{n}(d - 1) \right\rceil + 1$$

Figure 1.10: The index

5. If i calculated in number **3** is a whole number, simply pick that numbered item from the ordered data points. If the k-*th* cut point is not a whole number, find the numbered item that is lower than i, and the one after it. Multiply the difference between the numbered item and the one after it, and then multiply by the decimal portion of the index. Add this number to the lowest numbered item.

6. Repeat *Steps 2 to 5* with different values of k until you have calculated all the cut points.

These steps are a little complicated to understand by themselves, so let's work through an exercise. With most modern tools, including SQL, computers can quickly calculate quantiles with built-in functionality.

Exercise 2: Calculating the Quartiles for Add-on Sales

Before you start your new job, your new boss wants you to look at some data before you start on Monday, so that you have a better sense of one of the problems you will be working on – that is, the increasing sales of add-ons and upgrades for car purchases. Your boss sends over a list of 11 car purchases and how much they have spent on add-ons and upgrades to the base model of the new ZoomZoom Model Chi. In this exercise, we will classify the data and calculate the quartiles for the car purchase using Excel. The following are the values of **Add-on Sales ($)**: 5,000, 1,700, 8,200, 1,500, 3,300, 9,000, 2,000, 0, 0, 2,300, and 4,700.

> **Note**
>
> All the datasets used in this chapter, can be found on GitHub: https://github.com/TrainingByPackt/SQL-for-Data-Analytics/tree/master/Datasets.

Perform the following steps to complete the exercise:

1. Open Microsoft Excel to a blank workbook.

2. Go to the **Data** tab and click on **From Text**.

3. You can find the `auto_upgrades.csv` dataset file in the `Datasets` folder of the GitHub repository. Navigate to the file and click on **OK**.

4. Choose the **Delimited** option in the **Text Import Wizard** dialog box, and make sure to start the import at row **1**. Now, click on **Next**.

5. Select the delimiter for your file. As this file is only one column, it has no delimiters, although CSVs traditionally use commas as delimiters (in future, use whatever is appropriate for your dataset). Now, click on **Next**.

6. Select **General** for the **Column Data Format**. Now, click on **Finish**.

7. For the dialog box asking **Where do you want to put the data?**, select **Existing Sheet**, and leave what is in the textbox next to it as is. Now, click on **OK**.

8. Click on cell **A1**. Then, click on the **Data** tab, and then click on **Sort** from the tab.

9. A sorted dialog box will pop up. Now, click on **OK**. The values will now be sorted from lowest to highest. The list in *Figure 1.11* shows the sorted values:

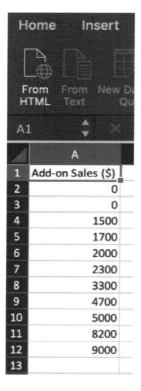

Figure 1.11: The Add-on Sales figures sorted

10. Now, determine the number of *n-quantiles* and cut points you need to calculate. Quartiles are equivalent to 4-tiles, as seen in *Figure* 1.9. Because the number of cut points is just 1 less than the number of *n-quantiles*, we know there will be 3 cut points.

11. Calculate the index for the first cut point. In this case, k=1; d, the number of data points, equals **10**; and n, the number of *n-quantiles*, equals 4. Plugging this into the equation from *Figure* 1.12, we get **3.5**:

12. Because index 3.5 is a non-integer, we first find the third and fourth items, which are 1,500 and 1,700, respectively. We find the difference between them, which is 200, and then multiply this by the decimal portion of 0.5, yielding 100. We add this to the third numbered item, 1,500, and get 1,600.

13. Repeat *Steps* 2 to 5 for k=2 and k=4 to calculate the second and third quartiles. You should get 2,300 and 4,850, respectively.

$$i = \left[\frac{k}{n}(d-1)\right] + 1$$
$$i = \left[\frac{1}{4}(11-1)\right] + 1$$
$$i = \frac{10}{4} + 1$$
$$i = \frac{10}{4} + 1$$
$$i = 2.5 + 1 = 3.5$$

Figure 1.12: Calculating the index for the first cut point

In this exercise, we learned how to classify the data and calculate the quartiles using Excel.

Central Tendency

One of the common questions asked of a variable in a dataset is what a typical value for that variable is. This value is often described as the **central tendency** of the variable. There are many numbers calculated from a dataset that are often used to describe its central tendency, each with their own advantages and disadvantages. Some of the ways to measure central tendency include the following:

- **Mode**: The mode is simply the value that comes up most often in the distribution of a variable. In *Figure* 1.2, the eye color example, the mode would be "brown eyes," because it occurs the most often in the dataset. If multiple values are tied for the most common variable, then the variable is called **multimodal** and all of the highest values are reported. If no value is repeated, then there is no mode for those sets of values. Mode tends to be useful when a variable can take on a small, fixed number of values. However, it is problematic to calculate when a variable is a continuous quantitative variable, such as in our height problem. With these variables, other calculations are more appropriate for determining the central tendency.

- **Average/Mean**: The average of a variable (also called the **mean**) is the value calculated when you take the sum of all values of the variable and divide by the number of data points. For example, let's say you had a small dataset of ages: 26, 25, 31, 35, and 29. The average of these ages would be 29.2, because that is the number you get when you sum the 5 numbers and then divide by 5, that is, the number of data points. The mean is easy to calculate, and generally does a good job of describing a "typical" value for a variable. No wonder it is one of the most commonly reported descriptive statistics in literature. The average as a central tendency, however, suffers from one major drawback – it is sensitive to **outliers**. Outliers are data that are significantly different in value from the rest of the data and occur very rarely. Outliers can often be identified by using graphical techniques (such as scatterplots and box plots) and identifying any data points that are very far from the rest of the data. When a dataset has an outlier, it is called a **skewed dataset**. Some common reasons why outliers occur include unclean data, extremely rare events, and problems with measurement instruments. Outliers often skew the average to a point when they are no longer representative of a typical value in the data.

- **Median**: The median (also called the second quartile and the fiftieth percentile) is sort of a strange measure of central tendency, but has some serious advantages compared with average. To calculate median, take the numbers for a variable and sort from the lowest to the highest, and then determine the middle number. For an odd number of data points, this number is simply the middle value of the ordered data. If there are an even number of data points, then take the average of the two middle numbers.

  While the median is a bit unwieldy to calculate, it is less affected by outliers, unlike mean. To illustrate this fact, we will calculate the median of the skewed age dataset of 26, 25, 31, 35, 29, and 82. This time, when we calculate the median of the dataset, we get the value of 30. This value is much closer to the typical value of the dataset than the average of 38. This robustness toward outliers is one of the major 'reasons why a median is calculated.

  As a general rule, it is a good idea to calculate both the mean and median of a variable. If there is a significant difference in the value of the mean and the median, then the dataset may have outliers.

Exercise 3: Calculating the Central Tendency of Add-on Sales

In this exercise, we will calculate the central tendency of the given data. To better understand the **Add-on Sales** data, you will need to gain an understanding of what the typical value for this variable is. We will calculate the mode, mean, and median of the **Add-on Sales** data. Here is the data for the 11 cars purchased: 5,000, 1,700, 8,200, 1,500, 3,300, 9,000, 2,000, 0, 0, 2,300, and 4,700.

Perform the following steps to implement the exercise:

1. To calculate the mode, find the most common value. Because 0 is the most common value in the dataset, the mode is 0.

2. To calculate the mean, sum the numbers in **Add-on Sales**, which should equal 37,700. Then, divide the sum by the number of values, 11, and you get the mean of 3,427.27.

3. Finally, calculate the median by sorting the data, as shown in *Figure 1.13*:

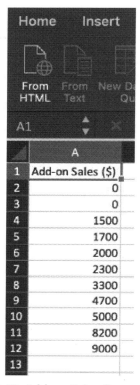

Figure 1.13: Add-on Sales figures sorted

Determine the middle value. Because there are 11 values, the middle value will be sixth in the list. We now take the sixth element in the ordered data and get a median of 2,300.

> **Note**
>
> When we compare the mean and the median, we see that there is a significant difference between the two. As previously mentioned, it is a sign that we have outliers in our dataset. We will discuss in future sections how to determine which values are outliers.

Dispersion

Another property that is of interest in a dataset is discovering how close together data points are in a variable. For example, the number sets [100, 100, 100] and [50, 100, 150] both have a mean of 100, but the numbers in the second group are spread out more than the first. This property of describing how the data is spread is called **dispersion**.

There are many ways to measure the dispersion of a variable. Here are some of the most common ways to evaluate dispersion:

- **Range**: The range is simply the difference between the highest and lowest values for a variable. It is incredibly easy to calculate but is very susceptible to outliers. It also does not provide much information about the spread of values in the middle of the dataset.

- **Standard Deviation/Variance**: Standard deviation is simply the square root of the average of the squared difference between each data point and the mean. The value of standard deviation ranges from 0 all the way to positive infinity. The closer the standard deviation is to 0, the less the numbers in the dataset vary. If the standard deviation is 0, this means that all the values for a dataset variable are the same.

    One subtle distinction to note is that there are two different formulas for standard deviation, which are shown in *Figure 1.14*. When the dataset represents the entire population, you should calculate the population standard deviation using formula A in *Figure 1.14*. If your sample represents a portion of the observations, then you should use formula B for the sample standard deviation, as displayed in *Figure 1.14*. When in doubt, use the sample variance, as it is considered more conservative. Also, in practice, the difference between the two formulas is very small when there are many data points.

    The standard deviation is generally the quantity used most often to describe dispersion. However, like range, it can also be affected by outliers, though not as extremely as the range is. It can also be fairly involved to calculate. Modern tools, however, usually make it very easy to calculate the standard deviation.

    One final note is that, occasionally, you may see a related value, variance, listed as well. This quantity is simply the square of the standard deviation:

$$A) \quad \sqrt{\frac{\sum_{i=1}^{n}(x_i - u_x)^2}{n}} \quad B) \sqrt{\frac{\sum_{i=1}^{n}(x_i - u_x)^2}{n-1}}$$

Figure 1.14: The standard deviation formulas for A) population and B) sample

- **Interquartile Range (IQR)**: The interquartile range is the difference between the first quartile, Q1 (this is also called the lower quartile), and the third quartile, Q3 (this is also called the upper quartile).

> **Note**
>
> For more information on calculating quantiles and quartiles, refer to the *Data Distribution* section in this chapter.

IQR, unlike range and standard deviation, is robust toward outliers, and so, while it is the most complicated of the functions to calculate, it provides a more robust way to measure the spread of datasets. In fact, IQR is often used to define outliers. If a value in a dataset is smaller than Q1 - 1.5 X IQR, or larger than Q3 + 1.5 X IQR, then the value is considered an outlier.

Exercise 4: Dispersion of Add-on Sales

To better understand the sales of additions and upgrades, you need to take a closer look at the dispersion of the data. In this exercise, we will calculate the range, standard deviation, IQR, and outliers of **Add-on Sales**. Here is the data for the 11 cars purchased: 5,000, 1,700, 8,200, 1,500, 3,300, 9,000, 2,000, 0, 0, 2,300, and 4,700.

Follow these steps to perform the exercise:

1. To calculate the range, we find the minimum value of the data, 0, and subtract it from the maximum value of the data, 9,000, yielding 9,000.

2. The standard deviation calculation requires you to do the following: Determine whether we want to calculate the sample standard deviation or the population standard deviation. As these 11 data points only represent a small portion of all purchases, we will calculate the sample standard deviation.

3. Next, find the mean of the dataset, which we calculated in *Exercise 2, Calculating the Quartiles for Add-on Sales*, to be 3,427.27.

4. Now, subtract each data point from the mean and square the result. The results are summarized in the following diagram:

Add-on Sales ($)	Difference with Mean	Difference with Mean Squared
5000	1572.727273	2473471.074
1700	-1727.272727	2983471.074
8200	4772.727273	22778925.62
1500	-1927.272727	3714380.165
3300	-127.2727273	16198.34711
9000	5572.727273	31055289.26
2000	-1427.272727	2037107.438
0	-3427.272727	11746198.35
0	-3427.272727	11746198.35
2300	-1127.272727	1270743.802
4700	1272.727273	1619834.711

Figure 1.15: The sum of the calculation of the square

5. Sum up the **Differences with Mean Squared** values, yielding 91,441,818.

6. Divide the sum by the number of data points minus 1, which, in this case, is 10, and take its square root. This calculation should result in 3,023.93 as the sample standard deviation.

7. To calculate the IQR, find the first and third quartiles. This calculation can be found in *Exercise 2, Calculating the Quartiles for Add-on Sales*, to give you 1,600 and 4,850. Then, subtract the two to get the value 3,250.

Bivariate Analysis

So far, we have talked about methods for describing a single variable. Now, we will discuss how to find patterns with two variables using bivariate analysis.

Scatterplots

A general principle you will find in analytics is that graphs are incredibly helpful in finding patterns. Just as histograms can help you to understand a single variable, scatterplots can help you to understand two variables. Scatterplots can be produced pretty easily using your favorite spreadsheet.

> **Note**
>
> Scatterplots are particularly helpful when there are only a small number of points, usually some number between 30 and 500. If you have a large number of points and plotting them appears to produce a giant blob in your scatterplot, take a random sample of 200 of those points and then plot them to help discern any interesting trends.

A lot of different patterns are worth looking out for within a scatterplot. The most common pattern people look for is an upward or downward trend between the two variables; that is, as one variable increases, does the other variable decrease? Such a trend indicates that there may be a predictable mathematical relationship between the two variables. *Figure 1.16* shows an example of a linear trend:

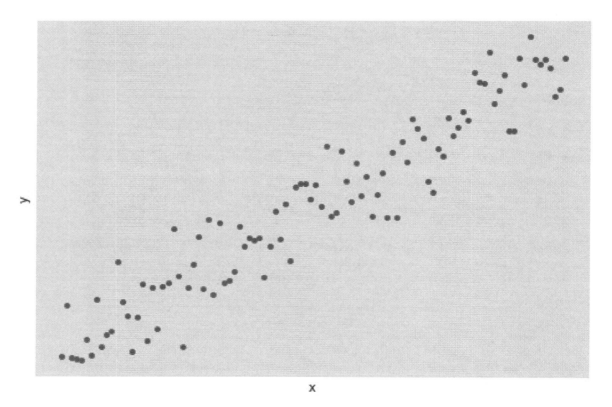

Figure 1.16: The upward linear trend of two variables, x and y

There are also many trends that are worth looking out for that are not linear, including quadratic, exponential, inverse, and logistic. The following diagram shows some of these trends and what they look like:

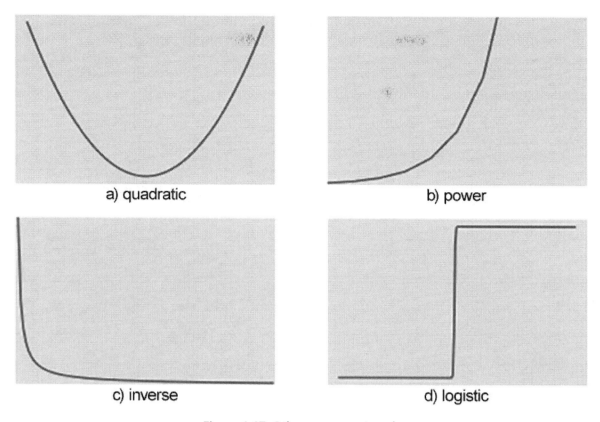

Figure 1.17: Other common trends

> **Note**
>
> The process of approximating a trend with a mathematical function is known as regression analysis. Regression analysis plays a critical part in analytics but is outside the scope of this book. For more information on regression analysis, refer to an advanced text, such as *Regression Modeling Strategies: With Applications to Linear Models, Logistic Regression, and Survival Analysis* by Frank E. Harrell Jr.

While trends are useful for understanding and predicting patterns, detecting changes in trends are often more important. Changes in trends usually indicate a critical change in whatever you are measuring and are worth examining further for an explanation. The following diagram shows an example of a change in a trend, where the linear trend wears off after **x=40**:

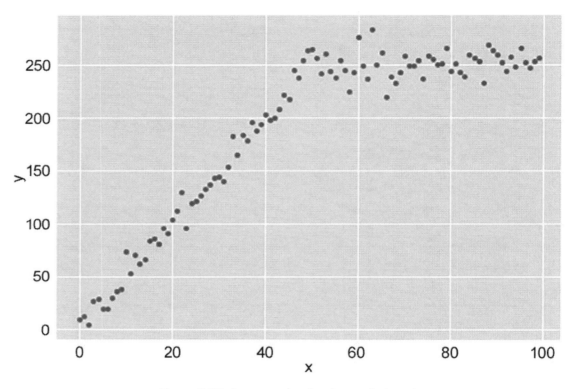

Figure 1.18: An example of a change in trend

Another pattern people tend to look for is periodicity, that is, repeating patterns in the data. Such patterns can indicate that two variables may have cyclical behavior and can be useful in making predictions. The following diagram shows an example of periodic behavior:

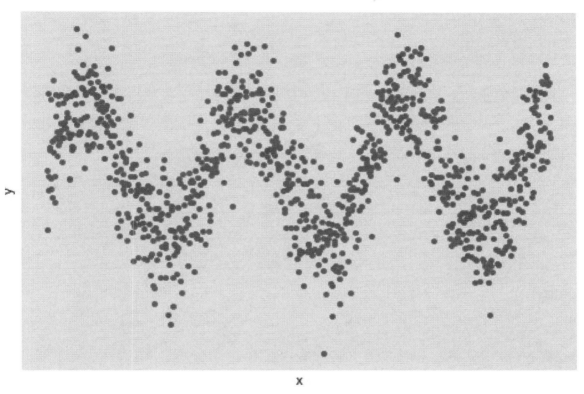

Figure 1.19: An example of periodic behavior

Another use of scatterplots is to help detect outliers. When most points in a graph appear to be in a specific region of the graph, but some points are quite far removed, this may indicate that those points are outliers with regard to the two variables. When performing further bivariate analysis, it may be wise to remove these points in order to reduce noise and produce better insights. The following diagram shows a case of points that may be considered outliers:

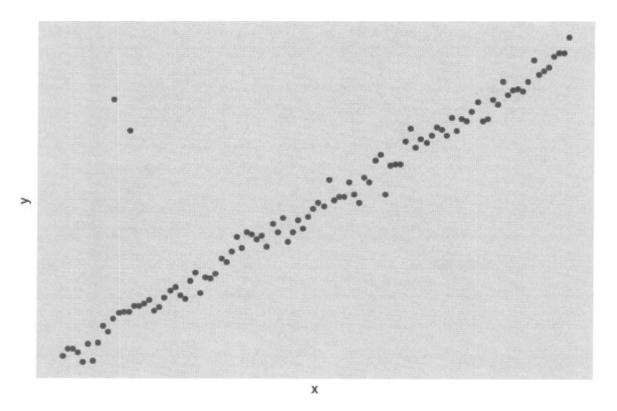

Figure 1.20: A scatterplot with two outliers

These techniques with scatterplots allow data professionals to understand the broader trends in their data and take the first steps to turn data into information.

Pearson Correlation Coefficient

One of the most common trends in analyzing bivariate data is linear trends. Often times though, some linear trends are weak, while other linear trends are strong in how well a linear trend fits the data. In *Figure 1.21* and *Figure 1.22*, we see examples of scatterplots with their line of best fit. This is a line calculated using a technique known as **Ordinary Least Square (OLS)** regression. Although OLS is beyond the scope of this book, understanding how well bivariate data fits a linear trend is an extraordinarily valuable tool for understanding the relationship between two variables:

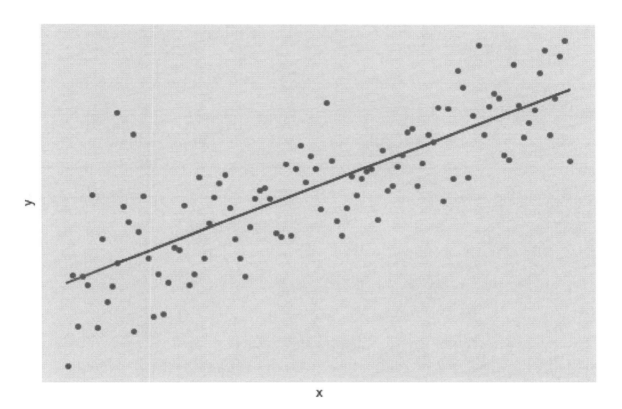

Figure 1.21: A scatterplot with a strong linear trend

The following diagram shows a scatterplot with a weak linear trend:

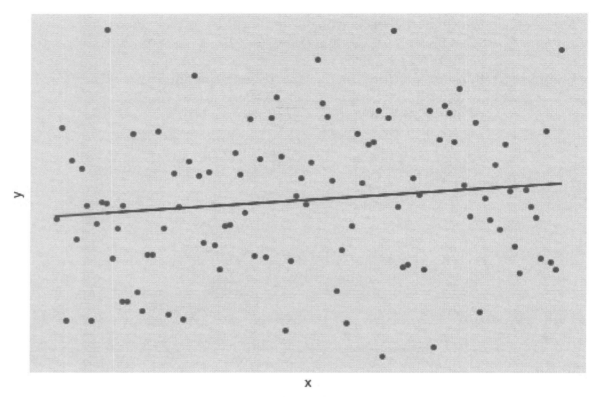

Figure 1.22: A scatterplot with a weak linear trend

> **Note**
>
> For more information on OLS regression, please refer to a statistics textbook, such as Statistics by David Freedman, Robert Pisani, and Roger Purves.

One method for quantifying linear correlation is to use what is called the Pearson correlation coefficient. The Pearson correlation coefficient, often represented by the letter r, is a number ranging from –1 to 1, indicating how well a scatterplot fits a linear trend. To calculate the Pearson correlation coefficient, **r**, we use the following formula:

$$r = \frac{\sum_{i=1}^{n}(x_i - \bar{x})(y - \bar{y})}{\sqrt{\sum_{i=1}^{n}(x_i - \bar{x})^2}\sqrt{\sum_{i=1}^{n}(y_i - \bar{y})^2}}$$

Figure 1.23: The formula for calculating the Pearson correlation coefficient

This formula is a bit heavy, so let's work through an example to turn the formula into specific steps.

Exercise 5: Calculating the Pearson Correlation Coefficient for Two Variables

Let's calculate the Pearson correlation coefficient for the relationship between **Hours Worked Per Week** and **Sales Per Week ($)**. In the following diagram, we have listed some data for 10 salesmen at a ZoomZoom dealership in Houston, and how much they netted in sales that week:

Hours Worked Per Week	Sales Per Week ($)
40	179,480.58
56	2,495,037.73
50	2,285,369.51
82	2,367,896.33
41	1,309,745.16
51	623,013.69
45	2,989,943.37
90	1,970,316.24
47	1,845,840.39
72	2,553,231.33

Figure 1.24: Data for 10 salesmen at a ZoomZoom dealership

Perform the following steps to complete the exercise:

1. First, create a scatterplot of the two variables in Excel by using the data given in the scenario. This will help us to get a rough estimate of what to expect for the Pearson correlation coefficient:

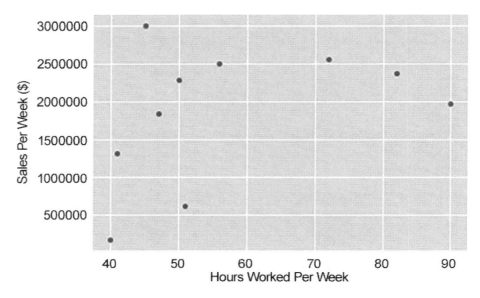

Figure 1.25: A scatterplot of Hours Worked Per Week and Sales Per Week

There does not appear to be a strong linear relationship, but there does appear to be a general increase in **Sales Per Week ($)** versus **Hours Worked Per Week**.

2. Now, calculate the mean of each variable. You should get 57.40 for **Hours Worked Per Week** and 1,861,987.3 for **Sales Per Week**. If you are not sure how to calculate the mean, refer to the *Central Tendency* section.

3. Now, for each row, calculate four values: the difference between each value and its mean, and the square of the difference between each value and its mean. Then, find the product of these differences. You should get a table of values, as shown in the following diagram:

Hours Worked Per Week	Sales Per Week ($)	x-mean(x)	(x-mean(x))^2	y-mean(y)	(y-mean(y))^2	[x-mean(x)][y-mean(y)]
40	179,480.58	-17.40	302.76	-1,682,506.85	2,830,829,303,631.31	29,275,619.21
56	2,495,037.73	-1.40	1.96	633,050.29	400,752,674,381.30	-886,270.41
50	2,285,369.51	-7.40	54.76	423,382.07	179,252,379,435.48	-3,133,027.34
82	2,367,896.33	24.60	605.16	505,908.90	255,943,812,657.79	12,445,358.88
41	1,309,745.16	-16.40	268.96	-552,242.27	304,971,527,314.18	9,056,773.27
51	623,013.69	-6.40	40.96	-1,238,973.75	1,535,055,945,620.25	7,929,431.98
45	2,989,943.37	-12.40	153.76	1,127,955.94	1,272,284,593,638.99	-13,986,653.61
90	1,970,316.24	32.60	1,062.76	108,328.81	11,735,131,115.82	3,531,519.21
47	1,845,840.39	-10.40	108.16	-16,147.04	260,726,862.48	167,929.20
72	2,553,231.33	14.60	213.16	691,243.90	477,818,127,736.76	10,092,160.92

Figure 1.26: Calculations for the Pearson correlation coefficient

4. Find the sum of the squared terms and the sum of the product of the differences. You should get 2,812.40 for **Hours Worked Per Week (x)**, 7,268,904,222,394.36 for **Sales Per Week (y)**, and 54,492,841.32 for the product of the differences.

5. Take the square root of the sum of the differences to get 53.03 for **Hours Worked Per Week (x)** and 2,696,090.54 for **Sales Per Week (y)**.

6. Input the values into the equation from *Figure* 1.27 to get **0.38**. The following diagram shows the calculation:

$$r = \frac{\sum_{i=1}^{n}(x_i - \bar{x})(y - \bar{y})}{\sqrt{\sum_{i=1}^{n}(x_i - \bar{x})^2}\sqrt{\sum_{i=1}^{n}(y_i - \bar{y})^2}} = \frac{54492841.32}{(53.03) * (2696090.54)} \approx 0.38$$

Figure 1.27: The final calculation of the Pearson correlation coefficient

We learned how to calculate the Pearson correlation coefficient for two variables in this exercise and got the final output as 0.38 after using the formula.

Interpreting and Analyzing the Correlation Coefficient

Calculating the correlation coefficient by hand can be very complicated. It is generally preferable to calculate it on the computer. As you will learn in *Chapter 3, SQL for Data Preparation*, it is possible to calculate the Pearson correlation coefficient using SQL.

To interpret the Pearson correlation coefficient, compare its value to the table in *Figure 1.28*. The closer to 0 the coefficient is, the weaker the correlation. The higher the absolute value of a Pearson correlation coefficient, the more likely it is that the points will fit a straight line:

Value of Correlation	Interpretation
-1.0 <= r <= -0.7	Very Strong Negative Correlation
-0.7<= r <= -0.4	Strong Negative Correlation
-0.4 < r < -0.2	Moderate Negative Correlation
-0.2 < r < 0.2	Weak to Non-Existent Correlation
0.2 < r < 0.4	Moderate Positive Correlation
0.4 < r < 0.7	Strong Positive Correlation
0.7 < r < 1.0	Very Strong Positive Correlation

Figure 1.28: Interpreting a Pearson correlation coefficient

There are a couple of things to watch out for when examining the correlation coefficient. The first thing to watch out for is that the correlation coefficient measures how well two variables fit a linear trend. Two variables may share a strong trend but have a relatively low Pearson correlation coefficient. For example, look at the points in *Figure 1.29*. If you calculate the correlation coefficient for these two variables, you will find it is -0.08. However, the curve has a very clear quadratic relationship. Therefore, when you look at the correlation coefficients of bivariate data, be on the lookout for non-linear relationships that may describe the relationship between the two variables:

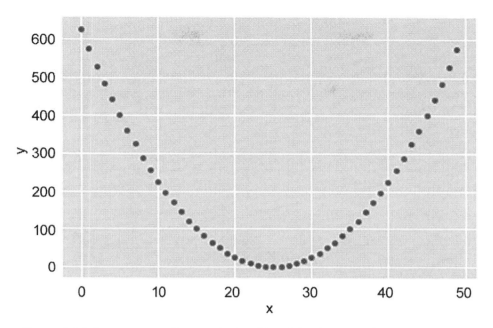

Figure 1.29: A strong non-linear relationship with a low correlation coefficient

Another point of importance is the number of points used to calculate a correlation. It only takes two points to define a perfectly straight line. Therefore, you may be able to calculate a high correlation coefficient when there are fewer points. However, this correlation coefficient may not hold when more data is presented into the bivariate data. As a rule of thumb, correlation coefficients calculated with fewer than 30 data points should be taken with a pinch of salt. Ideally, you should have as many good data points as you can in order to calculate the correlation.

Notice the use of the term "good data points." One of the recurring themes of this chapter has been the negative impact of outliers on various statistics. Indeed, with bivariate data, outliers can impact the correlation coefficient. Let's take a look at the graph in *Figure 1.30*. It has 11 points, one of which is an outlier. Due to that outlier, the Pearson correlation coefficient, r, for the data falls to 0.59, but without it, it equals 1.0. Therefore, care should be taken to remove outliers, especially from limited data:

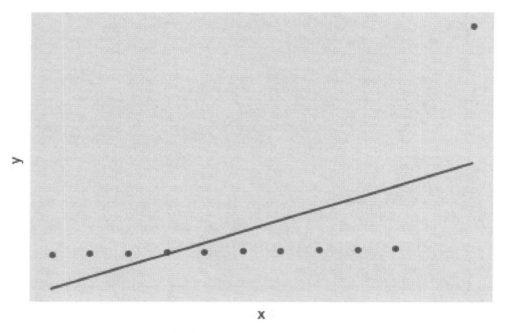

Figure 1.30: Calculating r for a scatterplot with an outlier

Finally, one of the major problems associated with calculating correlation is the logical fallacy of correlation implying causation. That is, just because x and y have a strong correlation does not mean that x causes y. Let's take our example of the number of hours worked versus the number of sales netted per week. Imagine that, after adding more data points, it turns out that the correlation is 0.5 between these two variables. Many beginner data professionals and experienced executives would conclude that more working hours net more sales and start making their sales team work nonstop. While it is possible that working more hours causes more sales, a high correlation coefficient is not hard evidence for that. Another possibility may even be a reverse set of causation; it is possible that because you produce more sales, there is more paperwork and, therefore, you need to stay longer at the office in order to complete it. In this scenario, working more hours may not cause more sales. Another possibility is that there is a third item responsible for the association between the two variables.

For example, it may actually be that experienced salespeople work longer hours, and experienced salespeople also do a better job of selling. Therefore, the real cause is having employees with lots of sales experience, and the recommendation should be to hire more experienced sales professionals. As analytics professional, you will be responsible for avoiding pitfalls such as correlation and causation, and critically think about all the possibilities that might be responsible for the results you see.

Time Series Data

One of the most important types of bivariate analysis is a time series. A time series is simply a bivariate relationship where the x-axis is time. An example of a time series can be found in *Figure* 1.31, which shows a time series from January 2010 to late 2012. While, at first glance, this may not seem to be the case, date and time information is quantitative in nature. Understanding how things change over time is one of the most important types of analysis done in organizations and provides a lot of information about the context of the business. All of the patterns discussed in the previous section can also be found in time series data. Time series are also important in organizations because they can be indicative of when specific changes happened. Such time points can be useful in determining what caused these changes:

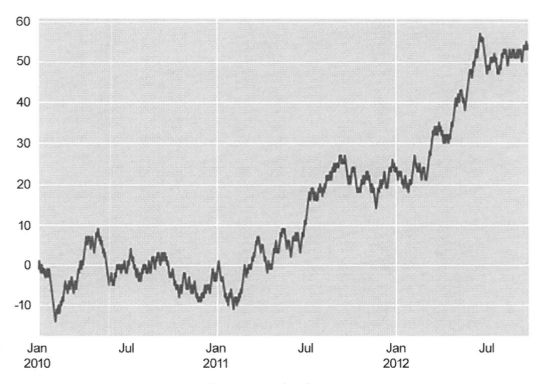

Figure 1.31: An example of a time series

Activity 2: Exploring Dealership Sales Data

In this activity, we will explore a dataset in full. It's your first day at ZoomZoom, where the company is hard at work building the world's best electric vehicles and scooters in order to stop climate change. You have been recently hired as the newest senior data analyst for the company. You're incredibly excited to start your job and are ready to help however you can. Your manager, the head of analytics is happy to see you, but unfortunately, can't help you get set up today because of a company emergency (something about the CEO having a meltdown on a podcast). You don't have access to a database, but he did email you a CSV file with some data about national dealerships on it. He wants you to do some high-level analysis on annual sales at dealerships across the country:

1. Open the **dealerships.csv** document in a spreadsheet or text editor. This can be found in the **Datasets** folder of the GitHub repository.

2. Make a frequency distribution of the number of female employees at a dealership.

3. Determine the average and median annual sales for a dealership.

4. Determine the standard deviation of sales.

5. Do any of the dealerships seem like an outlier? Explain your reasoning.

6. Calculate the quantiles of the annual sales.

7. Calculate the correlation coefficient of annual sales to female employees and interpret the result.

> **Note**
>
> The solution for this activity can be found on page 314.

Working with Missing Data

In all of our examples so far, our datasets have been very clean. However, real-world datasets are almost never this nice. One of the many problems you may have to deal with when working with datasets is missing values. We will discuss the specifics of preparing data further in *Chapter 3, SQL for Data Preparation*. Nonetheless, in this section, we would like to take some time to discuss some of the strategies you can use to handle missing data. Some of your options include the following:

- **Deleting Rows**: If a very small number of rows (that is, less than 5% of your dataset) are missing data, then the simplest solution may be to just delete the data points from your set. Such a result should not overly impact your results.

- **Mean/Median/Mode Imputation**: If 5% to 25% of your data for a variable is missing, another option is to take the mean, median, or mode of that column and fill in the blanks with that value. This may provide a small bias to your calculations, but it will allow you to complete more analysis without deleting valuable data.

- **Regression Imputation**: If possible, you may be able to build and use a model to impute missing values. This skill may be beyond the capability of most data analysts, but if you are working with a data scientist, this option could be viable.

- **Deleting Variables**: Ultimately, you cannot analyze data that does not exist. If you do not have a lot of data available, and a variable is missing most of its data, it may simply be better to remove that variable than to make too many assumptions and reach faulty conclusions.

You will also find that a decent portion of data analysis is more art than science. Working with missing data is one such area. With experience, you will find a combination of strategies that work well for different scenarios.

Statistical Significance Testing

Another piece of analysis that is useful in data analysis is statistical significance testing. Often times, an analyst is interested in comparing the statistical properties of two groups, or perhaps just one group before and after a change. Of course, the difference between these two groups may just be due to chance.

An example of where this comes up is in marketing A/B tests. Companies will often test two different types of landing pages for a product and measure the **click-through rate** (**CTR**). You may find that the CTR for variation A of the landing page is 10%, and the CTR for variation B is 11%. So, does that mean that variation B is 10% better than A, or is this just a result of day-to-day variance? Statistical testing helps us to determine just that.

In statistical testing, there are a couple of major parts you need to have (*Figure* 1.32). First, we have the **test statistic** we are examining. It may be a proportion, an average, the difference between two groups, or a distribution. The next necessary part is a **null hypothesis**, which is the idea that the results observed are the product of chance. You will then need an **alternative hypothesis**, which is the idea that the results seen cannot be explained by chance alone. Finally, a test needs a significance level, which is the value the test statistic needs to take before it is decided that the null hypothesis cannot explain the difference. All statistical significance tests have these four aspects, and it is simply a matter of how these components are calculated that differentiate significance tests:

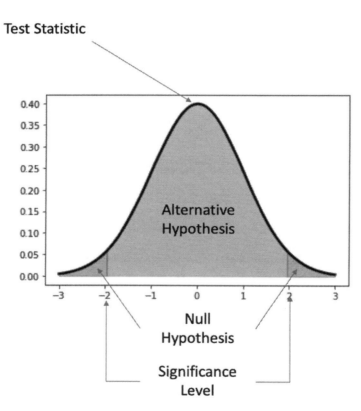

Figure 1.32: Parts of statistical significance testing

Common Statistical Significance Tests

Some common statistical significance tests include the following:

- **<u>Two-sample Z-test</u>**: A test to determine whether the averages of the two samples are different. This test assumes that both samples are drawn from a normal distribution with a known population standard deviation.

- **<u>Two-sample T-test</u>**: A test to determine whether the average of two samples is different when either the sample set is too small (that is, fewer than 30 data points per sample), or if the population standard deviation is unknown. The two samples are also generally drawn from distributions assumed to be normal.

- **<u>Pearson's Chi-Squared Test</u>**: A test to determine whether the distribution of data points to categories is different than what would be expected due to chance. This is the primary test for determining whether the proportions in tests, such as those in an A/B test, are beyond what would be expected from chance.

> **Note**
>
> To learn more about statistical significance, please refer to a statistics textbook, such as *Statistics by David Freedman, Robert Pisani, and Roger Purves*.

Summary

Data is a powerful method by which to understand the world. The ultimate goal for analytics is to turn data into information and knowledge. To accomplish this goal, statistics can be used to better understand data, especially descriptive statistics, and statistical significance testing.

One branch of descriptive statistics, univariate analysis, can be utilized to understand a single variable of data. Univariate analysis can be used to find the distribution of data by utilizing frequency distributions and quantiles. We can also find the central tendency of a variable by calculating the mean, median, and mode of data. It can also be used to find the dispersion of data using the range, standard deviation, and IQR. Univariate analysis can also be used to find outliers.

Bivariate analysis can also be used to understand the relationship between data. Using scatterplots, we can determine trends, changes in trends, periodic behavior, and anomalous points in regard to two variables. We can also use the Pearson correlation coefficient to measure the strength of a linear trend between the two variables. The Pearson correlation coefficient, however, is subject to scrutiny due to outliers or the number of data points used to calculate the coefficient. Additionally, just because two variables have a strong correlation coefficient does not mean that one variable causes the other variable.

Statistical significance testing can also provide important information about data. Statistical significance testing allows us to determine how likely certain outcomes are to occur by chance and can help us to understand whether the changes seen between groups are of consequence.

Now that we have the basic analytical tools necessary to understand data, we will now review SQL and how we can use it to manipulate a database in the next chapter.

The Basics of SQL for Analytics

Learning Objectives

By the end of this chapter, you will be able to:

- Describe the purpose of SQL
- Analyze how SQL can be used in an analytics workflow
- Apply the basics of a SQL database
- Perform operations to create, read, update, and delete a table

In this chapter, we will cover how SQL is used in data analytics. Then, we will learn the basics of SQL databases and perform CRUD (create, read, update, and delete) operations on a table.

Introduction

In *Chapter 1, Understanding and Describing Data*, we discussed analytics and how we can use data to obtain valuable information. While we could, in theory, analyze all data by hand, computers are far better at the task and are certainly the preferred tool for storing, organizing, and processing data. Among the most critical of these data tools is the relational database and the language used to access it, **Structured Query Language (SQL)**. These two technologies have been cornerstones of data processing and continue to be the data backbone of most companies that deal with substantial amounts of data.

Companies use SQL as the primary method for storing much of their data. Furthermore, companies now take much of this data and put it into specialized databases called **data warehouses** and **data lakes** so that they can perform advanced analytics on their data. Virtually all of these data warehouses and data lakes are accessed using SQL. We'll be looking at working with SQL using analytics platforms such as data warehouses.

We assume that every person following this chapter has had some basic exposure to SQL. However, for those users who have very limited exposure to SQL, or who have not used it for some time, this chapter will provide a basic refresher of what relational databases and SQL are, along with a basic review of SQL operations and syntax. We will also go over a number of practice exercises to help reinforce these concepts.

Relational Databases and SQL

A **relational database** is a database that utilizes the **relational model** of data. The relational model, invented by Edgar F. Codd in 1970, organizes data as relations, or sets of tuples. Each tuple consists of a series of attributes, which generally describe the tuple. For example, we could imagine a customer relation, where each tuple represents a customer. Each tuple would then have attributes describing a single customer, giving information such as first name, last name, and age, perhaps in the format (John, Smith, 27). One or more of the attributes is used to uniquely identify a tuple in a relation and is called the **relational key**. The relational model then allows logical operations to be performed between relations.

In a relational database, relations are usually implemented as tables, as in an Excel spreadsheet. Each row of the table is a tuple, and the attributes are represented as columns of the table. While not technically required, most tables in a relational database have a column referred to as the **primary key**, which uniquely identifies a row of the database. Every column also has a **data type**, which describes the data for the column.

Tables are then usually assimilated in common collections in databases called **schemas**. These tables usually are loaded via processes known as **Extract, Transform, and Load** jobs (**ETL**).

> **Note**
>
> Tables are usually referred to in queries in the format [schema].[table]. For example, a **product** table in the analytics schema would be generally referred to as **analytics.product**. However, there is also a special schema called **public**. This is a default schema where, if you do not explicitly mention a schema, the database uses the public schema, for example, the **public.products** table and **product** table are similar.

The software used to manage relational databases on a computer is referred to as a **relational database management system** (**RDBMS**). SQL is the language utilized by users of an RDBMS to access and interact with a relational database.

> **Note**
>
> Technically, virtually all relational databases that use SQL deviate from the relational model in some basic ways. For example, not every table has a specified relational key. Also, the relational model does not technically allow for duplicate rows, but you can have duplicate rows in a relational database. These differences are minor and will not matter for the vast majority of readers of this book. For more information on why most relational databases are not technically relational, refer to this article: https://www.periscopedata.com/blog/your-database-isnt-really-relational.

Advantages and Disadvantages of SQL Databases

Since the release of Oracle Database in 1979, SQL has become an industry standard for data in nearly all computer applications – and for good reason. SQL databases provide a ton of advantages that make it the de facto choice for many applications:

- **Intuitive**: Relations represented as tables is a common data structure that almost everyone understands. As such, working with and reasoning about relational databases is much easier than doing so with other models.

- **Efficient**: Using a technique known as normalization, relational databases allow the representation of data without unnecessarily repeating it. As such, relational databases can represent large amounts of information while utilizing less space. This reduced storage footprint also allows the database to reduce operation costs, making well-designed relational databases quick to process.

- **Declarative**: SQL is a declarative language, meaning that when you write code, you only need to tell the computer what data you want, and the RDBMS takes care of determining how to execute the SQL code. You never have to worry about telling the computer how to access and pull data in the table.

- **Robust**: Most popular SQL databases have a property known as **atomicity, consistency, isolation, and durability (ACID)** compliance, which guarantees the validity of the data, even if the hardware fails.

That said, there are still some downsides to SQL databases, which are as follows:

- **Lower specificity**: While SQL is declarative, its functionality can often be limited to what has already been programmed into it. Although most popular RDBMS software is updated constantly with new functionality being built all the time, it can be difficult to process and work with data structures and algorithms not programmed into an RDBMS.

- **Limited scalability**: SQL databases are incredibly robust, but this robustness comes at a cost. As the amount of information, you have doubles, the cost of resources more than doubles. When very large volumes of information are involved, other data stores, such as NoSQL databases, may actually be better.

- **Object-relation mismatch impedance**: While tables are a very intuitive data structure, they are not necessarily the best format for representing objects in a computer. This primarily occurs because objects often have attributes that have many-to-many relationships. For instance, a customer for a company may own multiple products, but each product may have multiple customers. For an object in a computer, we could easily represent this as a `list` attribute under the `customer` object. However, in a normalized database, a customer's products would potentially have to be represented using three different tables, each of which must be updated for every new purchase, recall, and return.

Basic Data Types of SQL

As previously mentioned, each column in a table has a data type. We review the major data types here.

Numeric

Numeric data types are data types that represent numbers. The following diagram provides an overview of some of the major types:

Name	Storage Size	Description	Range
smallint	2 bytes	Small-range integer	-32768 to +32767
integer	4 bytes	Typical choice for integer	-2147483648 to +2147483647
bigint	8 bytes	Large-range integer	-9223372036854775808 to +9223372036854775807
decimal	variable	User-specified precision, exact	Up to 131072 digits before the decimal point; up to 16383 digits after the decimal point
numeric	variable	User-specified precision, exact	Up to 131072 digits before the decimal point; up to 16383 digits after the decimal point
real	4 bytes	Variable precision, inexact	6 decimal digits precision
double precision	8 bytes	Variable precision, inexact	15 decimal digits precision
smallserial	2 bytes	Small autoincrementing integer	1 to 32767
serial	4 bytes	Autoincrementing integer	1 to 2147483647
bigserial	8 bytes	Large autoincrementing integer	1 to 9223372036854775807

Figure 2.1: Major numeric data types

Character

Character data types store text information. The following diagram summarizes the character data types:

Name	Description
character varying(n), varchar(n)	Variable length with limit
character(n), char(n)	Fixed length, blank padded
text	Variable unlimited length

Figure 2.2: Major character data types

Under the hood, all of the character data types use the same underlying data structure in PostgreSQL and many other SQL databases, and most modern developers do not use **char(n)**.

Boolean

Booleans are a data type used to represent **True** or **False**. The following table summarizes values that are represented as a Boolean when used in a query with a Boolean data column type:

Boolean Value	Accepted Values
True	t, true, y, yes, on, 1
False	f, false, n, no, off, 0

Figure 2.3: Accepted Boolean values

While all of these values are accepted, the values **True** and **False** are considered compliant with best practice. Booleans columns can also have **NULL** values.

Datetime

The **datetime** data type is used to store time-based information such as dates and times. The following are some of the datetime data types:

Name	Size	Description
Timestamp without timezone	8 bytes	both date and time (no time zone)
Timestamp with timezone	8 bytes	both date and time, with time zone
date	4 bytes	date (no time of day)
Time without timezone	8 bytes	time of day (no date)
Time with timezone	12 bytes	times of day only, with time zone
interval	16 bytes	time interval

Figure 2.4: Major datetime data types

We will discuss this data type more in *Chapter 7, Analytics Using Complex Data Types*.

Data Structures: JSON and Arrays

Many versions of modern SQL also support data structures such as **JavaScript Object Notation (JSON)** and arrays. Arrays are simply listing of data usually written as members enclosed in square brackets. For example, ['cat', 'dog', 'horse'] is an array. A JSON object is a series of key-value pairs that are separated by commas and enclosed in curly braces. For example, {'name': 'Bob', 'age': 27, 'city': 'New York'} is a valid JSON object. These data structures show up consistently in technology applications and being able to use them in a database makes it easier to perform many kinds of analysis work.

We will discuss data structures more in *Chapter 7, Analytics Using Complex Data Types*.

We will now look at the basic operations in an RDBMS using SQL.

Reading Tables: The SELECT Query

The most common operation in a database is reading data from a database. This is almost exclusively done through the use of the **SELECT** keyword.

Basic Anatomy and Working of a SELECT Query

Generally speaking, a query can be broken down into five parts:

- **Operation**: The first part of a query describes what is going to be done. In this case, this is the word **SELECT**, followed by the names of columns combined with functions.

- **Data**: The next part of the query is the data, which is the **FROM** keyword followed by one or more tables connected together with reserved keywords indicating what data should be scanned for filtering, selection, and calculation.

- **Conditional**: A part of the query that filters the data to only rows that meet a condition usually indicated with **WHERE**.

- **Grouping**: A special clause that takes the rows of a data source, assembles them together using a key created by a **GROUP BY** clause, and then calculates a value using the values from all rows with the same value. We will discuss this step more in *Chapter 4, Aggregate Functions for Data Analysis*.

- **Post-processing**: A part of the query that takes the results of the data and formats them by sorting and limiting the data, often using keywords such as **ORDER BY** and **LIMIT**.

The steps of a **SELECT** query are as follows:

1. Create a data source by taking one or more tables and combining them in one large table.

2. Filter the table based on the large data source created in step 1 by seeing which rows meet the **WHERE** clause.

3. Calculate values based on columns in the data source in step 1. If there is a **GROUP BY** clause, divide the rows into groups and then calculate an aggregate statistic for each group. Otherwise, return a column or value calculated by performing functions on one or more columns together.

4. Take the rows returned and reorganize them based on the query.

To break down these steps, let's look at a typical query and follow the logic we've described:

```
SELECT first_name
FROM customers
WHERE state='AZ'
ORDER BY first_name
```

The operation of this query follows a sequence:

1. We start with the **customers** table.

2. The **customers** table is filtered to where the **state** column equals **'AZ'**.

3. We capture the **first_name** column from the filtered table.

4. The **first_name** column is then ordered in alphabetical order.

Here, we've shown how a query can be broken down into a series of steps for the database to process.

We will now look at the query keywords and patterns found in a **SELECT** query.

Basic Keywords in a SELECT Query

SELECT and FROM

The most basic **SELECT** query follows the pattern **SELECT…FROM <table_name>;**. This query is the way to pull data from a single table. For example, if you want to pull all the data from the **products** table in our sample database, simply use this query:

```
SELECT *

FROM products;
```

This query will pull all data from a database. The * symbol seen here is shorthand to return all columns from a database. The semicolon operator (;) is used to tell the computer it has reached the end of the query, much like a period is used for a normal sentence. It's important to note that the rows will be returned in no specific order. If we want to return only specific columns from a query, we can simply replace the asterisk with the names of the columns we want to be separated in the order we want them to be returned in. For example, if we wanted to return the **product_id** column followed by the **model** column of the **products** table, we would write the following query:

```
SELECT product_id, model

FROM products;
```

If we wanted to return the **model** column first and the **product_id** column second, we would write this:

```
SELECT model, product_id
FROM products;
```

WHERE

The **WHERE** clause is a piece of conditional logic that limits the amount of data returned. All the rows returned in a **SELECT** statement with a **WHERE** clause in it meet the conditions of the **WHERE** clause. The **WHERE** clause can usually be found after the **FROM** clause of a single **SELECT** statement.

The condition in the **WHERE** clause is generally a Boolean statement that can either be **True** or **False** for every row. In the case of numeric columns, these Boolean statements can use equals, greater than, or less than operators to compare the columns against a value.

We will use an example to illustrate. Let's say we wanted to see the model names of our products with the model year of 2014 from our sample dataset. We would write the following query:

```
SELECT model
FROM products
WHERE year=2014;
```

AND/OR

The previous query had only one condition. We are often interested in multiple conditions being met at once. For this, we put multiple statements together using the **AND** or **OR** clause.

Now, we will illustrate this with an example. Let's say we wanted to return models that not only were built in 2014, but also have a **manufacturer's suggested retail price (MSRP)** of less than $1,000. We can write:

```
SELECT model
FROM products
WHERE year=2014
AND msrp<=1000;
```

Now, let's say we wanted to return models that were released in the year 2014 or had a product type of **automobile**. We would then write the following query:

```
SELECT model
FROM products
WHERE year=2014
OR product_type='automobile';
```

When using more than one **AND/OR** condition, use parentheses to separate and position pieces of logic together. This will make sure that your query works as expected and that it is as readable as possible. For example, if we wanted to get all products with models in the years between 2014 and 2016, as well as any products that are scooters, we could write:

```
SELECT *
FROM products
WHERE year>2014
AND year<2016
OR product_type='scooter';
```

However, to clarify the **WHERE** clause, it would be preferable to write:

```
SELECT *
FROM products
WHERE (year>2014 AND year<2016)
OR product_type='scooter';
```

IN/NOT IN

As mentioned earlier, Boolean statements can use equals signs to indicate that a column must equal a certain value. However, what if you are interested in returning rows where a row has a column that can be equal to any of a group of values? For instance, let's say you were interested in returning all models with the year 2014, 2016, or 2019. You could write a query such as this:

```
SELECT model
FROM products
WHERE year = 2014
OR year = 2016
OR year = 2019;
```

However, this is long and tedious to write. Using **IN**, you can instead write:

```
SELECT model
FROM products
WHERE year IN (2014, 2016, 2019);
```

This is much cleaner to write and makes it easier to understand what is going on.

Conversely, you can also use the **NOT IN** clause to return all values that are not in a list of values. For instance, if you wanted all products that were not produced in the years 2014, 2016, and 2019, you could write:

```
SELECT model
FROM products
WHERE year NOT IN (2014, 2016, 2019);
```

ORDER BY

As previously mentioned, SQL queries will order rows as the database finds them if more specific instructions to do otherwise are not given. For many use cases, this is acceptable. However, you will often want to see rows in a specific order. Let's say you want to see all of the products listed by the date when they were first produced, from earliest to latest. The method for doing this in SQL would be as follows:

```
SELECT model
FROM products
ORDER BY production_start_date;
```

If an order sequence is not explicitly mentioned, the rows will be returned in ascending order. Ascending order simply means the rows will be ordered from the smallest value to the highest value of the chosen column or columns. In the case of things such as text, this means alphabetical order. You can make the ascending order explicit by using the **ASC** keyword. For our last query, this would be achieved by writing:

```
SELECT model
FROM products
ORDER BY production_start_date ASC;
```

If you would like to extract data in greatest-to-least order, you can use the **DESC** keyword. If we wanted to fetch manufactured models ordered from newest to oldest, we would write:

```
SELECT model
FROM products
ORDER BY production_start_date DESC;
```

Also, instead of writing the name of the column you want to order by, you can instead refer to what number column it is in the natural order of the table. For instance, say you wanted to return all the models in the **products** table ordered by product ID. You could write:

```
SELECT model
FROM products
ORDER BY product_id;
```

However, because **product_id** is the first column in the table, you could instead write:

```
SELECT model
FROM products
ORDER BY 1;
```

Finally, you can order by multiple columns by adding additional columns after **ORDER BY** separated with commas. For instance, let's say we wanted to order all of the rows in the table first by the year of the model, from newest to oldest, and then by the MSRP from least to greatest. We would then write:

```
SELECT *
FROM products
ORDER BY year DESC, base_msrp ASC;
```

The following is the output of the preceding code:

product_id bigint	model text	year bigint	product_type text	base_msrp numeric	production_start_date timestamp without time zone	production_end_date timestamp without time zone
12	Lemon ...	2019	scooter	349.99	2019-02-04 00:00:00	[null]
11	Model ...	2019	automobile	95000.00	2019-02-04 00:00:00	[null]
8	Bat Limi...	2017	scooter	699.99	2017-02-15 00:00:00	[null]
9	Model E...	2017	automobile	35000.00	2017-02-15 00:00:00	[null]
10	Model ...	2017	automobile	85750.00	2017-02-15 00:00:00	[null]
7	Bat	2016	scooter	599.99	2016-10-10 00:00:00	[null]
6	Model S...	2015	automobile	65500.00	2015-04-15 00:00:00	2018-10-01 00:00:00
5	Blade	2014	scooter	699.99	2014-06-23 00:00:00	2015-01-27 00:00:00
4	Model ...	2014	automobile	115000.00	2014-06-23 00:00:00	2018-12-28 00:00:00
3	Lemon	2013	scooter	499.99	2013-05-01 00:00:00	2018-12-28 00:00:00
2	Lemon ...	2011	scooter	799.99	2011-01-03 00:00:00	2011-03-30 00:00:00

Figure 2.5: Ordering multiple columns using ORDER BY

LIMIT

Most tables in SQL databases tend to be quite large, and therefore returning every single row is unnecessary. Sometimes, you may want only the first few rows. For this scenario, the **LIMIT** keyword comes in handy. Let's imagine that you wanted to only get the first five products that were produced by the company. You could get this by using the following query:

```
SELECT model
FROM products
ORDER BY production_start_date
LIMIT 5;
```

As a general rule, you probably want to use a **LIMIT** keyword for a table or query you have not worked with.

IS NULL/IS NOT NULL

Often, some entries in a given column may be missing. This could be for a variety of reasons. Perhaps the data was not collected or not available at the time that the data was collected. Perhaps the ETL job failed to collect and load data into a column. It may also be possible that the absence of a value is representative of a certain state in the row and actually provides valuable information. Whatever the reason, we are often interested in finding rows where the data is not filled in for a certain value. In SQL, blank values are often represented by the **NULL** value. For instance, in the **products** table, the **production_end_date** column having a **NULL** value indicates that the product is still being made. In this case, if we want to list all products that are still being made, we can use the following query:

```
SELECT *
FROM products
WHERE production_end_date IS NULL
```

If we are only interested in products that are not being produced, we can use the **IS NOT NULL** clause, as in the following query:

```
SELECT *
FROM products
WHERE production_end_date IS NOT NULL
```

Exercise 6: Querying the Salespeople Table Using Basic Keywords in a SELECT Query

In this exercise, we will create various queries using basic keywords in a **SELECT** query. Let's say that, after a few days at your new job, you finally get access to the company database. Today, your boss has asked you to help a sales manager who does not know SQL particularly well. The sales manager would like a couple of different lists of salespeople. First, create a list of the online usernames of the first 10 female salespeople hired, ordered from the first hired to the latest hired.

> **Note**
>
> For all exercises in this book, we will be using pgAdmin 4. Codes for all the exercises and activities can also be found on GitHub: https://github.com/TrainingByPackt/SQL-for-Data-Analytics/tree/master/Lesson02.

Perform the following steps to complete the exercise:

1. Open your favorite SQL client and connect to the **sqlda** database.

2. Examine the schema for the **salespeople** table from the schema dropdown. Notice the names of the columns in the following diagram:

Figure 2.6: Schema of the salespeople table

3. Execute the following query to get the usernames of female salespeople sorted by their **hire_date** values and set **LIMIT** as **10**:

```
SELECT username
FROM salespeople
WHERE gender= 'Female'
ORDER BY hire_date
LIMIT 10
```

The following is the output of the preceding code:

	username text
1	nlie2l
2	adufaire3r
3	bgrimoldby4q
4	jmedgewick...
5	bhain3y
6	kclyburn54
7	adobbing4g
8	skinner1h
9	alimon7j

Figure 2.7: Usernames of female salespeople sorted by hire date

We now have a list of usernames for female salespeople ordered from the earliest hire to the most recent hire.

In this exercise, we used different basic keywords in a **SELECT** query to help the sales manager to get the list of salespeople as per their requirements.

Activity 3: Querying the customers Table Using Basic Keywords in a SELECT Query

One day, your manager at ZoomZoom calls you in and tells you that the marketing department has decided that they want to do a series of marketing campaigns to help promote a sale. You will need to send queries to the manager to pull the data. The following are the steps to complete the activity:

1. Open your favorite SQL client and connect to the **sqlda** database. Examine the schema for the **customers** table from the schema dropdown.

2. Write a query that pulls all emails for ZoomZoom customers in the state of Florida in alphabetical order.

3. Write a query that pulls all the first names, last names and email details for ZoomZoom customers in New York City in the state of New York. They should be ordered alphabetically by the last name followed by the first name.

4. Write a query that returns all customers with a phone number ordered by the date the customer was added to the database.

Expected Output:

customer_id bigint	title text	first_name text	last_name text	suffix text	email text	gender text	ip_address text	phone text	street_address text	city text	state text	postal_code text	latitude double precision	longitude double precision	date_added timestamp without time zon
2625	[null]	Binky	Dawtrey	[null]	bdawtr...	M	15.75.236.78	804-990...	0353 Iowa Road	Rich...	VA	23208	37.5593	-77.4471	2010-03-15 00:00:00
6173	[null]	Danila	Gristwood	[null]	dgrist...	F	254.239.58.1...	832-157...	79865 Hagen Terr...	Katy	TX	77493	29.8678	-95.8298	2010-03-15 00:00:00
13390	[null]	Danika	Lough	[null]	dlough...	F	188.19.7.207	212-769...	38463 Forest Dal...	New ...	NY	10019	40.7651	-73.9858	2010-03-15 00:00:00
7486	[null]	Ciro	Ferencowicz	[null]	cferen...	M	8.151.167.184	786-458...	61 Village Crossing	Miami	FL	33111	25.5584	-80.4582	2010-03-15 00:00:00
17099	[null]	Pearla	Halksworth	[null]	phalks...	F	114.138.62.24	541-198...	130 Maroy Crossi...	Euge...	OR	97405	44.0185	-123.0998	2010-03-15 00:00:00
18685	[null]	Ingram	Crossman	[null]	icross...	M	207.145.1.202	503-352...	86 Michigan Junc...	Salem	OR	97306	44.8685	-123.0438	2010-03-15 00:00:00
30046	[null]	Nanete	Hassur	[null]	nhassu...	F	232.115.170...	209-364...	13961 Steensland...	Stoc...	CA	95205	37.9625	-121.2624	2010-03-15 00:00:00
35583	[null]	Betleanne	Rulf	[null]	brulfrj6...	F	52.208.248.90	503-396...	1 Cordelia Crossing	Salem	OR	97306	44.8685	-123.0438	2010-03-15 00:00:00
22640	[null]	Shana	Nugent	[null]	snuge...	F	207.239.127...	202-378...	96725 Cordelia La...	Was...	DC	20010	38.9327	-77.0322	2010-03-16 00:00:00
34189	[null]	Devlin	Barhems	[null]	dbarhe...	M	180.175.21.2...	240-895...	0 Park Meadow St...	Rock...	MD	20851	39.0763	-77.1234	2010-03-16 00:00:00
46277	Mr	Salomon	Rillatt	[null]	srillatt...	M	83.205.86.187	504-700...	5799 Thackeray C...	New ...	LA	70179	30.033	-89.9826	2010-03-16 00:00:00

Figure 2.8: Customers with a phone number ordered by the date
the customer was added to the database

> **Note**
>
> The solution for the activity can be found on page 317.

In this activity, we used various basic keywords in a **SELECT** query and helped the marketing manager to get the data they needed.

Creating Tables

Now that we know how to read data from tables, we will now look at how to create new tables. There are fundamentally two ways to create tables: creating blank tables or using **SELECT** queries.

Creating Blank Tables

To create a new blank table, we use the **CREATE TABLE** statement. This statement takes the following structure:

```
CREATE TABLE {table_name} (

{column_name_1} {data_type_1} {column_constraint_1},

{column_name_2} {data_type_2} {column_constraint_2},

{column_name_3} {data_type_3} {column_constraint_3},

...

{column_name_last} {data_type_last} {column_constraint_last},

);
```

Here **{table_name}** is the name of the table, **{column_name}** is the name of the column, **{data_type}** is the data type of the column, and **{column_constraint}** is one or more optional keywords giving special properties to the column. Before we discuss how to use the **CREATE TABLE** query, we will first discuss column constraints.

Column Constraints

Column constraints are keywords that give special properties to a column. Some major column constraints are:

- **NOT NULL**: This constraint guarantees that no value in a column can be null.

- **UNIQUE**: This constraint guarantees that every single row for a column has a unique value and that no value is repeated.

- **PRIMARY KEY**: This is a special constraint that is unique for each row and helps to find the row quicker. Only one column in a table can be a primary key.

Suppose we want to create a table called **state_populations**, and it has columns with states' initials and populations. The query would look like this:

```
CREATE TABLE state_populations (^state VARCHAR(2) PRIMARY KEY,

population NUMERIC

);
```

> **Note**
>
> Sometimes, you may run a **CREATE TABLE** query and get the error "relation
> **{table_name}** already exists". This simply means that a table with the same name
> already exists. You will either have to delete the table with the same name or
> change the name of your table.

We will now discuss the next way to create a table, which is by using a SQL query.

Exercise 7: Creating a Table in SQL

In this exercise, we will create a table using the **CREATE TABLE** statement. The marketing team at ZoomZoom would like to create a table called **countries** to analyze the data of different countries. It should have four columns: an integer key column, a unique name column, a founding year column, and a capital column.

Perform the following steps to complete the exercise:

1. Open your favorite SQL client and connect to the **sqlda** database.

2. Run the following query to create the **countries** table:

   ```
   CREATE TABLE countries (
   key INT PRIMARY KEY,
   name text UNIQUE,
   founding_year INT,
   capital text
   );
   ```

   You should get a blank table as follows:

Figure 2.9: Blank countries' table with column names

In this exercise, we learned how to create a table using different column constraints and the **CREATE TABLE** statement.

Creating Tables with SELECT

We know how to create a table. However, say you wanted to create a table using data from an existing table. This can be done using a modification of the **CREATE TABLE** statement:

```
CREATE TABLE {table_name} AS (

{select_query}

);
```

Here, **{select_query}** is any **SELECT** query that can be run in your database. For instance, say you wanted to create a table based on the **products** table that only had products from the year 2014. Let's call this table **products_2014**. You could then write the following query:

```
CREATE TABLE products_2014 AS (

SELECT *

FROM products

WHERE year=2014

);
```

This can be done with any **SELECT** query, and the table will inherit all the properties of the output query.

Updating Tables

Over time, you may also need to modify a table by adding columns, adding new data, or updating existing rows. We will discuss how to do that in this section.

Adding and Removing Columns

To add new columns to an existing table, we use the **ADD COLUMN** statement as in the following query:

```
ALTER TABLE {table_name}
ADD COLUMN {column_name} {data_type};
```

Let's say, for example, that we wanted to add a new column to the **products** table that we will use to store the products' weight in kilograms called **weight**. We could do this by using the following query:

```
ALTER TABLE products
ADD COLUMN weight INT;
```

This query will make a new column called **weight** in the **products** table and will give it the integer data type so that only numbers can be stored within it.

If you want to remove a column from a table, you can use the **DROP** column statement:

```
ALTER TABLE {table_name}
DROP COLUMN {column_name};
```

Here, **{table_name}** is the name of the table you want to change, and **{column_name}** is the name of the column you want to drop.

Let's imagine that you decide to delete the **weight** column you just created. You could get rid of it using the following query:

```
ALTER TABLE products
DROP COLUMN weight;
```

Adding New Data

You can add new data in a table using several methods in SQL.

One method is to simply insert values straight into a table using the **INSERT INTO…VALUES** statement. It has the following structure:

```
INSERT INTO {table_name} ({column_1], {column_2}, …{column_last})
VALUES ({column_value_1}, {column_value_2}, … {column_value_last});
```

Here, **{table_name}** is the name of the table you want to insert your data into, **{column_1}, {column_2}, … {column_last}** is a list of the columns whose values you want to insert, and **{column_value_1}, {column_value_2}, … {column_value_last}** is the values of the rows you want to insert into the table. If a column in the table is not put into the **INSERT** statement, the column is assumed to have a **NULL** value.

As an example, let's say you wanted to insert a new scooter into the **products** table. This could be done with the following query:

```
INSERT INTO products (product_id, model, year, product_type, base_msrp,
production_start_date, production_end_date)
VALUES (13, "Nimbus 5000", 2019, 'scooter', 500.00, '2019-03-03', '2020-03-
03');
```

Another way to insert data into a table is to use the **INSERT** statement with a **SELECT** query using the following syntax:

```
INSERT INTO {table_name} ({column_1], {column_2}, …{column_last})

{select_query};
```

Here, **{table_name}** is the name of the table into which you want to insert the data, **{column_1}, {column_2}, … {column_last}** is a list of the columns whose values you want to insert, and **{select query}** is a query with the same structure as the values you want to insert into the table.

Take the example of the **products_2014** table we discussed earlier. Imagine that instead of creating it with a **SELECT** query, we created it as a blank table with the same structure as the **products** table. If we wanted to insert the same data as we did earlier, we could use the following query:

```
INSERT INTO products (product_id, model, year, product_type, base_msrp,
production_start_date, production_end_date)

SELECT *

FROM products

WHERE year=2014;
```

Updating Existing Rows

Sometimes, you may need to update the values of the data present in a table. To do this, you can use the **UPDATE** statement:

```
UPDATE {table_name}

SET {column_1} = {column_value_1},

    {column_2} = {column_value_2},

    . . .

    {column_last} = {{column_value_last}}

WHERE

  {conditional};
```

Here, **{table_name}** is the name of the table with data that will be changed, **{column_1}, {column_2},… {column_last}** is the columns whose values you want to change, **{column_value_1}, {column_value_2},… {column_value_last}** is the new values you want to insert into those columns, and **{WHERE}** is a conditional statement like one you would find in a SQL query.

To illustrate its use of the update statement, let's say that for the rest of the year, the company has decided to sell all scooter models before 2018 for $299.99. We could change the data in the **products** table using the following query:

```
UPDATE products

SET base_msrp = 299.99,

WHERE

product_type = 'scooter'

AND year<2018;
```

Exercise 8: Updating Tables in SQL

Our goal in this exercise is to update the data in a table using the **UPDATE** statement. Due to the higher cost of rare metals needed to manufacture an electric vehicle, the new 2019 Model Chi will need to undergo a price hike of 10%. Update the **products** table to increase the price of this product.

Perform the following steps to complete the exercise:

1. Open your favorite SQL client and connect to the **sqlda** database.

2. Run the following query to update the price of **Model Chi** in the **products** table:

```
UPDATE products
SET base_msrp = base_msrp*1.10
WHERE model='Model Chi'
and year=2019;
```

3. Now, write the **SELECT** query to check whether the price of **Model Chi** in **2019** has been updated:

```
SELECT *
FROM products
WHERE model='Model Chi'
AND year=2019;
```

The following is the output of the preceding code:

product_id	model	year	product_type	base_msrp	production_start_date	production_end_date
11	Model Chi	2019	automobile	104500	2019-02-04 00:00:00	NULL

Figure 2.10: The updated price of Model Chi in 2019

As seen in the output, the price of **Model Chi** is now **104,500**, which was previously $95,000.

In this exercise, we learned how to update a table using the **UPDATE** statement.

We will now discuss how to delete tables and data from tables.

Deleting Data and Tables

We often discover that data in a table is incorrect, and therefore can no longer be used. At such times, we need to delete data from a table.

Deleting Values from a Row

Often, we will be interested in deleting a value in a row. The easiest way to accomplish this task is to use the **UPDATE** structure we already discussed and to set the column value to **NULL** like so:

```
UPDATE {table_name}
SET {column_1} = NULL,
    {column_2} = NULL,
    ...
    {column_last} = NULL
WHERE
  {conditional};
```

Here, **{table_name}** is the name of the table with the data that needs to be changed, **{column_1}, {column_2},… {column_last}** is the columns whose values you want to delete, and **{WHERE}** is a conditional statement like one you would find in a SQL query.

Let's say, for instance, that we have the wrong email on file for the customer with the customer ID equal to **3**. To fix that, we can use the following query:

```
UPDATE customers
SET email = NULL
WHERE customer_id=3;
```

Deleting Rows from a Table

Deleting a row from a table can be done using the **DELETE** statement, which looks like this:

```
DELETE FROM {table_name}
WHERE {conditional};
DELETE FROM customers
WHERE email='bjordan2@geocities.com';
```

If we wanted to delete all the data in the **customers** table without deleting the table, we could write the following query:

```
DELETE FROM customers;
```

Alternatively, if you want to delete all the data in a query without deleting the table, you could use the **TRUNCATE** keyword as follows:

```
TRUNCATE TABLE customers;
```

Deleting Tables

To delete the table along with the data completely, you can just use the **DROP TABLE** statement with the following syntax:

```
DROP TABLE {table_name};
```

Here, **{table_name}** is the name of the table you want to delete. If we wanted to delete all the data in the **customers** table along with the table itself, we would write:

```
DROP TABLE customers;
```

Exercise 9: Unnecessary Reference Table

The marketing team has finished analyzing the potential number of customers they have in every state, and no longer need the **state_populations** table. To save space on the database, delete the table.

Perform the following steps to complete the exercise:

1. Open your favorite SQL client and connect to the **sqlda** database.

2. Run the following query to drop the **state_populations** table:

   ```
   DROP TABLE state_populations;
   ```

   The **state_populations** table should now be deleted from the database.

3. Since the table has just been dropped, a **SELECT** query on this table throws an error, as expected:

   ```
   SELECT * FROM state_populations;
   ```

   You will find the error shown in the following diagram:

   ```
   ERROR:  relation "state_populations" does not exist
   LINE 1: select * from state_populations;
                         ^
   ```

   Figure 2.11: Error shown as the state_populations table was dropped

In this exercise, we learned how to delete a table using the **DROP TABLE** statement.

Activity 4: Marketing Operations

You did a great job pulling data for the marketing team. However, the marketing manager, who you so graciously helped, realized that they had made a mistake. It turns out that instead of just the query, the manager needs to create a new table in the company's analytics database. Furthermore, they need to make some changes to the data that is present in the **customers** table. It is your job to help the marketing manager with the table:

1. Create a new table called **customers_nyc** that pulls all rows from the **customers** table where the customer lives in New York City in the state of New York.

2. Delete from the new table all customers in postal code **10014**. Due to local laws, they will not be eligible for marketing.

3. Add a new text column called **event**.

4. Set the value of the event to **thank-you party**.

    Expected Output:

customer_id bigint	title text	first_name text	last_name text	suffix text	email text	gender text	ip_address text	phone text	street_address text	city text	state text	postal_code text	latitude double precision	longitude double precision	date_added timestamp without time zone	event text
52	[null]	Giusto	Backe	[null]	gbacke...	M	26.56.68.189	212-959...	6 Onsgard Terrace	New ...	NY	10131	40.7808	-73.9772	2010-07-05 00:00:00	thank-you party
406	[null]	Rozina	Jeal	[null]	rjeal9...	F	50.235.32.29	917-610...	64653 Homewoo...	New ...	NY	10105	40.7628	-73.9785	2010-09-15 00:00:00	thank-you party
456	Rev	Cybil	Noke	[null]	cnokec...	F	5.31.139.106	212-306...	88 Sycamore Park...	New ...	NY	10260	40.7808	-73.9772	2017-01-21 00:00:00	thank-you party
472	[null]	Rawley	Yegorov	[null]	ryegor...	M	183.199.249...	212-560...	872 Old Shore Par...	New ...	NY	10094	40.8662	-73.9221	2014-11-24 00:00:00	thank-you party
496	[null]	Layton	Spoilton	[null]	lspolto...	M	108.112.9.165	646-900...	7 Old Gate Drive	New ...	NY	10024	40.7864	-73.9764	2010-12-20 00:00:00	thank-you party
1028	[null]	Issy	Andrieux	[null]	iandrie...	F	199.50.5.37	212-296...	33337 Dahle Way	New ...	NY	10115	40.8111	-73.9642	2017-11-27 00:00:00	thank-you party
1037	[null]	Magdalene	Veryard	[null]	mverya...	F	93.201.129.2...	[null]	41028 Katie Junct...	New ...	NY	10039	40.8265	-73.9383	2014-03-04 00:00:00	thank-you party
1063	[null]	Juliet	Bredles	[null]	jbesdle...	F	47.96.88.226	212-645...	34984 Goodland ...	New ...	NY	10120	40.7506	-73.9894	2014-08-17 00:00:00	thank-you party
1211	[null]	Gwyneth	McCobb	[null]	gmoco...	F	39.182.161.2...	[null]	4 Jana Park	New ...	NY	10160	40.7808	-73.9772	2014-01-08 00:00:00	thank-you party
1262	[null]	Conrado	Escoffier	[null]	cescofl...	M	28.126.12.44	646-523...	2 Atwood Court	New ...	NY	10060	40.7808	-73.9772	2015-02-17 00:00:00	thank-you party

Figure 2.12: The customers_nyc table with event set as 'thank-you party'

5. You've told the manager that you've completed these steps. He tells the marketing operations team, who then uses the data to launch a marketing campaign. The marketing manager thanks you and then asks you to delete the **customers_nyc** table.

> **Note**
>
> The solution for the activity can be found on page 319.

In this activity, we used different CRUD operations to modify a table as requested by the marketing manager. We will now come full circle to talk about how SQL and analytics connect.

SQL and Analytics

In this chapter, we went through the basics of SQL, tables, and queries. You may be wondering, then, what SQL has to do with analytics. You may have seen some parallels between the first two chapters. When we talk about a SQL table, it should be clear that it can be thought of as a dataset. Rows can be considered individual units of observation and columns can be considered features. If we view SQL tables in this way, we can see that SQL is a natural way to store datasets in a computer.

However, SQL can go further than just providing a convenient way to store datasets. Modern SQL implementations also provide tools for processing and analyzing data through various functions. Using SQL, we can clean data, transform data to more useful formats, and analyze data with statistics to find interesting patterns. The rest of this book will be dedicated to understanding how SQL can be used for these purposes productively and efficiently.

Summary

Relational databases are a mature and ubiquitous technology that is used to store and query data. Relational databases store data in the form of relations, also known as tables, which allow for an excellent combination of performance, efficiency, and ease of use. SQL is the language used to access relational databases. SQL is a declarative language that allows users to focus on what to create, as opposed to how to create it. SQL supports many different data types, including numeric data, text data, and even data structures.

When querying data, SQL allows a user to pick which fields to pull, as well as how to filter the data. This data can also be ordered, and SQL allows for as much or as little data as we need to be pulled. Creating, updating, and deleting data is also fairly simple and can be quite surgical.

Now that we have reviewed the basics of SQL, we will discuss how SQL can be used to perform the first step in data analytics, cleaning, and the transformation of data, in the next chapter.

3

SQL for Data Preparation

Learning Objectives

By the end of this chapter, you will be able to:

- Assemble multiple tables and queries together into a dataset

- Transform and clean data using SQL functions

- Remove duplicate data using DISTINCT and DISTINCT ON

In this chapter, we will learn to clean and prepare our data for analysis using SQL techniques.

Introduction

In the previous chapter, we discussed the basics of SQL and how to work with individual tables in SQL. We also used CRUD (create, read, update and delete) operations on a table. These tables are the foundation for all the work undertaken in analytics. One of the first tasks implemented in analytics is to create clean datasets. According to Forbes, it is estimated that, almost 80% of the time spent by analytics professionals involves preparing data for use in analysis and building models with unclean data which harms analysis by leading to poor conclusions. SQL can help in this tedious but important task, by providing ways to build datasets which are clean, in an efficient manner. We will start by discussing how to assemble data using **JOIN**s and **UNION**s. Then, we will use different functions, such as **CASE WHEN**, **COALESCE**, **NULLIF**, and **LEAST/GREATEST**, to clean data. We will then discuss how to transform and remove duplicate data from queries using the **DISTINCT** command.

Assembling Data

Connecting Tables Using JOIN

In *Chapter 2, The Basics of SQL for Analytics*, we discussed how we can query data from a table. However, the majority of the time, the data you are interested in is spread across multiple tables. Fortunately, SQL has methods for bringing related tables together using the **JOIN** keyword.

To illustrate, let's look at two tables in our database – dealerships and salespeople. In the salespeople table, we observe that we have a column called **dealership_id**. This **dealership_id** column is a direct reference to the **dealership_id** column in the dealerships table. When table A has a column that references the primary key of table B, the column is said to be a foreign key to table A. In this case, the **dealership_id** column in **salespeople** is a foreign key to the dealerships table.

> **Note**
>
> Foreign keys can also be added as a column constraint to a table in order to improve the integrity of the data by making sure that the foreign key never contains a value that cannot be found in the referenced table. This data property is known as **referential integrity**. Adding foreign key constraints can also help to improve performance in some databases. Foreign key constraints are beyond the scope of this book and, in most instances, your company's data engineers and database administrators will deal with these details. You can learn more about foreign key constraints in the PostgreSQL documentation at the following link: https://www.postgresql.org/docs/9.4/tutorial-fk.html.

As these tables are related, you can perform some interesting analyses with these two tables. For instance, you may be interested in determining which salespeople work at a dealership in California. One way of retrieving this information is to first query which dealerships are located in California using the following query:

```
SELECT *
FROM dealerships
WHERE state='CA';
```

This query should give you the following results:

	dealership_id bigint	street_address text	city text	state text	postal_code text	latitude double precision	longitude double precision	date_opened timestamp without time zone	date_closed timestamp without time zone
1	2	808 South Hobart...	Los ...	CA	90005	34.057754	-118.305423	2014-06-01 00:00:00	[null]
2	5	2210 Bunker Hill ...	San ...	CA	94402	37.524487	-122.343609	2014-06-01 00:00:00	[null]

Figure 3.1: Dealerships in California

Now that you know that the only two dealerships in California have IDs of **2** and **5**, respectively, you can then query the salespeople table as follows:

```
SELECT *
FROM salespeople
WHERE dealership_id in (2, 5)
ORDER BY 1;
```

The results will be similar to the following:

salesperson_id bigint	dealership_id bigint	title text	first_name text	last_name text	suffix text	username text	gender text	hire_date timestamp without time zone	termination_date timestamp without time zone
23	2	[null]	Beauregard	Peschke	[null]	bpeschkem	Male	2018-09-12 00:00:00	[null]
51	5	[null]	Lanette	Gerriessen	[null]	lgerriessen1e	Female	2018-06-24 00:00:00	[null]
57	5	[null]	Spense	Pithcock	[null]	spithcock1k	Male	2017-12-15 00:00:00	[null]
61	5	[null]	Ludvig	Baynam	[null]	lbaynam1o	Male	2016-08-25 00:00:00	[null]
62	2	[null]	Carroll	Pudan	[null]	cpudan1p	Female	2016-05-17 00:00:00	[null]
63	2	[null]	Adrianne	Otham	[null]	aotham1q	Female	2014-12-20 00:00:00	[null]
71	2	[null]	Georgianna	Bastian	[null]	gbastian1y	Female	2018-12-23 00:00:00	[null]
75	2	[null]	Saundra	Shoebottom	[null]	sshoebotto...	Female	2018-03-18 00:00:00	[null]
108	2	[null]	Hale	Brigshaw	[null]	hbrigshaw2z	Male	2015-07-30 00:00:00	[null]

Figure 3.2: Salespeople in California

While this method gives you the results you want, it is tedious to perform two queries to get these results. What would make this query easier would be to somehow add the information from the dealerships table to the salespeople table and then filter for users in California. SQL provides such a tool with the **JOIN** clause. The **JOIN** clause is a SQL clause that allows a user to join one or more tables together based on distinct conditions.

Types of Joins

In this chapter, we will discuss three fundamental joins, which are illustrated in *Figure 3.3*: inner joins, outer joins, and cross joins:

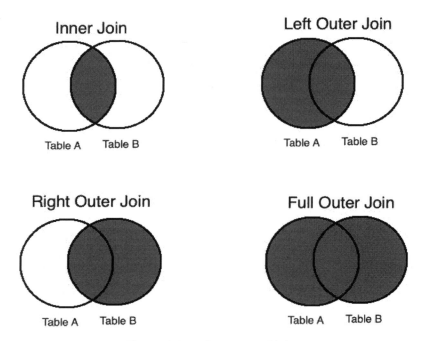

Figure 3.3: Major types of joins

INNER JOIN

The inner join connects rows in different tables together based on a condition known as the **join predicate**. In many cases, the join predicate is a logical condition of equality. Each row in the first table is compared against every other row in the second table. For row combinations that meet the inner join predicate, that row is returned in the query. Otherwise, the row combination is discarded.

Inner joins are usually written in the following form:

```
SELECT {columns}
FROM {table1}
INNER JOIN {table2} ON {table1}.{common_key_1}={table2}.{common_key_2}
```

Here, **{columns}** are the columns you want to get from the joined table, **{table1}** is the first table, **{table2}** is the second table, **{common_key_1}** is the column in **{table1}** you want to join on, and **{common_key_2}** is the column in **{table2}** to join on.

Now, let's go back to the two tables we discussed – dealerships and salespeople. As mentioned earlier, it would be good if we could append the information from the dealerships table to the salespeople table in order to know which state each dealer works in. For the time being, let's assume that all the salespeople IDs have a valid **dealership_id**.

> **Note**
>
> At this point in the book, you do not have the necessary skills to verify that every dealership ID is valid in the salespeople table, and so we assume it. However, in real-world scenarios, it will be important for you to validate these things on your own. Generally speaking, there are very few datasets and systems that guarantee clean data.

We can join the two tables using an equal's condition in the join predicate, as follows:

```
SELECT *

FROM salespeople

INNER JOIN dealerships

    ON salespeople.dealership_id = dealerships.dealership_id

ORDER BY 1;
```

This query will produce the following output:

salesperson_id bigint	dealership_id bigint	title text	first_name text	last_name text	suffix text	username text	gender text	hire_date timestamp without time zone	termination_date timestamp without time zone	dealership_id bigint	street_address text	city text	state text	postal_code text
1	17	[null]	Electra	Elleyne	[null]	eelleyne0	Female	2017-05-31 00:00:00	[null]	17	2120 Walnut Street	Phila...	PA	19092
2	6	[null]	Montague	Alcoran	[null]	malcoran1	Male	2018-12-31 00:00:00	[null]	6	7315 California A...	Seatt...	WA	98136
3	17	[null]	Ethyl	Sloss	IV	esloss2	Female	2016-08-10 00:00:00	[null]	17	2120 Walnut Street	Phila...	PA	19092
4	10	[null]	Nester	Dugood	[null]	ndugood3	Male	2017-06-03 00:00:00	[null]	10	7425 Wilson Aven...	Chic...	IL	60706
5	17	[null]	Cornall	Swanger	[null]	cswanger4	Male	2018-05-17 00:00:00	[null]	17	2120 Walnut Street	Phila...	PA	19092
6	8	[null]	Ellary	Nend	[null]	enend5	Male	2016-05-07 00:00:00	[null]	8	5938 Comfoot Ro...	Portl...	OR	97218
7	1	[null]	Granville	Fidell	[null]	gfidell6	Male	2017-06-17 00:00:00	[null]	1	52 Hillside Terrace	Millb...	NJ	07039
8	18	[null]	Lanie	Tisun	[null]	ltisun7	Male	2017-12-12 00:00:00	[null]	18	1447 Hardesty Av...	Kans...	MO	64195
9	14	[null]	Lamar	Treleven	[null]	ltreleven8	Male	2018-05-08 00:00:00	[null]	14	800 North Mays S...	Roun...	TX	78664

Figure 3.4: Salespeople table joined to the dealerships table

As you can see in the preceding output, the table is the result of joining the salespeople table to the dealerships table (note also that the first table listed in the query, salespeople, is on the left-hand side of the result, while the dealerships table is on the right-hand side. This is important to understand for the next section). More specifically, **dealership_id** in the **salespeople** table matches the **dealership_id**, in the dealerships table. This shows how the join predicate is met. By running this join query, we have effectively created a new "super dataset" consisting of the two tables merged together where the two **dealership_id** columns are equal.

We can now query this "super-dataset" the same way we would query one large table using the clauses and keywords from *Chapter 1*, *Understanding and Describing Data*. For example, going back to our multi-query issue to determine which sales query works in California, we can now address it with one easy query:

```
SELECT *

FROM salespeople

INNER JOIN dealerships

    ON salespeople.dealership_id = dealerships.dealership_id

WHERE dealerships.state = 'CA'

ORDER BY 1
```

This gives us the following output:

	salesperson_id bigint	dealership_id bigint	title text	first_name text	last_name text	suffix text	username text	gender text	hire_date timestamp without time zone	termination_date timestamp without time zone	dealership_id bigint	street_address text	city text
1	23	2	[null]	Beauregard	Peschke	[null]	bpeschkem	Male	2018-09-12 00:00:00	[null]	2	808 South Hobart...	Los ...
2	51	5	[null]	Lanette	Gerriessen	[null]	lgerriessen1e	Female	2018-06-24 00:00:00	[null]	5	2210 Bunker Hill ...	San ...
3	57	5	[null]	Spense	Pithcock	[null]	spithcock1k	Male	2017-12-15 00:00:00	[null]	5	2210 Bunker Hill ...	San ...
4	61	5	[null]	Ludvig	Baynam	[null]	lbaynam1o	Male	2016-08-25 00:00:00	[null]	5	2210 Bunker Hill ...	San ...
5	62	2	[null]	Carroll	Pudan	[null]	cpudan1p	Female	2016-05-17 00:00:00	[null]	2	808 South Hobart...	Los ...
6	63	2	[null]	Adrianne	Otham	[null]	aotham1q	Female	2014-12-20 00:00:00	[null]	2	808 South Hobart...	Los ...
7	71	2	[null]	Georgianna	Bastian	[null]	gbastian1y	Female	2018-12-23 00:00:00	[null]	2	808 South Hobart...	Los ...
8	75	2	[null]	Saundra	Shoebottom	[null]	sshoebotto...	Female	2018-03-18 00:00:00	[null]	2	808 South Hobart...	Los ...
9	108	2	[null]	Hale	Brigshaw	[null]	hbrigshaw2z	Male	2015-07-30 00:00:00	[null]	2	808 South Hobart...	Los ...

Figure 3.5: Salespeople in California with one query

Careful readers will observe that the output in *Figure* 3.2 and *Figure* 3.5 are nearly identical, with the exception being that the table in *Figure* 3.5 has dealerships' data appended as well. If we want to isolate just the salespeople table portion of this, we can select the salespeople columns using the following star syntax:

```
SELECT salespeople.*

FROM salespeople

INNER JOIN dealerships

    ON dealerships.dealership_id = salespeople.dealership_id

WHERE dealerships.state = 'CA'

ORDER BY 1;
```

There is one other shortcut that can help when writing statements with several join clauses: you can alias table names so that you do not have to type out the entire name of the table every time. Simply write the name of the alias after the first mention of the table after the join clause, and you can save a decent amount of typing. For instance, for the last preceding query, if we wanted to alias salespeople with **s** and dealerships with **d**, you could write the following statement:

```
SELECT s.*
FROM salespeople s
INNER JOIN dealerships d
    ON d.dealership_id = s.dealership_id
WHERE d.state = 'CA'
ORDER BY 1;
```

Alternatively, you can also put the **AS** keyword between the table name and alias to make the alias more explicit:

```
SELECT s.*
FROM salespeople AS s
INNER JOIN dealerships AS d
    ON d.dealership_id = s.dealership_id
WHERE d.state = 'CA'
ORDER BY 1;
```

Now that we have cleared up the basics of inner joins, we will discuss outer joins.

OUTER JOIN

As discussed, inner joins will only return rows from the two tables, and only if the join predicate is met for both rows. Otherwise, no rows from either table are returned. Sometimes, however, we want to return all rows from one of the tables regardless of whether the join predicate is met. In this case, the join predicate is not met; the row for the second table will be returned as **NULL**. These joins, where at least one table will be represented in every row after the join operation, are known as **<u>outer joins</u>**.

Outer joins can be classified into three categories: left outer joins, right outer joins, and full outer joins.

Left outer joins are where the left table (that is, the table mentioned first in a join clause) will have every row returned. If a row from the other table is not found, a row of **NULL** is returned. Left outer joins are performed by using the **LEFT OUTER JOIN** keywords followed by a join predicate. This can also be written in short as **LEFT JOIN**. To show how left outer joins work, let's examine two tables: the **customers** tables and the **emails** table. For the time being, assume that not every customer has been sent an email, and we want to mail all customers who have not received an email. We can use outer joins to make that happen. Let's do a left outer join between the customer table on the left and the **emails** table on the right. To help manage output, we will only limit it to the first 1,000 rows. The following code snippet is utilized:

```
SELECT *
FROM customers c
LEFT OUTER JOIN emails e ON e.customer_id=c.customer_id
ORDER BY c.customer_id
LIMIT 1000;
```

Following is the output of the preceding code:

customer_id bigint	title text	first_name text	last_name text	suffix text	email text	gender text	ip_address text	phone text	street_address text	city text	state text	postal_code text	latitude double precision	longitude double precision	date_added timestamp without time zone	email_id bigint
1	[null]	Arlena	Riveles	[null]	arivele...	F	98.36.172.246	[null]	[null]	[null]	[null]	[null]		[null]	2017-04-23 00:00:00	282584
1	[null]	Arlena	Riveles	[null]	arivele...	F	98.36.172.246	[null]	[null]	[null]	[null]	[null]		[null]	2017-04-23 00:00:00	370722
1	[null]	Arlena	Riveles	[null]	arivele...	F	98.36.172.246	[null]	[null]	[null]	[null]	[null]		[null]	2017-04-23 00:00:00	323983
2	Dr	Ode	Stovin	[null]	ostovin...	M	16.97.59.186	314-534...	2573 Fordem Par...	Saint...	MO	63116	38.5814	-90.2625	2014-10-02 00:00:00	323984
2	Dr	Ode	Stovin	[null]	ostovin...	M	16.97.59.186	314-534...	2573 Fordem Par...	Saint...	MO	63116	38.5814	-90.2625	2014-10-02 00:00:00	245816
2	Dr	Ode	Stovin	[null]	ostovin...	M	16.97.59.186	314-534...	2573 Fordem Par...	Saint...	MO	63116	38.5814	-90.2625	2014-10-02 00:00:00	144183
2	Dr	Ode	Stovin	[null]	ostovin...	M	16.97.59.186	314-534...	2573 Fordem Par...	Saint...	MO	63116	38.5814	-90.2625	2014-10-02 00:00:00	370723
2	Dr	Ode	Stovin	[null]	ostovin...	M	16.97.59.186	314-534...	2573 Fordem Par...	Saint...	MO	63116	38.5814	-90.2625	2014-10-02 00:00:00	282585
2	Dr	Ode	Stovin	[null]	ostovin...	M	16.97.59.186	314-534...	2573 Fordem Par...	Saint...	MO	63116	38.5814	-90.2625	2014-10-02 00:00:00	117146
2	Dr	Ode	Stovin	[null]	ostovin...	M	16.97.59.186	314-534...	2579 Fordem Par...	Saint...	MO	63116	38.5814	-90.2625	2014-10-02 00:00:00	209804
2	Dr	Ode	Stovin	[null]	ostovin...	M	16.97.59.186	314-534...	2573 Fordem Par...	Saint...	MO	63116	38.5814	-90.2625	2014-10-02 00:00:00	174737
2	Dr	Ode	Stovin	[null]	ostovin...	M	16.97.59.186	314-534...	2573 Fordem Par...	Saint...	MO	63116	38.5814	-90.2625	2014-10-02 00:00:00	91913
3	[null]	Braden	Jordan	[null]	bjorda...	M	192.86.248.59	[null]	5651 Kennedy Park	Pens...	FL	32590	30.6143	-87.2758	2018-10-27 00:00:00	323985

Figure 3.6: Customers left-joined to emails

When you look at the output of the query, you should see that entries from the customer table are present. However, for some of the rows, such as for customer row 27 which can be seen in *Figure* 3.7, the columns belonging to the **emails** table are completely full of nulls. This arrangement explains how the outer join is different from the inner join. If the inner join was used, the **customer_id** column would not be blank. This query, however, is still useful because we can now use it to find people who have never received an email. Because those customers who were never sent an email have a null **customer_id** column in the **emails** table, we can find all of these customers by checking the **customer_id** column in the **emails** table as follows:

```
SELECT *
FROM customers c
LEFT OUTER JOIN emails e ON c.customer_id = e.customer_id
WHERE e.customer_id IS NULL
```

```
ORDER BY c.customer_id

LIMIT 1000
```

We then get the following output:

customer_id bigint	title text	first_name text	last_name text	suffix text	email text	gender text	ip_address text	phone text	street_address text	city text	state text	postal_code text	latitude double preci	longitude double prec	date_added timestamp without time zone	email_id bigint	customer_id bigint	email_subjec text
27	[null]	Anson	Fellibrand	[null]	afellbr...	M	64.80.85.50	203-107...	65 Shelley Road	New ...	CT	06505	41.3057	-72.7799	2019-04-07 00:00:00	[null]	[null]	[null]
32	[null]	Hamnet	Purselowe	[null]	hpurse...	M	225.215.209...	239-462...	5 Johnson Way	Napl...	FL	34102	26.134	-81.7953	2019-02-07 00:00:00	[null]	[null]	[null]
70	[null]	Caty	Woolveridge	[null]	cwoolv...	F	104.21.118.34	757-238...	[null]	[null]	[null]	[null]	[null]	[null]	2019-04-09 00:00:00	[null]	[null]	[null]
77	[null]	Donal	Lattey	[null]	dlattey...	M	5.31.114.103	304-575...	48889 Laurel Pass	Charl...	WV	25326	38.2948	-81.5547	2019-05-25 00:00:00	[null]	[null]	[null]
112	[null]	Harcourt	Cripps	[null]	hcripp...	M	219.20.188.2...	951-922...	9 Hoard Place	San ...	CA	92410	34.1069	-117.2978	2019-02-21 00:00:00	[null]	[null]	[null]
113	[null]	Giffy	Bennington	Jr	gbenni...	M	181.117.182...	202-767...	7861 Michigan Po...	Was...	DC	20231	38.8933	-77.0146	2019-02-13 00:00:00	[null]	[null]	[null]
125	[null]	Bernard	Jirka	[null]	bjirka3...	M	124.58.237.8	[null]	112 Lunder Hill	Pitts...	PA	15215	40.5048	-79.9136	2019-03-17 00:00:00	[null]	[null]	[null]
192	[null]	Selina	Heerl	[null]	sheerl...	F	174.136.106...	585-208...	842 Moulton Court	Roch...	NY	14646	43.286	-77.6843	2019-04-09 00:00:00	[null]	[null]	[null]
199	[null]	Mercy	Martschik	[null]	mmart...	F	63.73.23.98	352-750...	66647 Stone Corn...	Broo...	FL	34605	28.5059	-82.4226	2019-04-01 00:00:00	[null]	[null]	[null]
212	[null]	Norma	Goldis	[null]	ngoldi...	F	90.182.242.61	215-737...	4865 Sauthoff Cir...	Phila...	PA	19125	39.9788	-75.1262	2019-03-26 00:00:00	[null]	[null]	[null]

Figure 3.7: Customers with no emails sent

As you can see, all entries are blank in the **customer_id** column, indicating that they have not received any emails. We could simply grab the emails from this join to get all customers who have not received an email.

A **right outer join** is very similar to a left join, except the table on the "right" (the second listed table) will now have every row show up, and the "left" table will have **NULLs** if the join condition is not met. To illustrate, let's "flip" the last query by right-joining the **emails** table to the **customers** table with the following query:

```
SELECT *

FROM emails e

RIGHT OUTER JOIN customers c ON e.customer_id=c.customer_id

ORDER BY c.customer_id

LIMIT 1000;
```

When you run this query, you will get something similar to the following result:

email_id bigint	customer_id bigint	email_subject text	opened text	clicked text	bounced text	sent_date timestamp without time zone	opened_date timestamp without time zone	clicked_date timestamp without time zone	customer_id bigint	title text	first_name text	last_name text	suffix text
282584	1	Black Friday. Gre...	t	f	f	2017-11-24 15:00:00	2017-11-26 01:12:32	[null]	1	[null]	Ariena	Riveles	[null]
370722	1	A New Year, And ...	f	f	f	2019-01-07 15:00:00	[null]	[null]	1	[null]	Ariena	Riveles	[null]
323983	1	Save the Planet ...	f	f	f	2018-11-23 15:00:00	[null]	[null]	1	[null]	Ariena	Riveles	[null]
323984	2	Save the Planet ...	f	f	f	2018-11-23 15:00:00	[null]	[null]	2	Dr	Ode	Stovin	[null]
245816	2	We Really Outdid...	t	f	f	2017-01-15 15:00:00	2017-01-16 09:23:16	[null]	2	Dr	Ode	Stovin	[null]
144183	2	Tis' the Season f...	f	f	f	2015-11-26 15:00:00	[null]	[null]	2	Dr	Ode	Stovin	[null]
370723	2	A New Year, And ...	f	f	f	2019-01-07 15:00:00	[null]	[null]	2	Dr	Ode	Stovin	[null]
282585	2	Black Friday. Gre...	f	f	f	2017-11-24 15:00:00	[null]	[null]	2	Dr	Ode	Stovin	[null]
117146	2	An Electric Car f...	f	f	f	2015-04-01 15:00:00	[null]	[null]	2	Dr	Ode	Stovin	[null]
209804	2	25% off all EVs. i...	f	f	f	2016-11-25 15:00:00	[null]	[null]	2	Dr	Ode	Stovin	[null]
174737	2	Like a Bat out of ...	f	f	f	2016-09-21 15:00:00	[null]	[null]	2	Dr	Ode	Stovin	[null]
91913	2	Zoom Zoom Bla...	f	f	f	2014-11-28 15:00:00	[null]	[null]	2	Dr	Ode	Stovin	[null]
323985	3	Save the Planet ...	f	f	f	2018-11-23 15:00:00	[null]	[null]	3	[null]	Braden	Jordan	[null]
370724	3	A New Year, And ...	f	f	f	2019-01-07 15:00:00	[null]	[null]	3	[null]	Braden	Jordan	[null]
323986	4	Save the Planet ...	f	f	f	2018-11-23 15:00:00	[null]	[null]	4	[null]	Jessika	Nussen	[null]
282586	4	Black Friday. Gre...	f	f	f	2017-11-24 15:00:00	[null]	[null]	4	[null]	Jessika	Nussen	[null]
370725	4	A New Year, And ...	f	f	f	2019-01-07 15:00:00	[null]	[null]	4	[null]	Jessika	Nussen	[null]
323987	5	Save the Planet ...	t	f	f	2018-11-23 15:00:00	2018-11-25 04:31:57	[null]	5	[null]	Lonnie	Rembaud	[null]
174738	5	Like a Bat out of ...	t	f	f	2016-09-21 15:00:00	2016-09-22 10:12:21	[null]	5	[null]	Lonnie	Rembaud	[null]

Figure 3.8: Emails right-joined to customers table

Notice that this output is similar to what was produced in *Figure* 3.7, except that the data from the `emails` table is now on the left-hand side, and the data from the `customers` table is on the right-hand side. Once again, `customer_id` 27 has `NULL` for the email. This shows the symmetry between a right join and a left join.

Finally, there is the **full outer join**. The full outer join will return all rows from the left and right tables, regardless of whether the join predicate is matched. For rows where the join predicate is met, the two rows are combined in a group. For rows where they are not met, the row has `NULL` filled in. The full outer join is invoked by using the `FULL OUTER JOIN` clause, followed by a join predicate. Here is the syntax of this join:

```
SELECT *
FROM email e
FULL OUTER JOIN customers c
ON e.customer_id=c.customer_id;
```

In this section, we learned how to implement three different outer joins. In the next section, we will work with the cross join.

CROSS JOIN

The final type of join we will discuss in this book is the cross join. The cross join is mathematically what is also referred to as the Cartesian product – it returns every possible combination of rows from the "left" table and the "right" table. It can be invoked using a `CROSS JOIN` clause, followed by the name of the other table. For instance, let's take the example of the `products` table.

Let's say we wanted to know every possible combination of two products you could create from a given set of products (like the one found in the `products` table) in order to create a two-month giveaway for marketing purposes. We can use a cross join to get the answer to the question using the following query:

```
SELECT p1.product_id, p1.model, p2.product_id, p2.model
FROM products p1 CROSS JOIN products p2;
```

The output of this query is as follows:

product_id bigint	model text	product_id bigint	model text
1	Lemon	1	Lemon
1	Lemon	2	Lemon Li...
1	Lemon	3	Lemon
1	Lemon	4	Model Chi
1	Lemon	5	Blade
1	Lemon	6	Model Sig...
1	Lemon	7	Bat
1	Lemon	8	Bat Limite...
1	Lemon	9	Model Ep...
1	Lemon	10	Model Ga...
1	Lemon	11	Model Chi
1	Lemon	12	Lemon Ze...
2	Lemon ...	1	Lemon

Figure 3.9: Cross join of a product to itself

You will observe that, in this particular case, we joined a table to itself. This is a perfectly valid operation and is also known as a **self join**. The result of the query has 144 rows, which is the equivalent of multiplying the 12 products by the same number (12 * 12). We can also see that there is no need for a join predicate; indeed, a cross join can simply be thought of as just an outer join with no conditions for joining.

In general, cross joins are not used in practice, and can also be very dangerous if you are not careful. Cross joining two large tables together can lead to the origination of hundreds of billions of rows, which can stall and crash a database. Take care when using them.

> **Note**
>
> To learn more about joins, check out the PostgreSQL documentation here: https://www.postgresql.org/docs/9.1/queries-table-expressions.html.

Up to this point, we have covered the basics of using joins to bring tables together. We will now talk about methods for joining queries together in a dataset.

Exercise 10: Using Joins to Analyze Sales Dealership

The head of sales at your company would like a list of all customers who bought a car. We need to create a query that will return all customer IDs, first names, last names, and valid phone numbers of customers who purchased a car.

> **Note**
>
> For all exercises in this book, we will be using pgAdmin 4. All the code files for the exercises and the activity in this chapter are also available on GitHub: https://github.com/TrainingByPackt/SQL-for-Data-Analytics/tree/master/Lesson03.

To solve this problem, do the following:

1. Open your favorite SQL client and connect to the **sqlda** database.

2. Use inner join to bring the tables' **sales** and **customers** together, which returns data for the following: customer IDs, first names, last names, and valid phone numbers:

```
SELECT c.customer_id,
c.first_name,
c.last_name,
c.phone
FROM sales s
INNER JOIN customers c ON c.customer_id=s.customer_id
INNER JOIN products p ON p.product_id=s.product_id
WHERE p.product_type='automobile'
AND c.phone IS NOT NULL
```

You should get an output similar to the following:

customer_id bigint	first_name text	last_name text	phone text
35824	Wyatan	Dickie	405-786...
13206	Stace	Tuison	810-769...
2958	Kirstyn	Draysay	208-534...
32636	Kile	Fishlee	937-207...
26730	Raina	Titterell	304-871...
23832	Harrietta	Leverette	803-298...
35844	Maura	Clyne	904-169...
43229	Field	Lopes	757-409...
6038	Carey	Swadling	727-426...

Figure 3.10: Customers who bought a car

We can see that after running the query, we were able to join the data from the tables **sales** and **customers** and obtain a list of customers who bought a car.

In this exercise, using joins, we were able to bring together related data easily and efficiently.

Subqueries

As of now, we have been pulling data from tables. However, you may have observed that all **SELECT** queries produce tables as an output. Knowing this, you may wonder whether there is some way to use the tables produced by **SELECT** queries instead of referencing an existing table in your database. The answer is yes. You can simply take a query, insert it between a pair of parentheses, and give it an alias. For example, if we wanted to find all the salespeople working in California, we could have written the query using the following alternative:

```
SELECT *
FROM salespeople
INNER JOIN (
    SELECT * FROM dealerships
    WHERE dealerships.state = 'CA'
```

```
    ) d
  ON d.dealership_id = salespeople.dealership_id
ORDER BY 1
```

Here, instead of joining the two tables and filtering for rows with the state equal to **'CA'**, we first find the dealerships where the state equals **'CA'** and then inner join the rows in that query to **salespeople**.

If a query only has one column, you can use a subquery with the **IN** keyword in a **WHERE** clause. For example, another way to extract the details from the salespeople table using the dealership ID for the state of California would be as follows:

```
SELECT *
FROM salespeople
WHERE dealership_id IN  (
    SELECT dealership_id FROM dealerships
    WHERE dealerships.state = 'CA'
    )
ORDER BY 1
```

As all these examples show, it's quite easy to write the same query using multiple techniques. In the next section, we will talk about unions.

Unions

So far, we have been talking about how to join data horizontally. That is, with joins, new columns are effectively added horizontally. However, we may be interested in putting multiple queries together vertically; that is, by keeping the same number of columns but adding multiple rows. An example may help to clarify this.

Let's say you wanted to visualize the addresses of dealerships and customers using Google Maps. To do this, you would need both the addresses of customers and dealerships You could build a query with all customer addresses as follows:

```
SELECT street_address, city, state, postal_code
FROM customers
WHERE street_address IS NOT NULL;
```

You could also retrieve dealership addresses with the following query:

```
SELECT street_address, city, state, postal_code
FROM dealerships
WHERE street_address IS NOT NULL;
```

However, it would be nice if we could assemble the two queries together into one list with one query. This is where the **UNION** keyword comes into play. Using the two previous queries, we could create the query:

```
(
SELECT street_address, city, state, postal_code
FROM customers
WHERE street_address IS NOT NULL
)
UNION
(
SELECT street_address, city, state, postal_code
FROM dealerships
WHERE street_address IS NOT NULL
)
ORDER BY 1;
```

This produces the following output:

street_address text	city text	state text	postal_code text
00003 Continenta...	Suff...	VA	23436
00003 Sullivan Ro...	Des ...	IA	50981
00006 Birchwood ...	Lake...	FL	33805
00006 Roth Plaza	Fort ...	AR	72916
00006 Vidon Place	Dallas	TX	75358
00027 Judy Place	Hou...	TX	77293
00031 Redwing D...	Minn...	MN	55446
0003 Novick Trail	Mont...	VT	05609
0004 Northport Al...	Boise	ID	83705
0004 Superior Alley	New ...	NJ	08922
0005 Eagle Crest ...	Ralei...	NC	27626

Figure 3.11: Union of Addresses

There are some caveats to using **UNION**. First, **UNION** requires that the subqueries therein have the same name columns and the same data types for the column. If it does not, the query will not run. Second, **UNION** technically may not return all the rows from its subqueries. **UNION**, by default, removes all duplicate rows in the output. If you want to retain the duplicate rows, it is preferable to use the **UNION ALL** keyword.

Exercise 11: Generating an Elite Customer Party Guest List using UNION

In this exercise, we will assemble two queries using unions. In order to help build up marketing awareness for the new Model Chi, the marketing team would like to throw a party for some of ZoomZoom's wealthiest customers in Los Angeles, CA. To help facilitate the party, they would like you to make a guest list with ZoomZoom customers who live in Los Angeles, CA, as well as salespeople who work at the ZoomZoom dealership in Los Angeles, CA. The guest list should include the first name, the last name, and whether the guest is a customer or an employee.

To solve this problem, execute the following:

1. Open your favorite SQL client and connect to the **sqlda** database.

2. Write a query that will make a list of ZoomZoom customers and company employees who live in Los Angeles, CA. The guest list should contain the first name, the last name, and whether the guest is a customer or an employee:

```
(
SELECT first_name, last_name, 'Customer' as guest_type
FROM customers
WHERE city='Los Angeles'
AND state='CA'
)
UNION
(
SELECT first_name, last_name, 'Employee' as guest_type
FROM salespeople s
INNER JOIN dealerships d ON d.dealership_id=s.dealership_id
WHERE d.city='Los Angeles'
AND d.state='CA'
)
```

You should get the following output:

first_name	last_name	guest_type
Euell	MacWhirter	Customer
Martainn	Tordoff	Customer
Truman	Cutmore	Customer
Asher	Drogan	Customer
Kelley	Christley	Customer
Megan	McCourtie	Customer
Free	Errol	Customer
Dick	Steward	Customer
Bing	Connal	Customer
Rea	Arnason	Customer
Powell	Sendley	Customer
Alastair	Blacklawe	Customer
Ada	Beeze	Customer
Orran	Worrall	Customer
Hyman	Gabbitus	Customer
Brandise	Yude	Customer
Barron	Dawney	Customer
Bob	Adamolli	Customer
Carroll	Pudan	Employee
Abbott	Poupard	Customer

Figure 3.12: Customer and employee guest list in Los Angeles, CA

We can see the guest list of customers and employees from Los Angeles, CA after running the UNION query.

In the exercise, we used the UNION keyword to combine rows from different queries effortlessly.

Common Table Expressions

Common table expressions are, in a certain sense, just a different version of subqueries. Common table expressions establish temporary tables by using the `WITH` clause. To understand this clause better, let's have a look at the following query:

```sql
SELECT *
FROM salespeople
INNER JOIN (
    SELECT * FROM dealerships
    WHERE dealerships.state = 'CA'
    ) d
  ON d.dealership_id = salespeople.dealership_id
ORDER BY 1
```

This could be written using common table expressions as follows:

```sql
WITH d as (
SELECT * FROM dealerships
    WHERE dealerships.state = 'CA'
    )
SELECT *
FROM salespeople
INNER JOIN d ON d.dealership_id = salespeople.dealership_id
ORDER BY 1;
```

The one advantage of common table expressions is that they are recursive. **Recursive common table expressions** can reference themselves. Because of this feature, we can use them to solve problems that other queries cannot. However, recursive common table expressions are beyond the scope of this book.

Now that we know several ways to join data together across a database, we will look at how to transform the data from these outputs.

Transforming Data

Often, the raw data presented in a query output may not be in the form we would like it to be. We may want to remove values, substitute values, or map values to other values. To accomplish these tasks, SQL provides a wide variety of statements and functions. Functions are keywords that take in inputs such as a column or a scalar value and change those inputs into some sort of output. We will discuss some very useful functions for cleaning data in the following sections.

CASE WHEN

CASE WHEN is a function that allows a query to map various values in a column to other values. The general format of a **CASE WHEN** statement is:

```
CASE WHEN condition1 THEN value1

WHEN condition2 THEN value2

…

WHEN conditionX THEN valueX

ELSE else_value END
```

Here, **condition1** and **condition2**, through **conditionX**, are Boolean conditions; **value1** and **value2**, through **valueX**, are values to map the Boolean conditions; and **else_value** is the value that is mapped if none of the Boolean conditions are met. For each row, the program starts at the top of the **CASE WHEN** statement and evaluates the first Boolean condition. The program then runs through each Boolean condition from the first one. For the first condition from the start of the statement that evaluates as true, the statement will return the value associated with that condition. If none of the statements evaluate as true, then the value associated with the **ELSE** statement will be returned.

As an example, let's say you wanted to return all rows for customers from the **customers** table. Additionally, you would like to add a column that labels a user as being an **Elite Customer** if they live in postal code **33111**, or as a **Premium Customer** if they live in postal code **33124**. Otherwise, it will mark the customer as a **Standard Customer**. This column will be called **customer_type**. We can create this table by using a **CASE WHEN** statement as sfollows:

```
SELECT *,
    CASE WHEN postal_code='33111' THEN 'Elite Customer'
    CASE WHEN postal_code='33124' THEN 'Premium Customer'
    ELSE 'Standard Customer' END
  AS customer_type
FROM customers;
```

This query will give the following output:

customer_id bigint	title text	first_name text	last_name text	suffix text	email text	gender text	ip_address text	phone text	street_address text	city text	state text	postal_code text	latitude double precision	longitude double precision	date_added timestamp without time zone	customer_type text
1	[null]	Arlena	Riveles	[null]	arivele...	F	98.36.172.246	[null]	[null]	[null]	[null]	[null]	[null]	[null]	2017-04-23 00:00:00	Standard Customer
2	Dr	Ode	Stovin	[null]	ostovin...	M	16.97.59.186	314-534...	2573 Fordem Par...	Saint...	MO	63116	38.5814	-90.2625	2014-10-02 00:00:00	Standard Customer
3	[null]	Braden	Jordan	[null]	bjorda...	M	192.86.248.59	[null]	5661 Kennedy Road	Pens...	FL	32590	30.6143	-87.2758	2018-10-27 00:00:00	Standard Customer
4	[null]	Jessika	Nussen	[null]	jnusse...	F	159.165.138...	615-824...	224 Village Circle	Nash...	TN	37215	36.0986	-86.8219	2017-09-03 00:00:00	Standard Customer
5	[null]	Lonnie	Rembaud	[null]	lremba...	F	18.131.58.65	786-499...	38 Lindbergh Way	Miami	FL	33124	25.5584	-80.4582	2014-03-05 00:00:00	Premium Customer
6	[null]	Cortie	Locksley	[null]	clocksl...	M	140.194.59.82	[null]	6537 Delladonna ...	Miami	FL	33158	25.6364	-80.3187	2013-03-31 00:00:00	Standard Customer
7	[null]	Wood	Kennham	[null]	wkenn...	M	191.190.135...	407-552...	001 Onagard Park	Orla...	FL	32891	28.5663	-81.2608	2011-08-25 00:00:00	Standard Customer
8	[null]	Rutger	Humblestone	[null]	rhumbl...	M	77.10.236.191	203-551...	21376 Esker Center	New...	CT	06510	41.3087	-72.9271	2013-12-15 00:00:00	Standard Customer
9	[null]	Melantha	Tibb	[null]	mtibb8...	F	155.176.37.1...	913-590...	05915 Havey Hill	Sha...	KS	66225	38.8999	-94.832	2016-02-11 00:00:00	Standard Customer
10	Ms	Barbara-anne	Gowlett	Jr	bgowle...	F	67.110.62.119	915-714...	9 Kim Point	El Pa...	TX	79940	31.6948	-106.3	2012-06-28 00:00:00	Standard Customer

Figure 3.13: Customer type query

As you can see in the preceding table, there is a column called **customer_type** indicating the type of customer a user is. The **CASE WHEN** statement effectively mapped a postal code to a string describing the customer type. Using a **CASE WHEN** statement, you can map values in any way you please.

Exercise 12: Using the CASE WHEN Function to Get Regional Lists

The aim is to create a query that will map various values in a column to other values. The head of sales has an idea to try and create specialized regional sales teams that will be able to sell scooters to customers in specific regions, as opposed to generic sales teams. To make his idea a reality, he would like a list of all customers mapped to regions. For customers from the states of MA, NH, VT, ME CT, or RI, he would like them labeled as **New England**. For customers from the states of GA, FL, MS, AL, LA, KY, VA, NC, SC, TN, VI, WV, or AR, he would like the customers labeled as **Southeast**. Customers from any other state should be labeled as **Other**:

1. Open your favorite SQL client and connect to the **sqlda** database.

2. Create a query that will produce a **customer_id** column and a column called **region**, with states categorized like in the following scenario:

```
SELECT c.customer_id,
CASE WHEN c.state in ('MA', 'NH', 'VT', 'ME', 'CT', 'RI') THEN 'New
England'
WHEN c.state in ('GA', 'FL', 'MS', 'AL', 'LA', 'KY', 'VA', 'NC', 'SC',
'TN', 'VI', 'WV', 'AR') THEN 'Southeast'
ELSE 'Other' END as region
FROM customers c
ORDER BY 1
```

This query will map a state to one of the regions based on whether the state is in the `CASE WHEN` condition listed for that line.

You should get output similar to the following:

customer_id bigint	region text
1	Other
2	Other
3	Southe…
4	Southe…
5	Southe…
6	Southe…
7	Southe…
8	New En…
9	Other
10	Other

Figure 3.14: Regional query output

In the preceding output, in the case of each customer, a region has been mapped based on the state where the customer resides.

In this exercise, we learned to map various values in a column to other values using the `CASE WHEN` function.

COALESCE

Another useful technique is to replace **NULL** values with a standard value. This can be accomplished easily by means of the **COALESCE** function. **COALESCE** allows you to list any number of columns and scalar values, and, if the first value in the list is **NULL**, it will try to fill it in with the second value. The **COALESCE** function will keep continuing down the list of values until it hits a **non-NULL** value. If all values in the **COALESCE** function are **NULL**, then the function returns **NULL**.

To illustrate a simple usage of the **COALESCE** function, let's return to the **customers** table. Let's say the marketing team would like a list of the first names, last names, and phone numbers of all male customers. However, for those customers with no phone number, they would like the table to instead write the value **'NO PHONE'**. We can accomplish this request with **COALESCE**:

```
SELECT first_name,

last_name,

COALESCE(phone, 'NO PHONE') as phone

FROM customers

ORDER BY 1;
```

This query produces the following results:

first_name text	last_name text	phone text
Aaren	Norrey	NO PHONE
Aaren	Sadat	504-559-3464
Aaren	Whelpdale	607-761-2568
Aaren	Lamlin	414-937-4628
Aaren	Deeman	NO PHONE
Aarika	Guerin	501-121-5841
Aarika	Danaher	904-175-3112
Aarika	Chadwell	915-856-7492
Aarika	Emmanuel	NO PHONE
Aarika	Mawhinney	205-355-4381

Figure 3.15: Coalesce query

When dealing with creating default values and avoiding **NULL**, **COALESCE** will always be helpful.

NULLIF

NULLIF is, in a sense, the opposite of **COALESCE**. **NULLIF** is a two-value function and will return **NULL** if the first value equals the second value.

As an example, imagine that the marketing department has created a new direct mail piece to send to the customer. One of the quirks of this new piece of advertising is that it cannot accept people who have titles longer than three letters.

In our database, the only known title longer than three characters is **'Honorable'**. Therefore, they would like you to create a mailing list that is just all the rows with valid street addresses and to blot out all titles with **NULL** that are spelled as **'Honorable'**. This could be done with the following query:

```
SELECT customer_id,
       NULLIF(title, 'Honorable') as title,
       first_name,
       last_name,
       suffix,
       email,
       gender,
       ip_address,
       phone,
       street_address,
       city,
       state,
       postal_code,
       latitude,
       longitude,
       date_added
  FROM customers c
  ORDER BY 1
```

This will blot out all mentions of **'Honorable'** from the title column.

LEAST/GREATEST

Two functions that come in handy for data preparation are the **LEAST** and **GREATEST** functions. Each function takes any number of values and returns the least or the greatest of the values, respectively.

A simple use of this variable would be to replace the value if it's too high or low. For example, the sales team may want to create a sales list where every scooter is $600 or less than that. We can create this using the following query:

```
SELECT product_id,
model,
year,
product_type,
LEAST(600.00, base_msrp) as base_msrp,
production_start_date,
production_end_date
FROM products
WHERE product_type='scooter'
ORDER BY 1;
```

This query will give the following output:

	product_id bigint	model text	year bigint	product_type text	base_msrp numeric	production_start_date timestamp without time zone	production_end_date timestamp without time zone
1	1	Lemon	2010	scooter	399.99	2010-03-03 00:00:00	2012-06-08 00:00:00
2	2	Lemon ...	2011	scooter	600.00	2011-01-03 00:00:00	2011-03-30 00:00:00
3	3	Lemon	2013	scooter	499.99	2013-05-01 00:00:00	2018-12-28 00:00:00
4	5	Blade	2014	scooter	600.00	2014-06-23 00:00:00	2015-01-27 00:00:00
5	7	Bat	2016	scooter	599.99	2016-10-10 00:00:00	[null]
6	8	Bat Limi...	2017	scooter	600.00	2017-02-15 00:00:00	[null]
7	12	Lemon ...	2019	scooter	349.99	2019-02-04 00:00:00	[null]

Figure 3.16: Cheaper scooters

Casting

Another useful data transformation is to change the data type of a column within a query. This is usually done to use a function only available to one data type, such as text, while working with a column that is in a different data type, such as a numeric. To change the data type of a column, you simply need to use the **column::datatype** format, where **column** is the column name, and **datatype** is the data type you want to change the column to. For example, to change the year in the **products** table to a text column in a query, use the following query:

```
SELECT product_id,
model,
year::TEXT,
product_type,
base_msrp,
production_start_date,
production_end_date
FROM products;
```

This will convert the year column to text. You can now apply text functions to this transformed column. There is one final catch; not every data type can be cast to a specific data type. For instance, **datetime** cannot be cast to float types. Your SQL client will throw an error if you ever make an unexpected strange conversion.

DISTINCT and DISTINCT ON

Often, when looking through a dataset, you may be interested in determining the unique values in a column or group of columns. This is the primary use case of the **DISTINCT** keyword. For example, if you wanted to know all the unique model years in the **products** table, you could use the following query:

```
SELECT DISTINCT year
FROM products
ORDER BY 1;
```

This gives the following result:

year bigint
2010
2011
2013
2014
2015
2016
2017
2019

Figure 3.17: Distinct model years

You can also use it with multiple columns to get all distinct column combinations present. For example, to find all distinct years and what product types were released for those model years, you can simply use the following:

```
SELECT DISTINCT year, product_type
FROM products
ORDER BY 1, 2;
```

This gives the following output:

year bigint	product_type text
2010	scooter
2011	scooter
2013	scooter
2014	automobile
2014	scooter
2015	automobile
2016	scooter
2017	automobile
2017	scooter
2019	automobile
2019	scooter

Figure 3.18: Distinct model years and product types

A keyword related to **DISTINCT** is **DISTINCT ON. DISTINCT ON** allows you to ensure that only one row is returned where one or more columns are always unique in the set. The general syntax of a **DISTINCT ON** query is:

```
SELECT DISTINCT ON (distinct_column)

column_1,

column_2,

…

column_n

FROM table

ORDER BY order_column;
```

Here, **dictinct_column** is the column or columns you want to be distinct in your query, **column_1** through **column_n** are the columns you want in the query, and **order_column** allows you to determine the first row that will be returned for a **DISTINCT ON** query if multiple columns have the same value for **distinct_column**. For **order_column**, the first column mentioned should be **distinct_column**. If an **ORDER BY** clause is not specified, the first row will be decided randomly. To clarify, let's say you wanted to get a unique list of salespeople where each salesperson has a unique first name. In the case that two salespeople have the same first name, we will return the one that started earlier. This query would look like this:

```
SELECT DISTINCT ON (first_name)

*

FROM salespeople

ORDER BY first_name, hire_date;
```

It will return the following:

salesperson_id bigint	dealership_id bigint	title text	first_name text	last_name text	suffix text	username text	gender text	hire_date timestamp without time zone	termination_date timestamp without time zone
189	17	[null]	Abby	Drewery	[null]	adrewery58	Male	2015-09-01 00:00:00	[null]
137	4	[null]	Abie	Brydell	[null]	abrydell3s	Male	2016-11-04 00:00:00	[null]
27	4	[null]	Ad	Loding	[null]	alodingq	Male	2017-06-27 00:00:00	[null]
63	2	[null]	Adrianne	Otham	[null]	aotham1q	Female	2014-12-20 00:00:00	[null]
272	7	[null]	Afton	Limon	[null]	alimon7j	Female	2014-09-01 00:00:00	[null]
35	17	[null]	Agnella	Linke	[null]	alinkey	Female	2018-10-23 00:00:00	[null]
161	18	[null]	Aile	Dobbing	[null]	adobbing4g	Female	2014-08-14 00:00:00	2016-10-03 00:00:00
136	3	[null]	Alanna	Dufaire	[null]	adufaire3r	Female	2014-06-27 00:00:00	[null]
147	6	[null]	Alaric	Sterrick	[null]	asterrick42	Male	2014-06-17 00:00:00	[null]
221	19	[null]	Alberik	Polglase	[null]	apolglase64	Male	2015-11-19 00:00:00	[null]
139	18	[null]	Alexina	Coatsworth	[null]	acoatswort...	Female	2015-07-27 00:00:00	[null]
100	18	[null]	Alie	Bellfield	[null]	abellfield2r	Female	2017-12-11 00:00:00	[null]
287	7	[null]	Allayne	Billingham	[null]	abillingham7y	Male	2014-08-06 00:00:00	[null]

Figure 3.19: DISTINCT ON first_name

This table now guarantees that every row has a distinct username and that the row returned if multiple users have a given first name is the person hired there with that first name. For example, if the **salespeople** table has multiple rows with the first name **'Abby'**, the row seen in *Figure* 3.19 with the name **'Abby'** (the first row in the outputs) was for the first person employed at the company with the name **'Abby'**.

Activity 5: Building a Sales Model Using SQL Techniques

The aim of this activity is to clean and prepare our data for analysis using SQL techniques. The data science team wants to build a new model to help predict which customers are the best prospects for remarketing. A new data scientist has joined their team and does not know the database well enough to pull a dataset for this new model. The responsibility has fallen to you to help the new data scientist prepare and build a dataset to be used to train a model. Write a query to assemble a dataset that will do the following:

1. Open a SQL client and connect to the database.

2. Use **INNER JOIN** to join the **customers** table to the **sales** table.

3. Use **INNER JOIN** to join the **products** table to the **sales** table.

4. Use **LEFT JOIN** to join the **dealerships** table to the **sales** table.

5. Now, return all columns of the **customers** table and the **products** table.

6. Then, return the **dealership_id** column from the **sales** table, but fill in **dealership_id** in sales with **-1** if it is **NULL**.

7. Add a column called **high_savings** that returns **1** if the sales amount was **500** less than **base_msrp** or lower. Otherwise, it returns **0**.

Expected Output:

customer_id bigint	title text	first_name text	last_name text	suffix text	email text	gender text	ip_address text	phone text	street_address text	city text	state text	postal_code text	latitude double precision	longitude double precision	date_added timestamp without time zone
1 [null]	Arlena	Riveles	[null]	arivelo...	F	98.36.172.246	[null]	[null]	[null]	[null]	[null]		[null]	2017-04-23 00:00:00
4 [null]	Jessika	Nussen	[null]	jnusse...	F	159.165.138...	615-824...	224 Village Circle	Nash...	TN	37215	36.0986	-86.8219	2017-09-03 00:00:00
5 [null]	Lonnie	Rembaud	[null]	lremba...	F	18.131.58.65	786-499...	38 Lindbergh Way	Miami	FL	33124	25.5584	-80.4582	2014-03-06 00:00:00
6 [null]	Cortie	Locksley	[null]	clocksl...	M	140.194.59.82	[null]	6537 Delladonna ...	Miami	FL	33158	25.6364	-80.3187	2018-03-31 00:00:00
7 [null]	Wood	Kennham	[null]	wkenn...	M	191.190.135...	407-552...	001 Onsgard Park	Orla...	FL	32891	28.5663	-81.2608	2011-08-25 00:00:00
7 [null]	Wood	Kennham	[null]	wkenn...	M	191.190.135...	407-552...	001 Onsgard Park	Orla...	FL	32891	28.5663	-81.2608	2011-08-25 00:00:00
7 [null]	Wood	Kennham	[null]	wkenn...	M	191.190.135...	407-552...	001 Onsgard Park	Orla...	FL	32891	28.5663	-81.2608	2011-08-25 00:00:00
11 Mrs	Urbano	Middlehurst	[null]	umiddl...	M	185.118.6.23	918-339...	5203 7th Trail	Tulsa	OK	74156	36.3024	-95.9605	2011-10-22 00:00:00
12 Mr	Tyne	Duggan	[null]	tdugga...	F	13.29.231.228	[null]	[null]	[null]	[null]	[null]	[null]	[null]	2017-10-25 00:00:00

Figure 3.20: Building a sales model query

> **Note**
>
> The solution for the activity can be found on page 321.

Summary

SQL provides us with many tools for mixing and cleaning data. We have learned how joins allow users to combine multiple tables, while **UNION** and subqueries allow us to combine multiple queries. We have also learned how SQL has a wide variety of functions and keywords that allow users to map new data, fill in missing data, and remove duplicate data. Keywords such as **CASE WHEN**, **COALESCE**, **NULLIF**, and **DISTINCT** allow us to make changes to data quickly and easily.

Now that we know how to prepare a dataset, we will learn how to start making analytical insights in the next chapter using aggregates.

Aggregate Functions for Data Analysis

Learning Objectives

By the end of this chapter, you will be able to:

- Explain the conceptual logic of aggregation
- Identify the common SQL aggregate functions
- Use the GROUP BY clause to aggregate and combine groups of data for analysis
- Use the HAVING clause to filter aggregates
- Use aggregate functions to clean data and examine data quality

In this chapter, we will cover SQL's aggregate functions, which are powerful functions for summarizing data.

Introduction

In the previous chapter, we discussed how to use SQL to prepare datasets for analysis. Once the data is prepared, the next step is to analyze the data. Generally, data scientists and analytics professionals will try to understand the data by summarizing it and trying to find high-level patterns in the data. SQL can help with this task primarily through the use of aggregate functions: functions that take rows as input and return one number for each row. In this chapter, we will discuss how to use basic aggregate functions and how to derive statistics and other useful information from data using aggregate functions with **GROUP BY**. We will then use the **HAVING** clause to filter aggregates and see how to clean data and examine data quality using aggregate functions. Finally, we look at how to use aggregates to understand data quality

Aggregate Functions

With data, we are often interested in understanding the properties of an entire column or table as opposed to just seeing individual rows of data. As a simple example, let's say you were wondering how many customers ZoomZoom has. You could select all the data from the table and then see how many rows were pulled back, but it would be incredibly tedious to do so. Luckily, there are functions provided by SQL that can be used to do calculations on large groups of rows. These functions are called **aggregate functions**. The aggregate function takes in one or more columns with multiple rows and returns a number based on those columns. As an illustration, we can use the **COUNT** function to count how many rows there are in the **customers** table to figure out how many customers ZoomZoom has:

```
SELECT COUNT(customer_id) FROM customers;
```

The **COUNT** function will return the number of rows without a **NULL** value in the column. As the **customer_id** column is a primary key and cannot be **NULL**, the **COUNT** function will return the number of rows in the table. In this case, the query will return:

Figure 4.1: Customer count table

As shown here, the **COUNT** function works with a single column and counts how many **non-NULL** values it has. However, if every single column has at least one **NULL** value, then it would be impossible to determine how many rows there are. To get a count of the number of rows in that situation, you could alternatively use the **COUNT** function with an asterisk, **(*)**, to get the total count of rows:

```
SELECT COUNT(*) FROM customers;
```

This query will also return **50,000**.

Let's say, however, that what you were interested in was the number of unique states in the customer list. This answer could be queried using **COUNT (DISTINCT expression)**:

```
SELECT COUNT(DISTINCT state) FROM customers;
```

This query creates the following output:

Figure 4.2: Count of distinct states

The following figure is a summary of the major aggregate functions used in SQL:

Function	Explanation
COUNT(columnX)	Counts the number of rows in columnX that have a non-NULL value.
COUNT(*)	Counts the number of rows in the output table.
MIN(columnX)	Returns the minimum value in columnX. For text columns, it returns the value that would appear first alphabetically.
MAX(columnX)	Returns the maximum value in columnX.
SUM(columnX)	Returns the sum of all values in columnX.
AVG(columnX)	Returns the average of all values in columnX.
STDDEV(columnX)	Returns the sample standard deviation of all values in columnX.
VAR(columnX)	Returns the sample variance of all values in columnX.
REGR_SLOPE(columnX, columnY)	Returns the slope of a linear regression for columnX as the response variable, and columnY as the predictor variable.
REGR_INTERCEPT(columnX, columnY)	Returns the intercept of a linear regression for columnX as the response variable, and columnY as the predictor variable.
CORR(columnX, columnY)	Calculates the Pearson correlation between columnX and columnY in the data.

Figure 4.3: Major aggregate functions

Aggregate functions can also be used with the **WHERE** clause in order to calculate aggregate values for specific subsets of data. For example, if you wanted to know how many customers ZoomZoom had in California, you could use the following query:

```
SELECT COUNT(*) FROM customers WHERE state='CA';
```

This gives the following result:

count
bigint

5038

Figure 4.4: The COUNT function used with the WHERE clause

You can also do arithmetic with aggregate functions. In the following query, you can divide the count of rows in the **customers** table by two like so:

```
SELECT COUNT(*)/2 FROM customers;
```

This query will return **25,000**.

You can also use the aggregate functions with each other in mathematical ways. In the following query, instead of using the **AVG** function to calculate the average MSRP of products at ZoomZoom, you could "build" the **AVG** function using **SUM** and **COUNT** as follows:

```
SELECT SUM(base_msrp)::FLOAT/COUNT(*) AS avg_base_msrp FROM products
```

You should get the following result:

avg_base_msrp
double precision

33358.3275

Figure 4.5: Average of the base MSRP

> **Note**
>
> The reason we have to cast the sum is that PostgreSQL treats integer division differently than float division. For example, dividing 7 by 2 as integers in PostgreSQL will give you 3. In order to get a more precise answer of 3.5, you have to cast one of the numbers to float.

Exercise 13: Using Aggregate Functions to Analyze Data

Here, we will analyze and calculate the price of a product using different aggregate functions. As you're always curious about the data at your company, you are interested in understanding some of the basic statistics around ZoomZoom product prices. You now want to calculate the lowest price, the highest price, the average price, and the standard deviation of the price for all the products the company has ever sold.

> **Note**
>
> For all exercises in this book, we will be using pgAdmin 4. All the exercises and activity are also available on GitHub: https://github.com/TrainingByPackt/SQL-for-Data-Analytics/tree/master/Lesson04.

To solve this problem, do the following:

1. Open your favorite SQL client and connect to the **sqlda** database.

2. Calculate the lowest, highest, average, and standard deviation of the price using the **MIN**, **MAX**, **AVG**, and **STDDEV** aggregate functions, respectively, from the **products** table:

```
SELECT MIN(base_msrp), MAX(base_msrp), AVG(base_msrp), STDDEV(base_msrp)
FROM products;
```

The following is the output of the preceding code:

min numeric	max numeric	avg numeric	stddev numeric
349.99	115000.00	33358.327500000000	44484.40866379

Figure 4.6: Statistics of the product price

We can see from the output that the minimum price is **349.99**, the maximum price is **115000.00**, the average price is **33358.32750**, and the standard deviation of the price is **44484.408**.

We have now used aggregate functions to understand the basic statistics of prices.

Aggregate Functions with GROUP BY

We have now used aggregate functions to calculate statistics for an entire column. However, often, we are not interested in the aggregate values for a whole table, but for smaller groups in the table. To illustrate, let's go back to the **customers** table. We know the total number of customers is 50,000. But we might want to know how many customers we have in each state. How would we calculate this?

We could determine how many states there are with the following query:

```
SELECT DISTINCT state FROM customers;
```

Once you have the list of states, you could then run the following query for each state:

```
SELECT COUNT(*) FROM customer WHERE state='{state}'
```

Although you can do this, it is incredibly tedious and can take an incredibly long time if there are many states. Is there a better way? There is, and it is through the use of the **GROUP BY** clause.

GROUP BY

GROUP BY is a clause that divides the rows of a dataset into multiple groups based on some sort of key specified in the **GROUP BY** clause. An aggregate function is then applied to all the rows within a single group to produce a single number. The **GROUP BY** key and the aggregate value for the group are then displayed in the SQL output. The following diagram illustrates this general process:

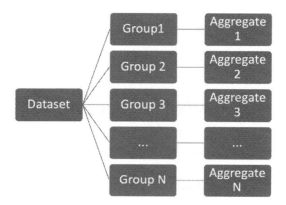

Figure 4.7: General GROUP BY computational model

In *Figure* 4.7, we can see that the dataset has multiple groups (**Group 1, Group 2, ...,
Group N**). Here, the **Aggregate 1** function is applied to all the rows in **Group1**, the
Aggregate 2 function is applied to all the rows in **Group 2**, and so on.

GROUP BY statements usually have the following structure:

```
SELECT {KEY}, {AGGFUNC(column1)} FROM {table1} GROUP BY {KEY}
```

Here, **{KEY}** is a column or a function on a column used to create individual groups,
{AGGFUNC(column1)} is an aggregate function on a column that is calculated for all the
rows within each group, and **{table}** is the table or set of joined tables from which rows
are separated into groups.

To better illustrate this point, let's count the number of customers in each US state
using a **GROUP BY** query. Using **GROUP BY**, a SQL user could count the number of
customers in each state by querying:

```
SELECT state, COUNT(*) FROM customers GROUP BY state
```

The computational model looks like the following:

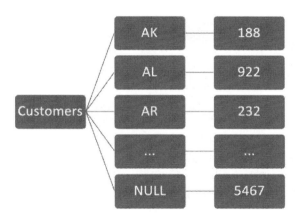

Figure 4.8: Customer count by the state computational model

Here, **AK**, **AL**, **AR**, and the other keys are abbreviations for US states.

You should get output similar to the following:

state text	count bigint
KS	619
[null]	5467
CA	5038
NH	77
OR	386
ND	93
TX	4865
NV	643
KY	598

Figure 4.9: Customer count by the state query output

You can also use the column number to perform a **GROUP BY** operation:

```
SELECT state, COUNT(*) FROM customers
GROUP BY 1
```

If you want to return the output in alphabetical order, simply use the following query:

```
SELECT state, COUNT(*) FROM customers GROUP BY state ORDER BY state
```

Alternatively, we can write:

```
SELECT state, COUNT(*) FROM customers GROUP BY 1ORDER BY 1
```

Either of these queries will give you the following result:

state text	count bigint
AK	188
AL	922
AR	232
AZ	931
CA	5038
CO	1042
CT	576
DC	1447
DE	149

Figure 4.10: Customer count by the state query output in alphabetical order

Often, though, you may be interested in ordering the aggregates themselves. The aggregates can be ordered using **ORDER BY** as follows:

```
SELECT state, COUNT(*) FROM customers GROUP BY state ORDER BY COUNT(*)
```

This query gives the following output:

state text	count bigint
VT	16
WY	23
ME	25
RI	47
NH	77
ND	93
MT	122
SD	124
DE	149

Figure 4.11: Customer count by the state query output in increasing order

You may also want to count only a subset of the data, such as the total number of male customers. To calculate the total number of male customers, you can use the following query:

```
SELECT state, COUNT(*) FROM customers WHERE gender='M' GROUP BY state ORDER
BY state
```

This gives you the following output:

| state | count |
text	bigint
AK	87
AL	489
AR	120
AZ	415
CA	2572
CO	526
CT	301
DC	713
DE	74

Figure 4.12: Male customer count by the state query output in alphabetical order

Multiple Column GROUP BY

While **GROUP BY** with one column is powerful, you can go even further and **GROUP BY** multiple columns. Let's say you wanted to get a count of not just the number of customers ZoomZoom had in each state, but also of how many male and female customers it had in each state. Multiple **GROUP BY** columns can query the answer as follows:

```
SELECT state, gender, COUNT(*) FROM customers GROUP BY state, genderORDER BY
state, gender
```

This gives the following result:

state text	gender text	count bigint
AK	F	101
AK	M	87
AL	F	433
AL	M	489
AR	F	112
AR	M	120
AZ	F	516
AZ	M	415
CA	F	2466

Figure 4.13: Customer count by the state and gender query outputs in alphabetical order

Any number of columns can be used in a GROUP BY operation in this fashion.

Exercise 14: Calculating the Cost by Product Type Using GROUP BY

In this exercise, we will analyze and calculate the cost of products using aggregate functions and the GROUP BY clause. The marketing manager wants to know the minimum, maximum, average, and standard deviation of the price for each product type that ZoomZoom sells, for a marketing campaign. Follow these steps:

1. Open your favorite SQL client and connect to the sample database, sqlda.

2. Calculate the lowest, highest, average, and standard deviation price using the MIN, MAX, AVG, and STDDEV aggregate functions, respectively, from the products table and use GROUP BY to check the price of all the different product types:

```
SELECT product_type, MIN(base_msrp), MAX(base_msrp), AVG(base_msrp),
STDDEV(base_msrp)
FROM products
GROUP BY 1
ORDER BY 1;
```

You should get the following result:

product_type text	min numeric	max numeric	avg numeric	stddev numeric
automobile	35000.00	115000.00	79250.000000000000	30477.45068079
scooter	349.99	799.99	578.5614285714285714	167.971085947212

Figure 4.14: Basic price statistics by product type

From the preceding output, the marketing manager can check and compare the price of various products that ZoomZoom sells for the campaign.

In this exercise, we calculated the basic statistics by product type using aggregate functions and the **GROUP BY** clause.

Grouping Sets

Now, let's say you wanted to count the total number of customers you have in each state, while simultaneously, in the same aggregate functions, counting the total number of male and female customers you have in each state. How could you accomplish that? One way is by using the **UNION ALL** keyword we discussed in *Chapter 2, The Basics of SQL for Analytics*, like so:

```
(
SELECT state, NULL as gender, COUNT(*)
FROM customers
GROUP BY 1, 2
ORDER BY 1, 2
)
UNION ALL
(
(
SELECT state, gender, COUNT(*)
FROM customers
GROUP BY 1, 2
```

```
ORDER BY 1, 2
)
)
ORDER BY 1, 2
```

The query produces the following result:

state text	gender text	count bigint
AK	F	101
AK	M	87
AK	[null]	188
AL	F	433
AL	M	489
AL	[null]	922
AR	F	112
AR	M	120
AR	[null]	232

Figure 4.15: Customer count by the state and gender query outputs in alphabetical order

However, using **UNION ALL** is tedious and can be very difficult to write. An alternative way is to use grouping sets. Grouping sets allow a user to create multiple categories of viewing, similar to the **UNION ALL** statement we just saw. For example, using the **GROUPING SETS** keyword, you could rewrite the previous **UNION ALL** query as:

```
SELECT state, gender, COUNT(*)
FROM customers
GROUP BY GROUPING SETS (
(state),
(gender),
(state, gender)
)
ORDER BY 1, 2
```

This creates the same output as the previous **UNION ALL** query.

Ordered Set Aggregates

Up to this point, all the aggregates we have discussed did not depend on the order of the data. Using **ORDER BY**, we can order the data, but it was not required. However, there are a subset of aggregates statistics that do depend on the order of the column to calculate. For instance, the median of a column is something that requires the order of the data to be specified. For calculating these use cases, SQL offers a series of functions called **ordered set aggregates** functions. The following figure lists the major ordered-set aggregate functions:

Function	Explanation
mode()	Returns the value that appears most often. In the case of a tie, returns the first value in order.
Percentile_cont(fraction)	Returns a value corresponding to the specified fraction in the ordering, interpolating between adjacent input items if needed.
Percentile_disc(fraction)	Returns the first input value whose position in the ordering equals or exceeds the specified fraction.

Figure 4.16: Major ordered set aggregate functions

The functions are used with the following format:

```
SELECT {ordered_set_function} WITHIN GROUP (ORDER BY {order_column})
FROM {table};
```

Where **{ordered_set_function}** is the ordered set aggregate function, **{order_column}** is the column to order results for the function by, and **{table}** is the table the column is in.

To illustrate, let's say you wanted to calculate the median price of the products table. You could use the following query:

```
SELECT PERCENTILE_CONT(0.5) WITHIN GROUP (ORDER BY base_msrp) AS median
from products;
```

The reason we use **0.5** is because the median is the 50th percentile, which is **0.5** as a fraction. This gives the following result:

Figure 4.17: Median of Product Prices

With ordered set aggregate functions, we now have tools for calculating virtually any aggregate statistic of interest for a data set. In the next section, we look at how to use aggregates to deal with data quality.

The HAVING Clause

We can now perform all sorts of aggregate operations using **GROUP BY**. Sometimes, though, certain rows in aggregate functions may not be useful, and you may like to remove them from the query output. For example, when doing the customer counts, perhaps you are only interested in places that have at least **1,000** customers. Your first instinct may be to write something such as this:

```
SELECT state, COUNT(*)
FROM customers
WHERE COUNT(*)>=1,000
GROUP BY state
ORDER BY state
```

However, you will find that the query does not work and gives you the following error:

```
ERROR:  aggregate functions are not allowed in WHERE
LINE 3: WHERE COUNT(*)>=1000
                    ^
SQL state: 42803
Character: 45
```

Figure 4.18: Error showing the query not working

In order to use filter on aggregate functions, you need to use a new clause, **HAVING**. The **HAVING** clause is similar to the **WHERE** clause, except it is specifically designed for **GROUP BY** queries. The general structure of a **GROUP BY** operation with a **HAVING** statement is:

```
SELECT {KEY}, {AGGFUNC(column1)}
FROM {table1}
GROUP BY {KEY}
HAVING {OTHER_AGGFUNC(column2)_CONDITION}
```

Here, **{KEY}** is a column or function on a column that is used to create individual groups, **{AGGFUNC(column1)}** is an aggregate function on a column that is calculated for all the rows within each group, **{table}** is the table or set of joined tables from which rows are separated into groups, and **{OTHER_AGGFUNC(column2)_CONDITION}** is a condition similar to what you would put in a **WHERE** clause involving an aggregate function.

Exercise 15: Calculating and Displaying Data Using the HAVING Clause

In this exercise, we will calculate and display data using the **HAVING** clause. The sales manager of ZoomZoom wants to know the customer count for the states that have at least 1,000 customers who have purchased any product from ZoomZoom. Help the manager to extract the data.

To solve this problem, do the following:

1. Open your favorite SQL client and connect to the **sqlda** database.

2. Calculate the customer count by the state with at least **1000** customers using the **HAVING** clause:

```
SELECT state, COUNT(*)
FROM customers
GROUP BY state
HAVING COUNT(*)>=1,000
ORDER BY state
```

This query will then give you the following output:

state text	count bigint
CA	5038
CO	1042
DC	1447
FL	3748
GA	1251
IL	1094
NC	1070
NY	2395
OH	1656

Figure 4.19: Customer count by the state with at least 1,000 customers

We can see the states that have more than 1,000 ZoomZoom customers, with CA having **5038**, the highest number of customers, and CO having **1042**, the lowest number of customers.

In this exercise, we used the **HAVING** clause to calculate and display data more efficiently.

Using Aggregates to Clean Data and Examine Data Quality

In *Chapter 2, The Basics of SQL for Analytics*, we discussed how SQL can be used to clean data. While the techniques in *Chapter 2, The Basics of SQL for Analytics for Analytics*, do an excellent job of cleaning data, aggregates add a number of techniques that can make cleaning data even easier and more comprehensive. In this section, we will look at some of these techniques.

Finding Missing Values with GROUP BY

As mentioned in *Chapter 2, The Basics of SQL for Analytics*, one of the biggest issues with cleaning data is dealing with missing values. While in *Chapter 2, The Basics of SQL for Analytics*, we discussed how to find missing values and how we could get rid of them, we did not say too much about how we could determine the extent of missing data in a dataset. Primarily, it was because we did not have the tools to deal with summarizing information in a dataset – that is, until this chapter.

Using aggregates, identifying the amount of missing data can tell you not only which columns have missing data, but also whether columns are even usable because so much of the data is missing. Depending on the extent of missing data, you will have to determine whether it makes the most sense to delete rows with missing data, fill in missing values, or to just delete columns as they do not have enough data to make definitive conclusions.

The easiest way to determine whether a column is missing values is to use a modified **CASE WHEN** statement with the **SUM** and **COUNT** functions to determine what percentage of data is missing. Generally speaking, the query looks as follows:

```
SELECT SUM(CASE WHEN {column1} IS NULL OR {column1} IN ({missing_values})
THEN 1 ELSE 0 END)::FLOAT/COUNT(*)
FROM {table1}
```

Here, **{column1}** is the column that you want to check for missing values, **{missing_values}** is a comma-separated list of values that are considered missing, and **{table1}** is the table or subquery with the missing values.

Based on the results of this query, you may have to vary your strategy for dealing with missing data. If a very small percentage of your data is missing (<1%), then you might consider just filtering out or deleting the missing data from your analysis. If some of your data is missing (<20%), you may consider filling in your missing data with a typical value, such as the mean or the mode, to perform an accurate analysis. If, however, more than 20% of your data is missing, you may have to remove the column from your data analysis, as there would not be enough accurate data to make accurate conclusions based on the values in the column.

Let's look at missing data in the **customers** table. Specifically, let's look at the missing data in the **street_address** column with the following query:

```
SELECT SUM(CASE WHEN state IS NULL OR state IN ('') THEN 1 ELSE 0
END)::FLOAT/COUNT(*)
     AS missing_state

FROM customers;
```

This gives the following output:

missing_state double precision
0.10934

Figure 4.20: Customer count by the state with at least 1,000 customers

As seen here, a little under 11% of the state data is missing. For analysis purposes, you may want to consider these customers are from CA, as CA is the most common state in the data. However, the far more accurate thing to do would be to find and fill in the missing data.

Measuring Data Quality with Aggregates

One of the major themes you will find in data analytics is that analysis is fundamentally only useful when there is a strong variation in data. A column where every value is exactly the same is not a particularly useful column. To this end, it often makes sense to determine how many distinct values there are in a column. To measure the number of distinct values in a column, we can use the **COUNT DISTINCT** function to find how many distinct values there are. The structure of such a query would look like this:

```
SELECT COUNT (DISTINCT {column1})

FROM {table1}
```

Here, **{column1}** is the column you want to count and **{table1}** is the table with the column.

Another common task that you might want to do is determine whether every value in a column is unique. While in many cases this can be solved by setting a column with a **PRIMARY KEY** constraint, this may not always be possible. To solve this problem, we can write the following query:

```
SELECT COUNT (DISTINCT {column1})=COUNT(*)

FROM {table1}
```

Here, **{column1}** is the column you want to count and **{table1}** is the table with the column. If this query returns **True**, then the column has a unique value for every single row; otherwise, at least one of the values is repeated. If values are repeated in a column that you are expecting to be unique, there may be some issues with data **ETL (Extract, Transform, Load)** or maybe there is a join that has caused a row to be repeated.

As a simple example, let's verify that the **customer_id** column in **customers** is unique:

```
SELECT COUNT (DISTINCT customer_id)=COUNT(*) AS equal_ids
FROM customers;
```

This query gives the following output:

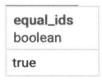

Figure 4.21: Checking whether every row has a unique customer ID

Activity 6: Analyzing Sales Data Using Aggregate Functions

The goal of this activity is to analyze data using aggregate functions. The CEO, COO, and CFO of ZoomZoom would like to gain some insights on what might be driving sales. Now that the company feels they have a strong enough analytics team with your arrival. The task has been given to you, and your boss has politely let you know that this project is the most important project the analytics team has worked on:

1. Open your favorite SQL client and connect to the **sqlda** database.

2. Calculate the total number of unit sales the company has done.

3. Calculate the total sales amount in dollars for each state.

4. Identify the top five best dealerships in terms of the most units sold (ignore internet sales).

5. Calculate the average sales amount for each channel, as seen in the **sales** table, and look at the average sales amount first by **channel** sales, then by **product_id**, and then by both together.

Expected Output:

channel text	product_id bigint	avg_sales_amount double precision
dealership	3	477.253737607644
dealership	4	109822.274881517
dealership	5	664.330132075472
dealership	6	62563.3763837638
dealership	7	573.744146637002
dealership	8	668.850500463391
dealership	9	33402.6845637584
dealership	10	81270.1121794872
dealership	11	91589.7435897436

Figure 4.22: Sales after the GROUPING SETS channel and product_id

> **Note**
>
> The solution for the activity can be found on page 322.

Summary

In this chapter, we learned about the incredible power of aggregate functions. We learned about several of the most common aggregate functions and how to use them. We then used the **GROUP BY** clause and saw how it can be used to divide datasets into groups and calculate summary statistics for each group. We then learned how to use the **HAVING** clause to further filter a query. Finally, we used aggregate functions to help us clean data and analyze data quality.

In the next chapter, we will learn about a close cousin of aggregate functions, window functions, and see how they can be utilized to understand data.

5

Window Functions for Data Analysis

Learning Objectives

By the end of this chapter, you will be able to:

- Explain what a window function is
- Write basic window functions
- Use common window functions to calculate statistics
- Analyze sales data using window functions and a window frame

In this chapter, we will cover window functions, functions similar to an aggregate function but that allow a new range of capabilities and insights.

Introduction

In the previous chapter, we discussed aggregate functions, functions that can take a large group of rows and output a single value for them. Often, being able to summarize a group of rows to a single value is important and useful. However, there are times when you want to keep the individual rows as well as gaining a summarizing value. To do this, in this chapter, we will introduce a new set of functions named **window functions**, which can calculate aggregate statistics while keeping individual rows. These functions are very useful for being able to calculate new types of statistics, such as ranks and rolling averages, with relative ease within SQL. In this chapter, we will learn about what window functions are, and how we can use them to calculate statistics.

Window Functions

Aggregate functions allow us to take many rows and convert those rows into one number. For example, the `COUNT` function takes in the rows of a table and returns the number of rows there are. However, we sometimes want to be able to calculate multiple rows but still keep all the rows following the calculation. For example, let's say you wanted to rank every user in order according to the time they became a customer, with the earliest customer being ranked 1, the second-earliest customer being ranked 2, and so on. You can get all the customers using the following query:

```
SELECT *
FROM customers
ORDER BY date_added;
```

You can order customers from the earliest to the most recent, but you can't assign them a number. You can use an aggregate function to get the dates and order them that way:

```
SELECT date_added, COUNT(*)
FROM customers
GROUP BY date_added
ORDER BY date_added
```

The following is the output of the preceding code:

date_added timestamp without time zone	count bigint
2010-03-15 00:00:00	11
2010-03-16 00:00:00	13
2010-03-17 00:00:00	12
2010-03-18 00:00:00	19
2010-03-19 00:00:00	23
2010-03-20 00:00:00	16
2010-03-21 00:00:00	20
2010-03-22 00:00:00	14
2010-03-23 00:00:00	11
2010-03-24 00:00:00	21
2010-03-25 00:00:00	15

Figure 5.1: Aggregate date-time ordering

While this gives the dates, it gets rid of the remainder of the columns, and still provides no rank information. What can we do? This is where window functions come into play. Window functions can take multiple rows of data and process them, but still retain all the information in the rows. For things such as ranks, this is exactly what you need.

For better understanding though, let's see what a windows function query looks like in the next section.

The Basics of Window Functions

The following is the basic syntax of a window function:

```
SELECT {columns},
{window_func} OVER (PARTITION BY {partition_key} ORDER BY {order_key})
FROM table1;
```

Where **{columns}** are the columns to retrieve from tables for the query, **{window_func}** is the window function you want to use, **{partition_key}** is the column or columns you want to partition on (more on this later), **{order_key}** is the column or columns you want to order by, and **table1** is the table or joined tables you want to pull data from. The **OVER** keyword indicates where the window definition starts.

To illustrate, let's use an example. You might be saying to yourself that you do not know any window functions, but the truth is, you do! All aggregate functions can be used as window functions. Let's use **COUNT(*)** in the following query:

```
SELECT customer_id, title, first_name, last_name, gender,
COUNT(*) OVER () as total_customers
FROM customers
ORDER BY customer_id;
```

This leads to the following results:

customer_id bigint	title text	first_name text	last_name text	gender text	total_customers bigint
1	[null]	Arlena	Riveles	F	50000
2	Dr	Ode	Stovin	M	50000
3	[null]	Braden	Jordan	M	50000
4	[null]	Jessika	Nussen	F	50000
5	[null]	Lonnie	Rembaud	F	50000
6	[null]	Cortie	Locksley	M	50000
7	[null]	Wood	Kennham	M	50000
8	[null]	Rutger	Humblestone	M	50000
9	[null]	Melantha	Tibb	F	50000
10	Ms	Barbara-anne	Gowlett	F	50000
11	Mrs	Urbano	Middlehurst	M	50000

Figure 5.2: Customers listed using the COUNT(*) window query

As can be seen in *Figure* 5.2, the **customers** query returns **title**, **first_name**, and **last_name**, just like a typical **SELECT** query. However, there is now a new column called **total_customers**. This column contains the count of users that would be created by the following query:

```
SELECT COUNT(*)
FROM customers;
```

This returns **50,000**. As discussed, the query returned both all of the rows and the **COUNT(*)** in the query, instead of just returning the **count** as a normal aggregate function would.

Now, let's examine the other parameters of the query. What happens if we use **PARTITION BY**, such as in the following query?

```
SELECT customer_id, title, first_name, last_name, gender,
COUNT(*) OVER (PARTITION BY gender) as total_customers
FROM customers
ORDER BY customer_id;
```

The following is the output of the preceding code:

customer_id bigint	title text	first_name text	last_name text	gender text	total_customers bigint
1	[null]	Arlena	Riveles	F	25044
2	Dr	Ode	Stovin	M	24956
3	[null]	Braden	Jordan	M	24956
4	[null]	Jessika	Nussen	F	25044
5	[null]	Lonnie	Rembaud	F	25044
6	[null]	Cortie	Locksley	M	24956
7	[null]	Wood	Kennham	M	24956
8	[null]	Rutger	Humblestone	M	24956
9	[null]	Melantha	Tibb	F	25044
10	Ms	Barbara-anne	Gowlett	F	25044
11	Mrs	Urbano	Middlehurst	M	24956

Figure 5.3: Customers listed using COUNT(*) partitioned by the gender window query

Here, you will see that **total_customers** have now changed counts to one of two values, **24,956** or **25,044**. These counts are the counts for each gender, which you can see with the following query:

```
SELECT gender, COUNT(*)
FROM customers
GROUP BY 1
```

For females, the count is equal to the female count, and for males, the count is equal to the male count. What happens now if we use **ORDER BY** in the partition, as follows?

```
SELECT customer_id, title, first_name, last_name, gender,
COUNT(*) OVER (ORDER BY customer_id) as total_customers
FROM customers
ORDER BY customer_id;
```

The following is the output of the preceding code:

customer_id bigint	title text	first_name text	last_name text	gender text	total_customers bigint
1	[null]	Arlena	Riveles	F	1
2	Dr	Ode	Stovin	M	2
3	[null]	Braden	Jordan	M	3
4	[null]	Jessika	Nussen	F	4
5	[null]	Lonnie	Rembaud	F	5
6	[null]	Cortie	Locksley	M	6
7	[null]	Wood	Kennham	M	7
8	[null]	Rutger	Humblestone	M	8
9	[null]	Melantha	Tibb	F	9
10	Ms	Barbara-anne	Gowlett	F	10
11	Mrs	Urbano	Middlehurst	M	11

Figure 5.4: Customers listed using COUNT(*) ordered by the customer_id window query

You will notice something akin to a running count for total customers. What is going on? This is where the "window" in window function comes from. When you use a window function, the query creates a "window" over the table on which it bases the count. **PARTITION BY** works like **GROUP BY**, dividing the dataset into multiple groups. For each group, a window is created. When **ORDER BY** is not specified, the window is assumed to be the entire group. However, when **ORDER BY** is specified, the rows in the group are ordered according to it, and for every row, a window is created over which a function is applied. Without specifying a window, the default behavior is to create a window to encompass every row from the first row based on **ORDER BY** to the current row being evaluated by a function, as shown in *Figure* 5.5. It is over this window that the function is applied.

As shown in *Figure 5.5*, the window for the first row contains one row and returns a count of **1**, the window for the second row contains two rows and returns a count of **2**, whereas the window for the third row contains three rows and thus returns a count of **3** in the **total_customers** column:

customer_id bigint	title text	first_name text	last_name text	gender text	total_customers bigint	
1	[null]	Arlena	Riveles	F	1	— Window for row 1
2	Dr	Ode	Stovin	M	2	— Window for row 2
3	[null]	Braden	Jordan	M	3	— Window for row 3

Figure 5.5: Windows for customers using COUNT(*) ordered by the customer_id window query

What happens when you combine **PARTITION BY** and **ORDER BY**? Let's look at the following query:

```
SELECT customer_id, title, first_name, last_name, gender,
COUNT(*) OVER (PARTITION BY gender ORDER BY customer_id) as total_customers
FROM customers
ORDER BY customer_id;
```

When you run the preceding query, you get the following result:

customer_id bigint	title text	first_name text	last_name text	gender text	total_customers bigint
1	[null]	Arlena	Riveles	F	1
2	Dr	Ode	Stovin	M	1
3	[null]	Braden	Jordan	M	2
4	[null]	Jessika	Nussen	F	2
5	[null]	Lonnie	Rembaud	F	3
6	[null]	Cortie	Locksley	M	3
7	[null]	Wood	Kennham	M	4
8	[null]	Rutger	Humblestone	M	5
9	[null]	Melantha	Tibb	F	4
10	Ms	Barbara-anne	Gowlett	F	5
11	Mrs	Urbano	Middlehurst	M	6

Figure 5.6: Customers listed using COUNT(*) partitioned by gender ordered by the customer_id window query

Like the previous query we ran, it appears to be some sort of rank. However, it seems to differ based on gender. What is this query doing? As discussed for the previous query, the query first divides the table into two subsets based on **PARTITION BY**. Each partition is then used as a basis for doing a count, with each partition having its own set of windows.

This process is illustrated in *Figure* 5.7. This process produces the count we see in *Figure* 5.7. The three keywords, **OVER()**, **PARTITION BY**, and **ORDER BY**, create the foundation to unlock the power of **WINDOW** functions.

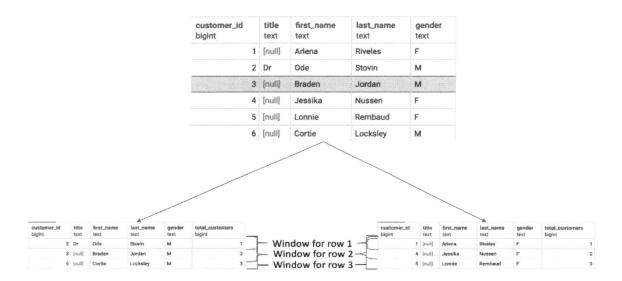

Figure 5.7: Windows for customers listed using COUNT(*) partitioned by gender ordered by the customer_id window query

Exercise 16: Analyzing Customer Data Fill Rates over Time

For the last 6 months, ZoomZoom has been experimenting with various features in order to encourage people to fill out all fields on the customer form, especially their address. To analyze this data, the company would like a running total of how many users have filled in their street address over time. Write a query to produce these results.

> **Note**
>
> For all exercises in this chapter, we will be using pgAdmin 4. All the exercise and activities in this chapter are also available on GitHub: https://github.com/TrainingByPackt/SQL-for-Data-Analytics/tree/master/Lesson05.

1. Open your favorite SQL client and connect to the **sqlda** database.

2. Use window functions and write a query that will return customer information and how many people have filled out their street address. Also, order the list as per the date. The query would look like:

```
SELECT customer_id, street_address, date_added::DATE,
COUNT(CASE WHEN street_address IS NOT NULL THEN customer_id ELSE NULL END)
    OVER (ORDER BY date_added::DATE) as total_customers_filled_street
FROM customers
ORDER BY date_added;
```

You should get the following result:

customer_id bigint	street_address text	date_added date	total_customers_filled_street bigint
2625	0353 Iowa Road	2010-03-15	10
17099	130 Marcy Crossing	2010-03-15	10
18685	86 Michigan Junction	2010-03-15	10
35683	1 Cordelia Crossing	2010-03-15	10
6173	79865 Hagan Terrace	2010-03-15	10
12484	[null]	2010-03-15	10
13390	38463 Forest Dale Way	2010-03-15	10
7486	61 Village Crossing	2010-03-15	10
30046	13961 Steensland Trail	2010-03-15	10
30555	294 Quincy Hill	2010-03-15	10
48307	8487 Warbler Plaza	2010-03-15	10
48229	943 Cody Trail	2010-03-16	22
42776	6010 Carey Drive	2010-03-16	22
46277	5799 Thackeray Crossing	2010-03-16	22
34189	0 Park Meadow Street	2010-03-16	22
8571	39223 Lunder Street	2010-03-16	22
17626	086 East Hill	2010-03-16	22
17832	62 Delladonna Road	2010-03-16	22

Figure 5.8: Street address filter ordered by the date_added window query

We now have every customer ordered by signup date and can see how the number of people filling out the street field changes over time.

In this exercise, we have learned how to use window functions to analyze data.

The WINDOW Keyword

Now that we understand the basics of window functions, we will introduce some syntax that will make it easier to write window functions. For some queries, you may be interested in calculating the exact same window for different functions. For example, you may be interested in calculating a running total number of customers and the number of customers with a title in each gender with the following query:

```
SELECT customer_id, title, first_name, last_name, gender,

COUNT(*) OVER (PARTITION BY gender ORDER BY customer_id) as total_customers,

SUM(CASE WHEN title IS NOT NULL THEN 1 ELSE 0 END)
    OVER (PARTITION BY gender ORDER BY customer_id) as total_customers_title

FROM customers

ORDER BY customer_id;
```

The following is the output of the preceding code:

customer_id bigint	title text	first_name text	last_name text	gender text	total_customers bigint	total_customers_title bigint
1	[null]	Arlena	Riveles	F	1	0
2	Dr	Ode	Stovin	M	1	1
3	[null]	Braden	Jordan	M	2	1
4	[null]	Jessika	Nussen	F	2	0
5	[null]	Lonnie	Rembaud	F	3	0
6	[null]	Cortie	Locksley	M	3	1
7	[null]	Wood	Kennham	M	4	1
8	[null]	Rutger	Humblestone	M	5	1
9	[null]	Melantha	Tibb	F	4	0
10	Ms	Barbara-anne	Gowlett	F	5	1
11	Mrs	Urbano	Middlehurst	M	6	2
12	Mr	Tyne	Duggan	F	6	2
13	[null]	Gannon	Braker	M	7	2
14	[null]	Derry	Lyburn	M	8	2
15	[null]	Nichols	Espinay	M	9	2

Figure 5.9: Running total of customers overall and with the title by gender window query

Although the query gives you the result, it can be tedious to write, especially the **WINDOW** clause. Is there a way in which we can simplify it? The answer is yes, and that is with another **WINDOW** clause. The **WINDOW** clause facilitates the aliasing of a window.

With our previous query, we can simplify the query by writing it as follows:

```
SELECT customer_id, title, first_name, last_name, gender,
COUNT(*) OVER w as total_customers,
SUM(CASE WHEN title IS NOT NULL THEN 1 ELSE 0 END)
    OVER w as total_customers_title
FROM customers
WINDOW w AS (PARTITION BY gender ORDER BY customer_id)
ORDER BY customer_id;
```

This query should give you the same result as seen in *Figure* 5.9. However, we did not have to write a long **PARTITION BY** and **ORDER BY** query for each window function. Instead, we simply made an alias with the defined **window w**.

Statistics with Window Functions

Now that we understand how window functions work, we can start using them to calculate useful statistics, such as ranks, percentiles, and rolling statistics.

In the following table, we have summarized a variety of statistical functions that are useful. It is also important to emphasize again that all aggregate functions can also be used as window functions (**AVG**, **SUM**, **COUNT**, and so on):

Function	Explanation
ROW_NUMBER()	Gives the current row number within a partition
RANK()	Gives a ranking within the partition based on ORDER BY, creating gaps when there are ties (for example, if row 1 and row 2 are both tied for 1, then row 3 will get the ranking 3)
DENSE_RANK()	Gives a ranking within the partition based on ORDER BY, creating no gaps when there are ties (for example, if row 1 and row 2 are both tied for 1, then row 3 will get the ranking 2)
NTILE(*num_buckets*)	Assigns an n-tile within a partition based on ORDER BY, where n is determined by the *num_buckets* integer
LAG(*column1*, *offset*)	Returns the value of *column 1* that is integer *offset* rows before the current row based on ORDER BY
LEAD(*column1*, *offset*)	Returns the value of *column 1* that is integer *offset* rows after the current row based on ORDER BY

Figure 5.10: Statistical window functions

Exercise 17: Rank Order of Hiring

ZoomZoom would like to promote salespeople at their regional dealerships to management and would like to consider tenure in their decision. Write a query that will rank the order of users according to their hire date for each dealership:

1. Open your favorite SQL client and connect to the **sqlda** database.

2. Calculate a rank for every salesperson, with a rank of 1 going to the first hire, 2 to the second hire, and so on, using the **RANK()** function:

```
SELECT *,
RANK() OVER (PARTITION BY dealership_id ORDER BY hire_date)
FROM salespeople
WHERE termination_date IS NULL;
```

The following is the output of the preceding code:

salesperson_id bigint	dealership_id bigint	title text	first_name text	last_name text	suffix text	username text	gender text	hire_date timestamp without time zone	termination_date timestamp without time zone	rank bigint
65	1	[null]	Dukie	Oxteby	[null]	doxteby1s	Male	2015-01-24 00:00:00	[null]	1
74	1	[null]	Marcos	Spong	[null]	mspong21	Male	2015-03-18 00:00:00	[null]	2
60	1	[null]	Eveleen	Mace	[null]	emace1n	Female	2015-07-15 00:00:00	[null]	3
87	1	[null]	Quent	Wogden	[null]	qwogden2e	Male	2015-08-17 00:00:00	[null]	4
98	1	[null]	Englebert	Loraine	[null]	eloraine2p	Male	2016-01-23 00:00:00	[null]	5
31	1	[null]	Lelia	Sheriff	[null]	lsheriffu	Female	2016-06-18 00:00:00	[null]	6
168	1	[null]	Sheff	McCoughan	[null]	smccougha...	Male	2016-07-22 00:00:00	[null]	7
49	1	[null]	Nadia	Rennick	[null]	nrennick1c	Female	2016-07-24 00:00:00	[null]	8
10	1	[null]	Jereme	Onele	[null]	jonele9	Male	2016-08-15 00:00:00	[null]	9
7	1	[null]	Granville	Fidell	[null]	gfidell6	Male	2017-06-17 00:00:00	[null]	10
155	1	[null]	Ira	Meere	[null]	imeere4e	Male	2017-09-11 00:00:00	[null]	11
297	1	[null]	Shay	Nafziger	Sr	snafziger88	Male	2017-12-03 00:00:00	[null]	12
183	1	[null]	Eleen	McAndie	[null]	emcandie52	Female	2018-07-08 00:00:00	[null]	13
170	1	[null]	Giselbert	Schule	[null]	gschule4p	Male	2018-08-01 00:00:00	[null]	14
162	1	[null]	Cristine	Gibbens	[null]	cgibbens4h	Female	2018-10-07 00:00:00	[null]	15
258	1	[null]	Dorie	Dosedale	[null]	ddosedale75	Male	2018-10-15 00:00:00	[null]	16
92	1	Rev	Sandye	Duny	[null]	sduny2j	Female	2019-01-03 00:00:00	[null]	17
39	1	[null]	Massimiliano	McSpirron	[null]	mmcspirron...	Male	2019-02-12 00:00:00	[null]	18

Figure 5.11: Salespeople rank-ordered by tenure

Here, you can see every salesperson with their info and rank in the **rank** column based on their hire date for each dealership.

In this exercise, we use the **RANK()** function to rank the data in a dataset in a certain order.

> **Note**
>
> **DENSE_RANK()** could also just be used as easily as **RANK()**.

Window Frame

When we discussed the basics of window functions, it was mentioned that, by default, a window is set for each row to encompass all rows from the first row in the partition to the current row, as seen in *Figure 5.5*. However, this is the default and can be adjusted using the **window frame** clause. A windows function query using the window frame clause would look like the following:

```
SELECT {columns},
{window_func} OVER (PARTITION BY {partition_key} ORDER BY {order_key}
{rangeorrows} BETWEEN {frame_start} AND {frame_end})
FROM {table1};
```

Here, **{columns}** are the columns to retrieve from tables for the query, **{window_func}** is the window function you want to use, **{partition_key}** is the column or columns you want to partition on (more on this later), **{order_key}** is the column or columns you want to order by, **{rangeorrows}** is either the keyword **RANGE** or the keyword **ROWS**, **{frame_start}** is a keyword indicating where to start the window frame, **{frame_end}** is a keyword indicating where to end the window frame, and **{table1}** is the table or joined tables you want to pull data from.

One point of difference to consider is the difference between using **RANGE** or **ROW** in a frame clause. **ROW** refer to actual rows and will take the rows before and after the current row to calculate values. **RANGE** differs when two rows have the same values based on the **ORDER BY** clause used in the window. If the current row used in the window calculation has the same value in the **ORDER BY** clause as one or more rows, then all of these rows will be added to the window frame.

Another point is to consider the values that **{frame_start}** and **{frame_end}** can take. To give further details, **{frame_start}** and **{frame_end}** can be one of the following values:

- **UNBOUNDED PRECEDING**: a keyword that, when used for **{frame_start}**, refers to the first record of the partition, and, when used for **{frame_end}**, refers to the last record of the partition

- **{offset} PRECEDING**: a keyword referring to integer **{offset}** rows or ranges before the current row

- **CURRENT ROW**: the current row

- **{offset} FOLLOWING**: a keyword referring to integer **{offset}** rows or ranges after the current row

By adjusting the window, various useful statistics can be calculated. One such useful statistic is the **rolling average**. The rolling average is simply the average for a statistic in a given time window. Let's say you want to calculate the 7-day rolling average of sales over time for ZoomZoom. This calculation could be accomplished with the following query:

```
WITH daily_sales as (
SELECT sales_transaction_date::DATE,
SUM(sales_amount) as total_sales
FROM sales
GROUP BY 1
),
moving_average_calculation_7 AS (
SELECT sales_transaction_date, total_sales,
AVG(total_sales) OVER (ORDER BY sales_transaction_date ROWS BETWEEN 7
PRECEDING and CURRENT ROW) AS sales_moving_average_7,
ROW_NUMBER() OVER (ORDER BY sales_transaction_date) as row_number
FROM daily_sales
ORDER BY 1)
SELECT sales_transaction_date,
CASE WHEN row_number>=7 THEN sales_moving_average_7 ELSE NULL END
    AS sales_moving_average_7
FROM moving_average_calculation_7;
```

The following is the output of the preceding code:

sales_transaction_date date	sales_moving_average_7 double precision
2010-03-10	[null]
2010-03-12	[null]
2010-03-15	[null]
2010-03-17	[null]
2010-03-18	[null]
2010-03-19	[null]
2010-03-21	394.275857142857
2010-03-23	394.990125
2010-03-24	399.99
2010-03-25	399.99
2010-03-29	449.98875
2010-04-01	544.986375
2010-04-02	594.985125
2010-04-03	594.985125
2010-04-04	589.98525
2010-04-05	589.98525
2010-04-06	639.984
2010-04-07	689.98275

Figure 5.12: The 7-day moving average of sales

The reason the first 7 rows are null is that the 7-day moving average is only defined if there are 7 days' worth of information, and the window calculation will still calculate values for the first 7 days using the first few days.

Exercise 18: Team Lunch Motivation

To help improve sales performance, the sales team has decided to buy lunch for all salespeople at the company every time they beat the figure for best daily total earnings achieved over the last 30 days. Write a query that produces the total sales in dollars for a given day and the target the salespeople have to beat for that day, starting from January 1, 2019:

1. Open your favorite SQL client and connect to the **sqlda** database.

2. Calculate the total sales for a given day and the target using the following query:

```
WITH daily_sales as (
SELECT sales_transaction_date::DATE,
SUM(sales_amount) as total_sales
FROM sales
GROUP BY 1
),

sales_stats_30 AS (
SELECT sales_transaction_date, total_sales,
MAX(total_sales) OVER (ORDER BY sales_transaction_date ROWS BETWEEN 30
PRECEDING and 1 PRECEDING)
AS max_sales_30
FROM daily_sales
ORDER BY 1)

SELECT sales_transaction_date,
total_sales,
max_sales_30
FROM sales_stats_30
WHERE sales_transaction_date>='2019-01-01';
```

You should get the following results:

sales_transaction_date date	total_sales double precision	max_sales_30 double precision
2019-01-01	87694.844	316464.847
2019-01-02	76149.854	316464.847
2019-01-03	161269.809	316464.847
2019-01-04	193209.912	316464.847
2019-01-05	49469.77	316464.847
2019-01-06	96319.835	316464.847
2019-01-07	42239.837	316464.847
2019-01-08	101729.748	316464.847
2019-01-09	118634.902	316464.847
2019-01-10	100089.78	316464.847
2019-01-11	183209.871	283849.84

Figure 5.13: Best sales over the last 30 days

Notice the use of a window frame from `30 PRECEDING` to `1 PRECEDING` to remove the current row from the calculation.

As can be seen in this exercise, window frames make calculating moving statistics simple, and even kind of fun!

Activity 7: Analyzing Sales Using Window Frames and Window Functions

It's the holidays, and it's time to give out Christmas bonuses at ZoomZoom. Sales team want to see how the company has performed overall, as well as how individual dealerships have performed within the company. To achieve this, ZoomZoom's head of Sales would like you to run an analysis for them:

1. Open your favorite SQL client and connect to the **sqlda** database.

2. Calculate the total sales amount by day for all of the days in the year 2018 (that is, before the date January 1, 2019).

3. Calculate the rolling 30-day average for the daily number of sales deals.

4. Calculate what decile each dealership would be in compared to other dealerships based on their total sales amount.

Expected Output:

dealership_id double precision	total_sales_amount double precision	ntile integer
13	538079.414	1
9	618263.995	1
8	671619.251	2
4	905158.609	2
17	907058.842	3
20	949849.053	3
12	1086033.376	4
15	1197118.234	4
6	1316253.465	5
14	1551108.481	5
3	1622872.801	6
16	1981062.341	6

Figure 5.14: Decile for dealership sales amount

> **Note**
>
> The solution for the activity can be found on page 325.

Summary

In this chapter, we learned about the power of window functions. We looked at how to construct a basic window function using **OVER**, **PARTITION BY**, and **ORDER BY**. We then looked at how to calculate statistics using window functions, and how to adjust a window frame to calculate rolling statistics.

In the next chapter, we will look at how to import and export data in order to utilize SQL with other programs. We will use the **COPY** command to upload data to your database in bulk. We will also use Excel to process data from your database and then simplify your code using SQLAlchemy.

Importing and Exporting Data

Learning Objectives

By the end of this chapter, you will be able to:

- Use psql at the command line to efficiently interact with your database
- Use the COPY command to upload data to your database in bulk
- Use Excel to process data from your database
- Simplify your code using SQLAlchemy in Python
- Upload and download data to and from your database in bulk with R and Python

This chapter covers how to move data between your database and other analytics processing pipelines.

Introduction

In order to extract insights from your database, you need data. And, while it's possible that some of that data will be populated and updated for you, there are always going to be scenarios where you need more data that is not yet in your database. In this chapter, we are going to explore how we can efficiently upload data to our centralized database for further analysis.

Not only will we want to upload data to our database for further analysis, but there are also going to be times where we want to download data from our database for further processing. We will also explore the process of extracting data from our database.

One of the primary reasons you would want to upload or download data to or from your database is because you have other analytics tools that you want to use. You will often want to use other software to analyze your data. In this chapter, we will also look at how you can integrate your workflows with two specific programming languages that are frequently used for analytics: Python and R. These languages are powerful because they are easy to use, allow for advanced functionality, are open source, and have large communities supporting them as a result of their popularity. We will look at how large datasets can be passed between our programming languages and our databases efficiently so that we can have workflows that take advantage of all of the tools available to us.

With this in mind, we will start by looking at the bulk uploading and downloading functionality in the Postgres command-line client, **psql**, and then move on to importing and exporting data using Python and R.

The COPY Command

At this point, you are probably pretty familiar with the **SELECT** statement (covered in *Chapter 2, The Basics of SQL for Analytics*), which allows us to retrieve data from our database. While this command is useful for small datasets that can be scanned quickly, we will often want to save a large dataset to a file. By saving these datasets to files, we can further process or analyze the data locally using Excel, Python, or R. In order to retrieve these large datasets, we can use the Postgres **COPY** command, which efficiently transfers data from a database to a file, or from a file to a database.

Getting Started with COPY

The **COPY** statement retrieves data from your database and dumps it in the file format of your choosing. For example, take the following statement:

```
COPY (SELECT * FROM customers LIMIT 5) TO STDOUT WITH CSV HEADER;
```

```
customer_id,title,first_name,last_name,suffix,email,gender,ip_address,phone,street_address,city,state,postal_code,latitude,longitude,date_added
1,,Arlena,Riveles,,ariveles0@stumbleupon.com,F,98.36.172.246,,,,,,,,2017-04-23 00:00:00
2,Dr,Ode,Stovin,,ostovin1@npr.org,M,16.97.59.186,314-534-4361,2573 Fordem Parkway,Saint Louis,MO,63116,38.5814,-90.2625,2014-10-02 00:00:00
3,,Braden,Jordan,,bjordan2@geocities.com,M,192.86.248.59,,5651 Kennedy Park,Pensacola,FL,32590,30.6143,-87.2758,2018-10-27 00:00:00
4,,Jessika,Nussen,,jnussen3@salon.com,F,159.165.138.166,615-824-2506,224 Village Circle,Nashville,TN,37215,36.0986,-86.8219,2017-09-03 00:00:00
5,,Lonnie,Rembaud,,lrembaud4@discovery.com,F,18.131.58.65,786-499-3431,38 Lindbergh Way,Miami,FL,33124,25.5584,-80.4582,2014-03-06 00:00:00
```

Figure 6.1: Using COPY to print results to STDOUT in a CSV file format

This statement returns five rows from the table, with each record on a new line, and each value separated by a comma, in a typical **.csv** file format. The header is also included at the top.

Here is the breakdown of this command and the parameters that were passed in:

- **COPY** is simply the command used to transfer data to a file format.

- **(SELECT * FROM customers LIMIT 5)** is the query that we want to copy.

- **TO STDOUT** indicates that the results should be printed rather than saved to a file on the hard drive. "Standard Out" is the common term for displaying output in a command-line terminal environment.

- **WITH** is an optional keyword used to separate the parameters that we will use in the database-to-file transfer.

- **CSV** indicates that we will use the **CSV** file format. We could have also specified **BINARY** or left this out altogether and received the output in text format.

- **HEADER** indicates that we want the header printed as well.

> **Note**
>
> You can learn more about the parameters available for the **COPY** command in the Postgres documentation: https://www.postgresql.org/docs/current/sql-copy.html.

While the **STDOUT** option is useful, often, we will want to save data to a file. The **COPY** command offers functionality to do this, but data is saved locally on the **Postgres server**. You must specify the full file path (relative file paths are not permitted). If you have your **Postgres** database running on your computer, you can test this out using the following command:

```
COPY (SELECT * FROM customers LIMIT 5) TO '/path/to/my_file.csv' WITH CSV
HEADER;
```

Copying Data with psql

While you have probably been using a frontend client to access your Postgres database, you might not have known that one of the first Postgres clients was actually a command-line program called **psql**. This interface is still in use today, and **psql** offers some great functionality for running Postgres scripts and interacting with the local computing environment. It allows for the **COPY** command to be called remotely using the **psql**-specific **\copy** instruction, which invokes **COPY**.

To launch **psql**, you can run the following command in the Terminal:

```
psql -h my_host -p 5432 -d my_database -U my_username
```

In this command, we pass in flags that provide the information needed to make the database connection. In this case:

- **-h** is the flag for the hostname. The string that comes after it (separated by a space) should be the hostname for your database.

- **-p** is the flag for the database port. Usually, this is **5432** for Postgres databases.

- **-d** is the flag for the database name. The string that comes after it should be the database name.

- **-U** is the flag for the username. It is succeeded by the username.

Once you have connected to your database using **psql**, you can test out the **\copy** instruction by using the following command:

```
\copy (SELECT * FROM customers LIMIT 5) TO 'my_file.csv' WITH CSV HEADER;
```

```
COPY 5
Time: 22.208 ms
```

Figure 6.2: Using \copy from psql to print results to a CSV file format

Here is the breakdown of this command and the parameters that were passed in:

- **\copy** is invoking the Postgres **COPY ... TO STDOUT...** command to output the data.

- **(SELECT * FROM customers LIMIT 5)** is the query that we want to copy.

- **TO 'my_file.csv'** indicates that **psql** should save the output from standard into **my_file.csv**.

- The **WITH CSV HEADER** parameters operate the same as before.

We can also take a look at **my_file.csv**:

```
customer_id,title,first_name,last_name,suffix,email,gender,ip_address,phone,street_address,city,state,postal_code,latitude,longitude,date_added
1,,Arlena,Riveles,,ariveles0@stumbleupon.com,F,98.36.172.246,,,,,,,,2017-04-23 00:00:00
2,Dr,Ode,Stovin,,ostovin1@npr.org,M,16.97.59.186,314-534-4361,2573 Fordem Parkway,Saint Louis,MO,63116,38.5814,-90.2625,2014-10-02 00:00:00
3,,Braden,Jordan,,bjordan2@geocities.com,M,192.86.248.59,,5651 Kennedy Park,Pensacola,FL,32590,30.6143,-87.2758,2018-10-27 00:00:00
4,,Jessika,Nussen,,jnussen3@salon.com,F,159.165.138.166,615-824-2506,224 Village Circle,Nashville,TN,37215,36.0986,-86.8219,2017-09-03 00:00:00
5,,Lonnie,Rembaud,,lrembaud4@discovery.com,F,18.131.58.65,786-499-3431,38 Lindbergh Way,Miami,FL,33124,25.5584,-80.4582,2014-03-06 00:00:00
[sqlda] #
```

Figure 6.3: The CSV file that we created using our \copy command

It is worth noting here that the formatting can look a little messy for the **\copy** command, because it does not allow for commands with new lines. A simple way around this is to create a view containing your data before the **\copy** command and drop the view after your **\copy** command has finished. For example:

```
CREATE TEMP VIEW customers_sample AS (
    SELECT *
    FROM customers
    LIMIT 5
);
\copy customers_sample TO 'my_file.csv' WITH CSV HEADER
DROP VIEW customers_sample;
```

While you can perform this action either way, for readability purposes, we will use the latter format in this book for longer queries.

Configuring COPY and \copy

There are several options to configure the **COPY** and **\copy** commands:

- **FORMAT format_name** can be used to specify the format. The options for **format_name** are **csv**, **text**, or **binary**. Alternatively, you can simply specify **CSV** or **BINARY** without the **FORMAT** keyword, or not specify the format at all and let the output default to a text file format.

- **DELIMITER 'delimiter_character'** can be used to specify the delimiter character for CSV or text files (for example ',' for CSV files, or '|' for pipe-separated files)

- **NULL 'null_string'** can be used to specify how null values should be represented (for example, ' ' if blanks represent null values, or **'NULL'** if that's how missing values should be represented in the data).

- **HEADER** specifies that the header should be output.

- **QUOTE 'quote_character'** can be used to specify how fields with special characters (for example, a comma in a text value within a CSV file) can be wrapped in quotes so that they are ignored by **COPY**.

- **ESCAPE 'escape_character'** specifies the character that can be used to escape the following character.

- **ENCODING 'encoding_name'** allows specification of the encoding, which is particularly useful when you are dealing with foreign languages that contain special characters or user input.

Using COPY and \copy to Bulk Upload Data to Your Database

As we have seen, the copy commands can be used to efficiently download data, but they can also be used to upload data.

The **COPY** and **\copy** commands are far more efficient at uploading data than an **INSERT** statement. There are a few reasons for this:

- When using **COPY**, there is only one commit, which occurs after all of the rows have been inserted.

- There is less communication between the database and the client, so there is less network latency.

- Postgres includes optimizations for **COPY** that would not be available through **INSERT**.

  Here's an example of using the **\copy** command to copy rows into the table from a file:

  ```
  \copy customers FROM 'my_file.csv' CSV HEADER DELIMITER ',';
  ```

Here is the breakdown of this command and the parameters that were passed in:

- **\copy** is invoking the Postgres **COPY ... FROM STDOUT...** command to load the data into the database.

- **Customers** specifies the name of the table that we want to append to.

- **FROM 'my_file.csv'** specifies that we are uploading records from **my_file.csv** – the **FROM** keyword specifies that we are uploading records as opposed to the **TO** keyword that we used to download records.

- The **WITH CSV HEADER** parameters operate the same as before.

- **DELIMITER ','** specifies what the delimiter is in the file. For a CSV file, this is assumed to be a comma, so we do not need this parameter. However, for readability, it might be useful to explicitly define this parameter, for no other reason than to remind yourself how the file has been formatted.

> **Note**
>
> While **COPY** and **\copy** are great for exporting data to other tools, there is additional functionality in Postgres for exporting a database backup. For these maintenance tasks, you can use **pg_dump** for a specific table and **pg_dumpall** for an entire database or schema. These commands even let you save data in compressed (**tar**) format, which saves space. Unfortunately, the output format from these commands is typically SQL, and it cannot be readily consumed outside of Postgres. Therefore, it does not help us with importing or exporting data to and from other analytics tools, such as Python and R.

Exercise 19: Exporting Data to a File for Further Processing in Excel

In this exercise, we will be saving a file containing the cities with the highest number of ZoomZoom customers. This analysis will help the ZoomZoom executive committee to decide where they might want to open the next dealership.

> **Note**
>
> For the exercises and activities in this chapter, you will need to be able to access your database with **psql**. https://github.com/TrainingByPackt/SQL-for-Data-Analytics/tree/master/Lesson07.

1. Open a **command-line tool** to implement this exercise, such as cmd for Windows or Terminal for Mac.

2. In your command-line interface, connect to your database using the **psql** command.

3. Copy the **customers** table from your **zoomzoom** database to a local file in .csv format. You can do this with the following command:

```
CREATE TEMP VIEW top_cities AS (
    SELECT city,
           count(1) AS number_of_customers
    FROM customers
    WHERE city IS NOT NULL
    GROUP BY 1
    ORDER BY 2 DESC
    LIMIT 10
);
\copy top_cities TO 'top_cities.csv' WITH CSV HEADER DELIMITER ','
DROP VIEW top_cities;
```

Here's a breakdown for these statements:

CREATE TEMP VIEW top_cities AS (…) indicates that we are creating a new view. A view is similar to a table, except that the data is not created. Instead, every time the view is referenced, the underlying query is executed. The **TEMP** keyword indicates that the view can be removed automatically at the end of the session.

SELECT city, count(1) AS number_of_customers … is a query that gives us the number of customers for each city. Because we add the **LIMIT 10** statement, we only grab the top 10 cities, as ordered by the second column (number of customers). We also filter out customers without a city filled in.

\copy … copies data from this view to the **top_cities.csv** file on our local computer.

DROP VIEW top_cities; deletes the view because we no longer need it.

If you open the **top_cities.csv** text file, you should see output that looks like this:

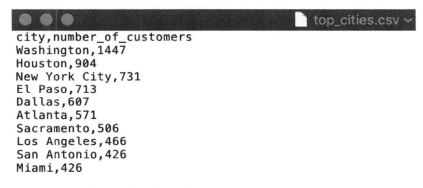

```
city,number_of_customers
Washington,1447
Houston,904
New York City,731
El Paso,713
Dallas,607
Atlanta,571
Sacramento,506
Los Angeles,466
San Antonio,426
Miami,426
```

Figure 6.4: Output from the \copy command

> **Note**
>
> Here, the output file is **top_cities.csv**. We will be using this file in the exercises to come in this chapter.

Now that we have the output from our database in a CSV file format, we can open it with a spreadsheet program, such as Excel.

4. Using Microsoft Excel or your favorite spreadsheet software or text editor, open the **top_cities.csv** file:

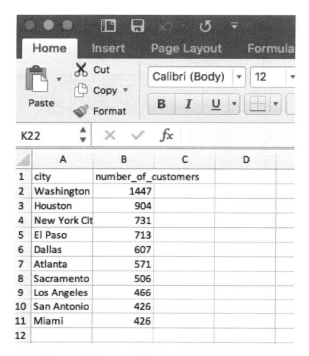

Figure 6.5: top_cities.csv open in Excel

5. Next, select the data from cell A1 to cell B11.

	A	B	C
1	city	number_of_	customers
2	Washington	1447	
3	Houston	904	
4	New York Cit	731	
5	El Paso	713	
6	Dallas	607	
7	Atlanta	571	
8	Sacramento	506	
9	Los Angeles	466	
10	San Antonio	426	
11	Miami	426	
12			

Figure 6.6: Select the entire dataset by clicking and dragging from A1 to B11

6. Next, in the top menu, go to **Insert** and then click on the bar chart icon (▮▮▮ ▾) to create a **2-D Column** chart:

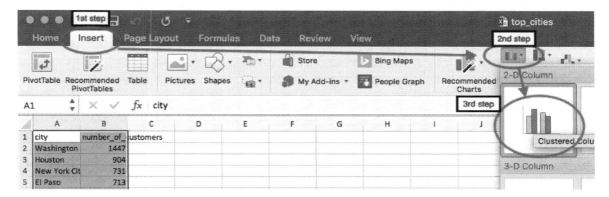

Figure 6.7: Insert a bar chart to visualize the selected data

7. Finally, you should end up with output like this:

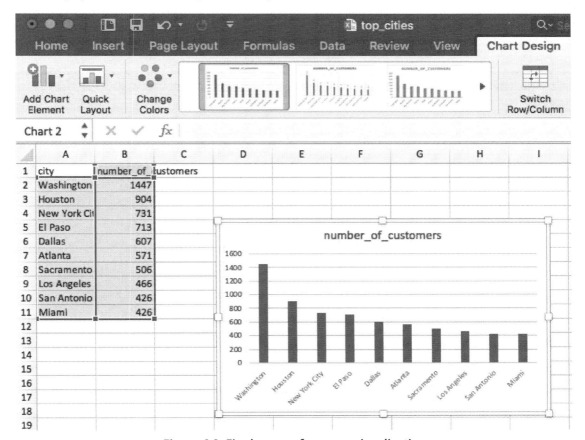

Figure 6.8: Final output from our visualization

We can see from this chart that Washington D.C. seems to have a very high number of customers. Based on this simple analysis, Washington D.C. would probably be the obvious next target for ZoomZoom expansion!

Using R with Our Database

At this point, you can now copy data to and from a database. This gives you the freedom to expand beyond SQL to other data analytics tools and incorporate any program that can read a CSV file as input into your pipeline. While just about every analytics tool that you would need can read a CSV file, there's still the extra step needed in which you download the data. Adding more steps to your analytics pipeline can make your workflow more complex. Complexity can be undesirable, both because it necessitates additional maintenance, and because it increases the number of failure points.

Another approach is to connect to your database directly in your analytics code. In this part of the chapter, we are going to look at how to do this in R, a programming language designed specifically for statistical computing. Later in the chapter, we will look at integrating our data pipelines with Python as well.

Why Use R?

While we have managed to perform aggregate-level descriptive statistics on our data using pure SQL, R allows us to perform other statistical analysis, including machine learning, regression analysis, and significance testing. R also allows us to create data visualizations that make trends clear and easier to interpret. R has arguably more statistical functionality than just about any other analytics software available.

Getting Started with R

Because R is an open source language with support for Windows, macOS X, and Linux, it is very easy to get started. Here are the steps to quickly set up your R environment:

1. Download the latest version of R from https://cran.r-project.org/.

2. Once you have installed R, you can download and install RStudio, an **Integrated Development Environment** (**IDE**) for R programming, from http://rstudio.org/download/desktop.

3. Next, we are going to install the **RPostgreSQL** package in R. We can do this in RStudio by navigating to the **Packages** tab and clicking the **Install** icon:

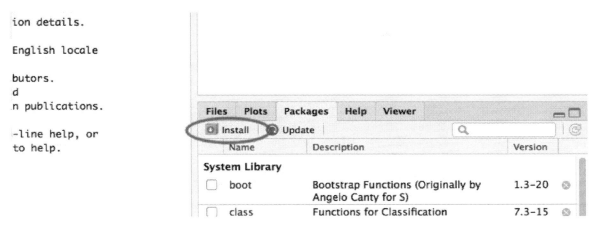

Figure 6.9: Install R packages in RStudio in the Packages pane

4. Next, we will search for the **RPostgreSQL** package in the **Install Packages** window and install the package:

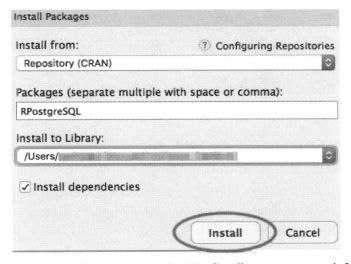

Figure 6.10: The Install Packages prompt in RStudio allows us to search for a package

5. Next, we can use the **RPostgreSQL** package to load some data into R. You can use the following commands:

```
library(RPostgreSQL)
con <- dbConnect(PostgreSQL(), host="my_host", user="my_username",
password="my password", dbname="zoomzoom", port=5432)
result <- dbGetQuery(con, "select * from customers limit 10;")
result
```

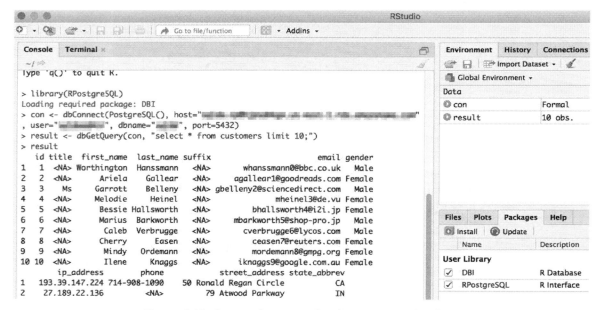

Figure 6.11: Output from our database connection in R

Here is a breakdown of these commands:

library(RPostgreSQL) is the syntax for loading a library in R.

con <- dbConnect(PostgreSQL(), host="my_host", user="my_username ", password="my_password", dbname="zoomzoom", port=5432) establishes the connection to the database. All of the database parameters are entered here, so you should replace the parameters as needed for your setup. If you have set up a **.pgpass** file, you can leave out the **password** parameter.

result <- dbGetQuery(con, "select * from customers limit 10;") is where we run a simple query to test our connection and check the result. The data is then stored in the result variable as an R dataframe.

In the last line, **result** is simply the name of the variable that stores our DataFrame, and the R terminal will print the contents of a variable or expression if there is no assignment.

At this point, we have successfully exported data from our database into R. This will lay the foundation for just about any analysis that you might want to perform. After you have loaded your data in R, you can continue processing data by researching other packages and techniques using other R packages. For example, `dplyr` can be used for data manipulation and transformation, and the `ggplot2` package can be used for data visualization.

Using Python with Our Database

While R has a breadth of functionality, many data scientists and data analysts are starting to use Python. Why? Because Python offers a similarly high-level language that can be easily used to process data. While the number of statistical packages and functionality in R can still have an edge on Python, Python is growing fast, and has generally overtaken R in most of the recent polls. A lot of the Python functionality is also faster than R, in part because so much of it is written in C, a lower-level programming language.

The other large advantage that Python has is that it is very versatile. While R is generally only used in the research and statistical analysis communities, Python can be used to do anything from statistical analysis to standing up a web server. As a result, the developer community is much larger for Python. A larger development community is a big advantage because there is better community support (for example, on StackOverflow), and there are more Python packages and modules being developed every day. The last major benefit of Python is that, because it is a general programming language, it can be easier to deploy Python code to a production environment, and certain controls (such as Python namespaces) make Python less susceptible to errors.

As a result of these advantages, it might be preferable to learn Python, unless the functionality that you require is only available in R, or if the rest of your team is using R.

Why Use Python?

While SQL can perform aggregate-level descriptive statistics, Python (like R) allows us to perform other statistical analysis and data visualizations. On top of these advantages, Python can be used to create repeatable pipelines that can be deployed to production, and it can also be used to create interactive analytics web servers. Whereas R is a specialist programming language, Python is a generalist programming language – a jack of all trades. Whatever your analytics requirements are, you can almost always complete your task using the tools available in Python.

Getting Started with Python

While there are many ways to get Python, we are going to start with the Anaconda distribution of Python, which comes with a lot of the commonly used analytics packages pre-installed.

Exercise 20: Exporting Data from a Database within Python

1. Download and install Anaconda: https://www.anaconda.com/distribution/

2. Once it's installed, open Terminal for Mac or cmd for Windows. Type **python** on the command line, and check that you can access the Python interpreter, which should look like this:

```
bash:~$ python
Python 3.6.3 |Anaconda custom (64-bit)| (default, Oct  6 2017, 12:04:38)
[GCC 4.2.1 Compatible Clang 4.0.1 (tags/RELEASE_401/final)] on darwin
Type "help", "copyright", "credits" or "license" for more information.
>>>
```

Figure 6.12: The Python interpreter is now available and ready for input

> **Note**
>
> If you get an error, it may be because you need to specify your Python path. You can enter **quit()** to exit.

3. Next, we will want to install the PostgreSQL database client for Python, **psycopg2**. We can download and install this package using the Anaconda package manager, **conda**. You can enter the following command at the command line to install the Postgres database client:

```
conda install psycopg2
```

We can break down this command as follows:

conda is the command for the **conda** package manager.

install specifies that we want to install a new Python package.

4. Now, we can open the Python interpreter and load in some data from the database

   Type **python** at the command line to open the Python interpreter.

5. Next, we can start writing the Python script to load data:

```
import psycopg2
with psycopg2.connect(host="my_host", user="my_username", password="my_
password", dbname="zoomzoom", port=5432) as conn:
    with conn.cursor() as cur:
        cur.execute("SELECT * FROM customers LIMIT 5")
            records = cur.fetchall()


records
```

```
[(1, None, 'Arlena', 'Riveles', None, 'ariveles0@stumbleupon.com', 'F', '98.36.172.246', None, None, No
ne, None, None, None, None, datetime.datetime(2017, 4, 23, 0, 0)), (2, 'Dr', 'Ode', 'Stovin', None, 'os
tovin1@npr.org', 'M', '16.97.59.186', '314-534-4361', '2573 Fordem Parkway', 'Saint Louis', 'MO', '6311
6', 38.5814, -90.2625, datetime.datetime(2014, 10, 2, 0, 0)), (3, None, 'Braden', 'Jordan', None, 'bjor
dan2@geocities.com', 'M', '192.86.248.59', None, '5651 Kennedy Park', 'Pensacola', 'FL', '32590', 30.61
43, -87.2758, datetime.datetime(2018, 10, 27, 0, 0)), (4, None, 'Jessika', 'Nussen', None, 'jnussen3@sa
lon.com', 'F', '159.165.138.166', '615-824-2506', '224 Village Circle', 'Nashville', 'TN', '37215', 36.
0986, -86.8219, datetime.datetime(2017, 9, 3, 0, 0)), (5, None, 'Lonnie', 'Rembaud', None, 'lrembaud4@d
iscovery.com', 'F', '18.131.58.65', '786-499-3431', '38 Lindbergh Way', 'Miami', 'FL', '33124', 25.5584
, -80.4582, datetime.datetime(2014, 3, 6, 0, 0))]
>>>
```

Figure 6.13: Output from our database connection in Python

These commands can be broken down as follows:

First, we import the **psycopg2** package using the following command: **import psycopg2**. Next, we set up our connection object using **psycopg2.connect(host="my_host", user="my_username", password="my_password", dbname="zoomzoom", port=5432)**.

All of the database parameters are entered here, so you should replace the parameters as required for your setup. If you have set up a **.pgpass** file, you can leave out the **password** parameter. This is wrapped in **with .. as conn** in Python; the **with** statement automatically tears down the object (in this case, the connection) when the indentation returns. This is particularly useful for database connection, where an idle connection could inadvertently consume database resources. We can store this connection object in a conn variable using the **as conn** statement.

Now that we have a connection, we need to create a **cursor** object, which will let us read from the database. `conn.cursor()` creates the database **cursor** object, which allows us to execute SQL in the database connection, and the `with` statement allows us to automatically tear down the cursor when we no longer need it.

`cur.execute("SELECT * FROM customers LIMIT 5")` sends the query `"SELECT * FROM customers LIMIT 5"` to the database and executes it.

`records = cur.fetchall()` fetches all of the remaining rows in a query result and assigns those rows to the **records** variable.

Now that we have sent the query to the database and received the records, we can reset the indentation level. We can view our result by entering the expression (in this case, just the variable name **records**) and hitting *Enter*. This output is the five customer records that we have collected.

While we were able to connect to the database and read data, there were several steps, and the syntax was a little bit more complex than that for some of the other approaches we have tried. While **psycopg2** can be powerful, it can be helpful to use some of the other packages in Python to facilitate interfacing with the database.

Improving Postgres Access in Python with SQLAlchemy and Pandas

While **psycopg2** is a powerful database client for accessing Postgres from Python, we can simplify the code by using a few other packages, namely, Pandas and SQLAlchemy.

First, we will look at SQLAlchemy, a Python SQL toolkit and object relational mapper that maps representations of objects to database tables. In particular, we will be looking at the SQLAlchemy database engine and some of the advantages that it offers. This will enable us to access our database seamlessly without worrying about connections and cursors.

Next, we can look at Pandas – a Python package that can perform data manipulation and facilitate data analysis. The **pandas** package allows us to represent our data table structure (called a **DataFrame**) in memory. Pandas also has high-level APIs that will enable us to read data from our database in just a few lines of code:

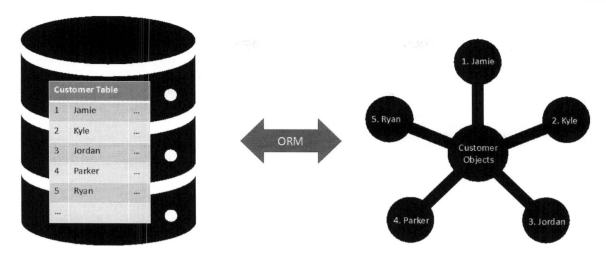

Figure 6.14: An object relational mapper maps rows in a database to objects in memory

While both of these packages are powerful, it is worth noting that they still use the **psycopg2** package in order to connect to the database and execute queries. The big advantage that these packages provide is that they abstract some of the complexities of connecting to the database. By abstracting these complexities, we can connect to the database without worrying that we might forget to close a connection or tear down a cursor.

What is SQLAlchemy?

SQLAlchemy is a SQL toolkit. While it offers some great functionality, the key benefit that we will focus on here is the SQLAlchemy **Engine** object.

A SQLAlchemy **Engine** object contains information about the type of database (in our case, PostgreSQL) and a connection pool. The connection pool allows for multiple connections to the database that operate simultaneously. The connection pool is also beneficial because it does not create a connection until a query is sent to be executed. Because these connections are not formed until the query is being executed, the **Engine** object is said to exhibit *lazy initialization*. The term "lazy" is used to indicate that nothing happens (the connection is not formed) until a request is made. This is advantageous because it minimizes the time of the connection and reduces the load on the database.

Another advantage of the SQLAlchemy **Engine** is that it automatically commits (autocommits) changes to the database due to **CREATE TABLE**, **UPDATE**, **INSERT**, or other statements that modify our database.

In our case, we will want to use it because it provides a robust **Engine** to access databases. If the connection is dropped, a SQLAlchemy **Engine** can instantiate that connection because it has a connection pool. It also provides a nice interface that works well with other packages (such as pandas).

Using Python with Jupyter Notebooks

In addition to interactively using Python at the command line, we can use Python in a notebook form in our web browser. This is useful for displaying visualizations and running exploratory analyses.

In this section, we are going to use Jupyter notebooks that were installed as part of the Anaconda installation. At the command line, run the following command:

```
jupyter notebook
```

You should see something like this pop up in your default browser:

Figure 6.15: Jupyter notebook pop-up screen in your browser

Next, we will create a new notebook:

Figure 6.16: Opening a new Python 3 Jupyter notebook

At the prompt, enter the following **import** statements:

```
from sqlalchemy import create_engine
import pandas as pd
```

You'll notice that we are importing two packages here – the first is the **create_engine** module within the **sqlalchemy** package, and the second is **pandas**, which we rename to **pd** because this is the standard convention (and it is fewer characters). Using these two packages, we will be able to read and write data to and from our database and visualize the output.

Hit *Shift+Enter* to run these commands. A new active cell should pop up:

```
In [1]:  from sqlalchemy import create_engine
         import pandas

In [ ]:
```

Figure 6.17: Running our first cell in the Jupyter notebook

Next, we will configure our notebook to display plots and visualizations inline. We can do this with the following command:

```
% matplotlib inline
```

This tells the **matplotlib** package (which is a dependency of pandas) to create plots and visualizations inline in our notebook. Hit *Shift + Enter* again to jump to the next cell.

In this cell, we will define our connection string:

```
cnxn_string = ("postgresql+psycopg2://{username}:{pswd}"
               "@{host}:{port}/{database}")

print(cnxn_string)
```

Press *Shift + Enter* again, and you should now see our connection string printed. Next, we need to fill in our parameters and create the database **Engine**. You can replace the strings starting with **your_** with the parameters specific to your connection:

```
engine = create_engine(cnxn_string.format(
    username="your_username",
    pswd="your_password",
    host="your_host",
    port=5432,
    database="your_database_name"))
```

In this command, we run **create_engine** to create our database **Engine** object. We pass in our connection string and we format it for our specific database connection by filling in the placeholders for **{username}**, **{pswd}**, **{host}**, **{port}**, and **{database}**.

Because SQLAlchemy is lazy, we will not know whether our database connection was successful until we try to send a command. We can test whether this database **Engine** works by running the following command and hitting *Shift + Enter*:

```
engine.execute("SELECT * FROM customers LIMIT 2;").fetchall()
```

We should see something like this:

```
Out[4]: [(1, None, 'Arlena', 'Riveles', None, 'ariveles0@stumbleupon.com', 'F', '98.36.172.246', None, None, None, None, None
        , None, None, datetime.datetime(2017, 4, 23, 0, 0)),
         (2, 'Dr', 'Ode', 'Stovin', None, 'ostovin1@npr.org', 'M', '16.97.59.186', '314-534-4361', '2573 Fordem Parkway', 'Sa
        int Louis', 'MO', '63116', 38.5814, -90.2625, datetime.datetime(2014, 10, 2, 0, 0))]
```

Figure 6.18: Executing a query within Python

The output of this command is a Python list containing rows from our database in tuples. While we have successfully read data from our database, we will probably find it more practical to read our data into a Pandas DataFrame in the next section.

Reading and Writing to our Database with Pandas

Python comes with great data structures, including lists, dictionaries, and tuples. While these are useful, our data can often be represented in a table form, with rows and columns, similar to how we would store data in our database. For these purposes, the DataFrame object in Pandas can be particularly useful.

In addition to providing powerful data structures, Pandas also offers:

- Functionality to read data in directly from a database

- Data visualization

- Data analysis tools

If we continue from where we left off with our Jupyter notebook, we can use the SQLAlchemy **Engine** object to read data into a Pandas DataFrame:

```
customers_data = pd.read_sql_table('customers', engine)
```

We have now stored our entire **customers** table as a Pandas DataFrame in the **customers_data** variable. The Pandas **read_sql_table** function requires two parameters: the name of a table and the connectable database (in this case, the SQLAlchemy **Engine**). Alternatively, we can use the **read_sql_query** function, which takes a query string instead of a table name.

Here's an example of what your notebook might look like at this point:

```
In [1]:  from sqlalchemy import create_engine
         import pandas as pd
         % matplotlib inline

In [2]:  cnxn_string = ("postgresql+psycopg2://{username}:{pswd}"
                         "@{host}:{port}/{database}")
         print(cnxn_string)

         postgresql+psycopg2://{username}:{pswd}@{host}:{port}/{database}

In [3]:  engine = create_engine(cnxn_string.format(
             username="            ",
             pswd="                          ",
             host="                                              ",
             port=5432,
             database="        "))

In [4]:  engine.execute("SELECT * FROM customers LIMIT 2;").fetchall()

Out[4]:  [(1, None, 'Arlena', 'Riveles', None, 'ariveles0@stumbleupon.com', 'F', '98.36.172.246', None, None, None, None, None
         , None, None, datetime.datetime(2017, 4, 23, 0, 0)),
          (2, 'Dr', 'Ode', 'Stovin', None, 'ostovin1@npr.org', 'M', '16.97.59.186', '314-534-4361', '2573 Fordem Parkway', 'Sa
         int Louis', 'MO', '63116', 38.5814, -90.2625, datetime.datetime(2014, 10, 2, 0, 0))]

In [5]:  customers_data = pd.read_sql_table('customers', engine)

In [ ]:  |
```

Figure 6.19: The entirety of our Jupyter notebook

Performing Data Visualization with Pandas

Now that we know how to read data from the database, we can start to do some basic analysis and visualization.

Exercise 21: Reading Data and Visualizing Data in Python

In this exercise, we will be reading data from the database output and visualizing the results using Python, Jupyter notebooks, SQLAlchemy, and Pandas. We will be analyzing the demographic information of customers by city to better understand our target audience.

1. Open the Jupyter notebook from the previous section and click on the last empty cell.

2. Enter the following query surrounded by triple quotes (triple quotes allow for strings that span multiple lines in Python):

```
query = """
    SELECT city,
           COUNT(1) AS number_of_customers,
           COUNT(NULLIF(gender, 'M')) AS female,
           COUNT(NULLIF(gender, 'F')) AS male
    FROM customers
    WHERE city IS NOT NULL
    GROUP BY 1
```

```
    ORDER BY 2 DESC
    LIMIT 10
"""
```

For each city, this query calculates the count of customers, and calculates the count for each gender. It also removes customers with missing city information and aggregates our customer data by the first column (the city). In addition, it sorts the data by the second column (the count of customers) from largest to smallest (descending). Then, it limits the output to the top 10 (the 10 cities with the highest number of customers).

3. Read the query result into a Pandas DataFrame with the following command and execute the cells using *Shift + Enter*:

    ```
    top_cities_data = pd.read_sql_query(query, engine)
    ```

4. You can view the data in **top_cities_data** by entering it in a new cell and simply hitting *Shift + Enter*. Just as with the Python interpreter, entering a variable or expression will display the value. You will notice that Pandas also numbers the rows by default – in Pandas, this is called an index.

```
Out[7]:
```

	city	number_of_customers	female	male
0	Washington	1447	734	713
1	Houston	904	446	458
2	New York City	731	369	362
3	El Paso	713	369	344
4	Dallas	607	309	298
5	Atlanta	571	292	279
6	Sacramento	506	244	262
7	Los Angeles	466	241	225
8	San Antonio	426	207	219
9	Miami	426	195	231

Figure 6.20: storing the result of a query as a pandas dataframe

5. Now, we will plot the number of men and women in each of the top 10 cities. Because we want to view the stats for each city separately, we can use a simple bar plot to view the data:

```
ax = top_cities_data.plot.bar('city', y=['female', 'male'], title='Number
of Customers by Gender and City')
```

Here is a screenshot of what our resulting output notebook should look like:

Figure 6.21: Data visualization in the Jupyter notebook

The results show that there is no significant difference in customer gender for the cities that we are considering expanding into.

Writing Data to the Database Using Python

There will also be many scenarios in which we will want to use Python to write data back to the database, and, luckily for us, Pandas and SQLAlchemy make this relatively easy.

If we have our data in a Pandas DataFrame, we can write data back to the database using the Pandas **to_sql(…)** function, which requires two parameters: the name of the table to write to and the connection. Best of all, the **to_sql(…)** function also creates the target table for us by inferring column types using a DataFrame's data types.

We can test out this functionality using the **top_cities_data** DataFrame that we created earlier. Let's use the following **to_sql(…)** command in our existing Jupyter notebook:

```
top_cities_data.to_sql('top_cities_data', engine,
                       index=False, if_exists='replace')
```

In addition to the two required parameters, we added two optional parameters to this function – the **index** parameter specifies whether we want the index to be a column in our database table as well (a value of **False** means that we will not include it), and the **if_exists** parameter allows us to specify how to handle a scenario in which there is already a table with data in the database. In this case, we want to drop that table and replace it with the new data, so we use the **'replace'** option. In general, you should exercise caution when using the **'replace'** option as you can inadvertently lose your existing data.

Now, we can query this data from any database client, including **psql**. Here is the result when we try to query this new table in our database:

```
      city       | number_of_customers | female | male
-----------------+---------------------+--------+------
 Washington      |                1447 |    734 |  713
 Houston         |                 904 |    446 |  458
 New York City   |                 731 |    369 |  362
 El Paso         |                 713 |    369 |  344
 Dallas          |                 607 |    309 |  298
 Atlanta         |                 571 |    292 |  279
 Sacramento      |                 506 |    244 |  262
 Los Angeles     |                 466 |    241 |  225
 San Antonio     |                 426 |    207 |  219
 Miami           |                 426 |    195 |  231
(10 rows)
```

Figure 6.22: Data created in Python that has now been imported into our database

Improving Python Write Speed with COPY

While this functionality is simple and works as intended, it is using **insert** statements to send data to the database. For a small table of 10 rows, this is OK, but for larger tables, the **psql \copy** command is going to be much faster.

We can actually use the **COPY** command in conjunction with Python, SQLAlchemy, and Pandas to deliver the same speed that we get with **\copy**. Say we define the following function:

```python
import csv
from io import StringIO


def psql_insert_copy(table, conn, keys, data_iter):
    # gets a DBAPI connection that can provide a cursor
```

```
dbapi_conn = conn.connection
with dbapi_conn.cursor() as cur:
    s_buf = StringIO()
    writer = csv.writer(s_buf)
    writer.writerows(data_iter)
    s_buf.seek(0)

    columns = ', '.join('"{}"'.format(k) for k in keys)
    if table.schema:
        table_name = '{}.{}'.format(table.schema, table.name)
    else:
        table_name = table.name

    sql = 'COPY {} ({}) FROM STDIN WITH CSV'.format(
        table_name, columns)
    cur.copy_expert(sql=sql, file=s_buf)
```

We can then leverage the method parameter in **to_sql**, as shown here:

```
top_cities_data.to_sql('top_cities_data', engine,
                       index=False, if_exists='replace',
                       method=psql_insert_copy)
```

The **psql_insert_copy** function defined here can be used without modification in any of your PostgreSQL imports from Pandas. Here is a breakdown of what this code does:

1. After performing some necessary imports, we begin by defining the function using the **def** keyword followed by the function name (**psql_insert_copy**) and the parameters (**table**, **conn**, **keys**, and **data_iter**).

2. Next, we establish a connection (**dbapi_conn**) and cursor (**cur**) that we can use for execution.

3. Next, we write all of the data in our rows (represented in **data_iter**) to a string buffer (**s_buf**) that is formatted like a CSV file, but that exists in memory and not in a file on our hard drive.

4. Then, we define the column names (**columns**) and table name (**table_name**).

5. Lastly, we execute the **COPY** statement by streaming the CSV file contents through Standard input (**STDIN**).

Reading and Writing CSV Files with Python

In addition to reading and writing data to our database, we can use Python to read and write data from our local filesystem. The commands for reading and writing CSV files with Pandas are very similar to those used for reading and writing from our database:

For writing, **pandas.DataFrame.to_csv(file_path, index=False)** would write the DataFrame to your local filesystem using the supplied **file_path**.

For reading, **pandas.read_csv(file_path, dtype={})** would return a DataFrame representation of the data supplied in the CSV file located at **file_path**.

When reading a CSV file, Pandas will infer the correct data type based on the values in the file. For example, if the column contains only integer numbers, it will create the column with an **int64** data type.

Similarly, it can infer whether a column contains floats, timestamps, or strings. Pandas can also infer whether or not there is a header for the file, and generally, this functionality works pretty well. If there is a column that is not read in correctly (for example, a five-digit US zip code might get read in as an integer causing leading zeros to fall off – "07123" would become 7123 without leading zeros), you can specify the column type directly using the **dtype** parameter. For example, if you have a **zip_code** column in your dataset, you could specify that it is a string using **dtype={'zip_code': str}**.

> **Note**
>
> There are many different ways in which a CSV file might be formatted. While pandas can generally infer the correct header and data types, there are many parameters offered to customize the reading and writing of a CSV file for your needs.

Using the **top_cities_data** in our notebook, we can test out this functionality:

```
top_cities_data.to_csv('top_cities_analysis.csv', index=False)
my_data = pd.read_csv('top_cities_analysis.csv')
my_data
```

my_data now contains the data that we wrote to a CSV and then read it back in. We do not need to specify the optional **dtype** parameter in this case because our columns could be inferred correctly using pandas. You should see an identical copy of the data that is in **top_cities_data**:

Out[13]:

	city	number_of_customers	female	male
0	Washington	1447	734	713
1	Houston	904	446	458
2	New York City	731	369	362
3	El Paso	713	369	344

Figure 6.23: Checking that we can write and read CSV files in pandas

Best Practices for Importing and Exporting Data

At this point, we have seen several different methods for reading and writing data between our computer and our database. Each method has its own use case and purpose. Generally, there are going to be two key factors that should guide your decision-making process:

- You should try to access the database with the same tool that you will use to analyze the data. As you add more steps to get your data from the database to your analytics tool, you increase the ways in which new errors can arise. When you can't access the database using the same tool that you will use to process the data, you should use **psql** to read and write CSV files to your database.

- When writing data, you can save time by using the **COPY** or **\copy** commands.

Going Password-Less

In addition to everything mentioned so far, it is also a good idea to set up a **.pgpass** file. A **.pgpass** file specifies the parameters that you use to connect to your database, including your password. All of the programmatic methods of accessing the database discussed in this chapter (using **psql**, R, and Python) will allow you to skip the **password** parameter if your **.pgpass** file contains the password for the matching hostname, database, and username.

On Unix-based systems and macOS X, you can create the **.pgpass** file in your home directory. On Windows, you can create the file in **%APPDATA%\postgresql\pgpass.conf**. The file should contain one line for every database connection that you want to store, and it should follow this format (customized for your database parameters):

```
hostname:port:database:username:password
```

For Unix and Mac users, you will need to change the permissions on the file using the following command on the command line (in the Terminal):

```
chmod 0600 ~/.pgpass
```

For Windows users, it is assumed that you have secured the permissions of the file so that other users cannot access it. Once you have created the file, you can test that it works by calling **psql** as follows in the terminal:

```
psql -h my_host -p 5432 -d my_database -U my_username
```

If the **.pgpass** file was created successfully, you will not be prompted for your password.

Activity 8: Using an External Dataset to Discover Sales Trends

In this activity, we are going to use United States Census data on public transportation usage by zip code to see whether the level of use of public transport has any correlation to ZoomZoom sales in a given location.

1. Download the public transportation according to zip code dataset from GitHub:

   https://github.com/TrainingByPackt/SQL-for-Data-Analytics/blob/master/Datasets/public_transportation_statistics_by_zip_code.csv

   This dataset contains three columns:

   zip_code: This is the five-digit United States postal code that is used to identify the region.

   public_transportation_pct: This is the percentage of the population in a postal code that has been identified as using public transportation to commute to work.

   public_transportation_population: This is the raw number of people in a zip code that use public transportation to commute to work.

2. Copy the data from the public transportation dataset to the ZoomZoom customer database by creating a table for it in the ZoomZoom dataset.

3. Find the maximum and minimum percentages in this data. Values below 0 will most likely indicate missing data.

4. Calculate the average sales amounts for customers that live in high public transportation regions (over 10%) as well as low public transportation usage (less than, or equal to, 10%).

5. Read the data into pandas and plot a histogram of the distribution (hint: you can use `my_data.plot.hist(y='public_transportation_pct')` to plot a histogram if you read the data into a my_data pandas DataFrame).

6. Using pandas, test using the `to_sql` function with and without the `method=psql_insert_copy` parameter. How do the speeds compare? (Hint: In a Jupyter notebook, you can add `%time` in front of your command to see how long it takes.)

7. Group customers based on their zip code public transportation usage, rounded to the nearest 10%, and look at the average number of transactions per customer. Export this data to Excel and create a scatterplot to better understand the relationship between public transportation usage and sales.

8. Based on this analysis, what recommendations would you have for the executive team at ZoomZoom when considering expansion opportunities?

> **Note**
>
> The solution to this activity can be found on page 328.

Summary

In this chapter, we learned how to interface our database with other analytical tools for further analysis and visualization. While SQL is powerful, there are always going to be some analyses that need to be undertaken in other systems and being able to transfer data in and out of the database enables us to do just about anything we want with our data.

In the next chapter, we will examine data structures that can be used to store complex relationships in our data. We will learn how to mine insights from text data, as well as look at the JSON and ARRAY data types so that we can make full use of all of the information available to us.

Analytics Using Complex Data Types

Learning Objectives

By the end of this chapter, you will be able to:

- Perform descriptive analytics on time series data using DATETIME

- Use geospatial data to identify relationships

- Use complex data types (arrays, JSON, and JSONB)

- Perform text analytics

This chapter covers how to make the most of your data by analyzing complex and alternative data types.

Introduction

In the previous chapter, we looked at how we can import and export data into other analytical tools in order to leverage analytical tools outside of our database. It is often easiest to analyze numbers, but in the real world, data is frequently found in other formats: words, locations, dates, and sometimes complex data structures. In this chapter, we will look at these other formats, and see how we can use this data in our analysis.

First, we will look at two commonly found column types: `datetime` columns and `latitude` and `longitude` columns. These data types will give us a foundational understanding of how to understand our data from both a temporal and a geospatial perspective. Next, we will look at complex data types, such as arrays and JSON, and learn how to extract data points from these complex data types. These data structures are often used for alternative data, or log-level data, such as website logs. Finally, we will look at how we can extract meaning out of text in our database and use text data to extract insights.

By the end of the chapter, you will have broadened your analysis capabilities so that you can leverage just about any type of data available to you.

Date and Time Data Types for Analysis

We are all familiar with dates and times, but we don't often think about how these quantitative measures are represented. Yes, they are represented using numbers, but not with a single number. Instead, they are measured with a set of numbers, one for the year, one for the month, one for the day of the month, one for the hour, one for the minute, and so on.

What we might not realize, though, is that this is a complex representation, comprising several different components. For example, knowing the current minute without knowing the current hour is useless. Additionally, there are complex ways of interacting with dates and times, for example, different points in time can be subtracted from one another. Additionally, the current time can be represented differently depending on where you are in the world.

As a result of these intricacies, we need to take special care when working with this type of data. In fact, Postgres, like most databases, offers special data types that can represent these types of values. We'll start by examining the **date** type.

Starting with the Date Type

Dates can be easily represented using strings, for example, "January 1, 2000," which clearly represents a specific date, but dates are a special form of text in that they represent a quantitative and sequential value. You can add a week to the current date, for example. A given date has many different properties that you might want to use in your analysis, for instance, the year or the day of the week that the date represents. Working with dates is also necessary for time series analysis, which is one of the most common types of analysis that come up.

The SQL standard includes a **DATE** data type, and PostgreSQL offers great functionality for interacting with this data type. First, we can set our database to display dates in the format that we are most familiar with. PostgreSQL uses the **DateStyle** parameter to configure these settings. To see your current settings, you can use the following command:

```
SHOW DateStyle;
```

The following is the output of the preceding query:

Figure 7.1: Displaying the current DateStyle configuration

The first parameter specifies the **International Organization Standardization (ISO)** output format, which displays the date as *Year, Month, Day* and the second parameter specifies the ordering (for example, *Month, Day, Year* versus *Day, Month, Year*) for input or output. You can configure the output for your database using the following command:

```
SET DateStyle='ISO, MDY';
```

For example, if you wanted to set it to the European format of *Day, Month, Year*, you would set **DateStyle** to **'GERMAN, DMY'**. For this chapter, we will use the ISO display format (*Year, Month, Day*) and the *Month, Day, Year* input format. You can configure this format by using the preceding command.

Let's start by testing out the **date** format:

```
# SELECT '1/8/1999'::DATE;


     date
 ------------
  1999-01-08
(1 row)
```

As we can see, when we input a string, **'1/8/1999'**, using the *Month, Day, Year* format, Postgres understands that this is January 8, 1999 (and not August 1, 1999). It displays the date using the ISO format specified previously, in the form YYYY-MM-DD.

Similarly, we could use the following formats with dashes and periods to separate the date components:

```
# SELECT '1-8-1999'::DATE;


     date
 ------------
  1999-01-08
(1 row)


# SELECT '1.8.1999'::DATE;


     date
 ------------
  1999-01-08
(1 row)
```

In addition to displaying dates that are input as strings, we can display the current date very simply using the **current_date** keywords in Postgres:

```
# SELECT current_date;


  current_date
 --------------
  2019-04-28
(1 row)
```

In addition to the **DATE** data type, the SQL standard offers a **TIMESTAMP** data type. A timestamp represents a date and a time, down to a microsecond.

We can see the current timestamp using the **now()** function, and we can specify our time zone using **AT TIME ZONE 'UTC'**. Here's an example of the **now()** function with the Eastern Standard time zone specified:

```
# SELECT now() AT TIME ZONE 'EST';


           timezone

    ----------------------------

     2019-04-28 13:47:44.472096

    (1 row)
```

We can also use the timestamp data type without time zone specified. You can grab the current time zone with the **now()** function:

```
# SELECT now();


              now

    -------------------------------

     2019-04-28 19:16:31.670096+00

    (1 row)
```

> **Note**
>
> In general, it is recommended that you use a timestamp with the time zone specified. If you do not specify the time zone, the value of the timestamp could be questionable (for example, the time could be represented in the time zone where the company is located, in Universal Time Coordinated (UTC) time, or the customer's time zone).

The date and timestamp data types are helpful not only because they display dates in a readable format, but also because they store these values using fewer bytes than the equivalent string representation (a date type value requires only 4 bytes, while the equivalent text representation might be 8 bytes for an 8-character representation such as **'20160101'**). Additionally, Postgres provides special functionality to manipulate and transform dates, and this is particularly useful for data analytics.

Transforming Date Types

Often, we will want to decompose our dates into their component parts. For example, we may be interested in only the year and month, but not the day, for the monthly analysis of our data. To do this, we can use **EXTRACT(component FROM date)**. Here's an example:

```
# SELECT current_date,
     EXTRACT(year FROM current_date) AS year,
     EXTRACT(month FROM current_date) AS month,
     EXTRACT(day FROM current_date) AS day;


 current_date | year | month | day
--------------+------+-------+-----
 2019-04-28   | 2019 |     4 |  28
(1 row)
```

Similarly, we can abbreviate these components as **y**, **mon**, and **d**, and Postgres will understand what we want:

```
# SELECT current_date,
     EXTRACT(y FROM current_date) AS year,
     EXTRACT(mon FROM current_date) AS month,
     EXTRACT(d FROM current_date) AS day;


 current_date | year | month | day
--------------+------+-------+-----
 2019-04-28   | 2019 |     4 |  28
(1 row)
```

In addition to the year, month, and day, we will sometimes want additional components, such as day of the week, week of the year, or quarter. You can also extract these date parts as follows:

```
# SELECT current_date,
    EXTRACT(dow FROM current_date) AS day_of_week,
    EXTRACT(week FROM current_date) AS week_of_year,
    EXTRACT(quarter FROM current_date) AS quarter;


 current_date | day_of_week | week | quarter
--------------+-------------+------+---------
 2019-04-28   |           0 |   17 |       2
(1 row)
```

Note that **EXTRACT** always outputs a number, so in this case, **day_of_week** starts at 0 (Sunday) and goes up to 6 (Saturday). Instead of **dow**, you can use **isodow**, which starts at 1 (Monday) and goes up to 7 (Sunday).

In addition to extracting date parts from a date, we may want to simply truncate our date or timestamp. For example, we may want to simply truncate our date to the year and month. We can do this using the **DATE_TRUNC()** function:

```
[datalake] # SELECT NOW(), DATE_TRUNC('month', NOW());
             now             |      date_trunc
-----------------------------+-----------------------
 2019-04-28 19:40:08.691618+00 | 2019-04-01 00:00:00+00
(1 row)
```

Notice that the **DATE_TRUNC (...)** function does not round off the value. Instead, it outputs the greatest rounded value less than or equal to the date value that you input.

> **Note**
>
> The **DATE_TRUNC(…)** function is similar to the flooring function in mathematics, which outputs the greatest integer less than or equal to the input (for example, 5.7 would be floored to 5).

The **DATE_TRUNC (...)** function is particularly useful for **GROUP BY** statements. For example, you can use it to group sales by quarter, and get the total quarterly sales:

```
SELECT DATE_TRUNC('quarter', NOW()) AS quarter,
    SUM(sales_amount) AS total_quarterly_sales
FROM sales
GROUP BY 1
ORDER BY 1 DESC;
```

> **Note**
>
> **DATE_TRUNC(...)** requires a string representing the field you want to truncate to, while **EXTRACT(...)** accepts either the string representation (with quotes) or the field name (without quotes).

Intervals

In addition to representing dates, we can also represent fixed time intervals using the interval data type. This is useful if we want to analyze how long something takes, for example, if we want to know how long it takes a customer to make a purchase.

Here's an example:

```
# SELECT INTERVAL '5 days';
  interval
 ----------
  5 days
(1 row)
```

Intervals are useful for subtracting timestamps, for example:

```
# SELECT TIMESTAMP '2016-03-01 00:00:00' - TIMESTAMP '2016-02-01 00:00:00'
AS days_in_feb;
  days_in_feb
 -------------
  29 days
(1 row)
```

Or, alternatively, intervals can be used to add the number of days to a timestamp:

```
# SELECT TIMESTAMP '2016-03-01 00:00:00' + INTERVAL '7 days' AS new_date;
      new_date
--------------------
 2016-03-08 00:00:00
(1 row)
```

While intervals offer a precise method for doing timestamp arithmetic, the **DATE** format can be used with integers to accomplish a similar result. In the following example, we simply add 7 (an integer) to the date to calculate the new date:

```
# SELECT DATE '2016-03-01' + 7 AS new_date;
  new_date
------------
 2016-03-08
(1 row)
```

Similarly, we can subtract two dates and get an integer result:

```
# SELECT DATE '2016-03-01' - DATE '2016-02-01' AS days_in_feb;

 days_in_feb
-------------
          29
(1 row)
```

While the date data type offers ease of use, the timestamp with the time zone data type offers precision. If you need your date/time field to be precisely the same as the time at which the action occurred, you should use the timestamp with the time zone. If not, you can use the date field.

Exercise 22: Analytics with Time Series Data

In this exercise, we will perform basic analysis using time series data to derive insights into how ZoomZoom has ramped up its efforts to sell more vehicles during the year 2018 by using the ZoomZoom database.

> **Note**
>
> All the exercises and activity codes of this chapter can also be found on GitHub: https://github.com/TrainingByPackt/SQL-for-Data-Analytics/tree/master/Lesson07.

Perform the following steps to complete the exercise:

1. First, let's look at the number of monthly sales. We can use the following aggregate query using the **DATE_TRUNC** method:

    ```
    SELECT
        DATE_TRUNC('month', sales_transaction_date)
            AS month_date,
        COUNT(1) AS number_of_sales
    FROM sales
    WHERE EXTRACT(year FROM sales_transaction_date) = 2018
    GROUP BY 1
    ORDER BY 1;
    ```

    After running this SQL, we get the following result:

month_date	number_of_sales
2018-01-01 00:00:00	504
2018-02-01 00:00:00	487
2018-03-01 00:00:00	624
2018-04-01 00:00:00	755
2018-05-01 00:00:00	945
2018-06-01 00:00:00	993
2018-07-01 00:00:00	1119
2018-08-01 00:00:00	1046
2018-09-01 00:00:00	867
2018-10-01 00:00:00	780
2018-11-01 00:00:00	801
2018-12-01 00:00:00	596

(12 rows)

Figure 7.2: Monthly number of sales

2. Next, we can look at how this compares with the number of new customers joining each month:

```
SELECT
    DATE_TRUNC('month', date_added)
        AS month_date,
    COUNT(1) AS number_of_new_customers
FROM customers
WHERE EXTRACT(year FROM date_added) = 2018
GROUP BY 1
ORDER BY 1;
```

The following is the output of the preceding query:

month_date	number_of_new_customers
2018-01-01 00:00:00	430
2018-02-01 00:00:00	415
2018-03-01 00:00:00	450
2018-04-01 00:00:00	423
2018-05-01 00:00:00	454
2018-06-01 00:00:00	456
2018-07-01 00:00:00	478
2018-08-01 00:00:00	448
2018-09-01 00:00:00	440
2018-10-01 00:00:00	464
2018-11-01 00:00:00	460
2018-12-01 00:00:00	473
(12 rows)	

Figure 7.3: Number of new customer sign-ups every month

We can probably deduce that customers are not being entered into our database during their purchase, but instead, they are signing up with us before they make a purchase. The flow of new potential customers is fairly steady, and hovers around 400-500 new customer sign-ups every month, while the number of sales (as queried in *step 1*) varies considerably – in July, we have 2.3 times as many sales (1,119) as we have new customers (478).

From this exercise, we can see that we get a steady number of customers entering our database, but sales transactions vary considerably from month to month.

Performing Geospatial Analysis in Postgres

In addition to looking at time series data to better understand trends, we can also use geospatial information – such as city, country, or latitude and longitude – to better understand our customers. For example, governments use geospatial analysis to better understand regional economic differences, while a ride-sharing platform might use geospatial data to find the closest driver for a given customer.

We can represent a geospatial location using latitude and longitude coordinates, and this will be the fundamental building block for us to begin geospatial analysis.

Latitude and Longitude

When we think about locations, we often think about it in terms of the address – the city, state, country, or postal code that is assigned to the location that we are interested in. From an analytics perspective, this is sometimes OK – for example, you can look at the sales volume by city and come up with meaningful results about which cities are performing well.

Often, however, we need to understand geospatial relationships numerically, to understand the distances between two points, or to understand relationships that vary based on where you are on a map. After all, if you live on the border between two cities, it's rare that your behavior would suddenly change if you move to the other city.

Latitude and longitude allow us to look at the location in a continuous context. This allows us to analyze the numeric relationships between location and other factors (for example, sales). latitude and longitude also enable us to look at the distances between two locations.

Latitude tells us how far north or south a point is. A point at +90° latitude is at the North Pole, while a point at 0° latitude is at the equator, and a point at -90° is at the South Pole. On a map, lines of constant latitude run east and west.

Longitude tells us how far east, or west, a point is. On a map, lines of constant latitude run east and west. Greenwich, England, is the point of 0° longitude. Points can be defined using longitude as west (-) or east (+) of this point, and values range from -180° west to +180° east. These values are actually equivalent because they both point to the vertical line that runs through the Pacific Ocean, which is halfway around the world from Greenwich, England.

Representing Latitude and Longitude in Postgres

In Postgres, we can represent latitude and longitude using two floating-point numbers. In fact, this is how latitude and longitude are represented in the ZoomZoom **customers** table:

```
SELECT
      latitude,
      longitude
FROM customers
LIMIT 10;
```

Here is the output of the preceding query:

```
 latitude | longitude
----------+----------
     NULL |      NULL
  38.5814 |  -90.2625
  30.6143 |  -87.2758
  36.0986 |  -86.8219
  25.5584 |  -80.4582
  25.6364 |  -80.3187
  28.5663 |  -81.2608
  41.3087 |  -72.9271
  38.8999 |   -94.832
  31.6948 |    -106.3
(10 rows)
```

Figure 7.4: Latitudes and longitudes of ZoomZoom customers

Here, we can see that all of the latitudes are positive because the United States is north of the equator. All of the longitudes are negative because the United States is west of Greenwich, England. We can also see that some customers do not have latitude and longitude values filled in, because their location is unknown.

While these values can give us the exact location of a customer, we cannot do much with that information, because distance calculations require trigonometry, and make simplifying assumptions about the shape of the Earth.

Thankfully, Postgres has tools to solve this problem. We can calculate distances in Postgres by installing these packages:

```
CREATE EXTENSION cube;
CREATE EXTENSION earthdistance;
```

These two extensions only need to be installed once, by running the two preceding commands. The **earthdistance** module depends on the **cube** module. Once we install the **earthdistance** module, we can define a **point**:

```
SELECT
    point(longitude, latitude)
FROM customers
LIMIT 10;
```

Here is the output of the preceding query:

```
           point
--------------------------
 NULL
 (-90.2625,38.5814)
 (-87.2758,30.6143)
 (-86.8219,36.0986)
 (-80.4582,25.5584)
 (-80.3187,25.6364)
 (-81.2608,28.5663)
 (-72.9271,41.3087)
 (-94.832,38.8999)
 (-106.3,31.6948)
(10 rows)
```

Figure 7.5: Customer latitude and longitude represented as points in Postgres

> **Note**
>
> A point is defined with longitude first and then latitude. This is contrary to the convention of latitude first and then longitude. The rationale behind this is that longitude more closely represents points along an x-axis, and latitude more closely represents points on the y-axis, and in mathematics, graphed points are usually noted by their x coordinate followed by their y coordinate.

The **earthdistance** module also allows us to calculate the distance between points in miles:

```
SELECT
    point(-90, 38) <@> point(-91, 37) AS distance_in_miles;
```

Here is the output of the preceding query:

```
distance_in_miles
------------------
 88.1949338379752
(1 row)
```

Figure 7.6: The distance (in miles) between two points separated by 1° longitude and 1° latitude

In this example, we defined two points, (38° N, 90° W) and (37° N, 91° W), and we were able to calculate the distance between these points using the **<@>** operator, which calculates the distance in miles (in this case, these two points are **88.2** miles apart).

In the following exercise, we will see how we can use these distance calculations in a practical business context.

Exercise 23: Geospatial Analysis

In this exercise, we will identify the closest dealership for each customer. ZoomZoom marketers are trying to increase customer engagement by helping customers find their nearest dealership. The product team is also interested to know what the average distance is between each customer and their closest dealership.

Follow these steps to implement the exercise:

1. First, we will create a table with the longitude and latitude points for every customer:

```
CREATE TEMP TABLE customer_points AS (
    SELECT
        customer_id,
        point(longitude, latitude) AS lng_lat_point
    FROM customers
    WHERE longitude IS NOT NULL
    AND latitude IS NOT NULL
);
```

2. Next, we can create a similar table for every dealership:

```
CREATE TEMP TABLE dealership_points AS (
    SELECT
        dealership_id,
        point(longitude, latitude) AS lng_lat_point
    FROM dealerships
);
```

3. Now we can cross join these tables to calculate the distance from each customer to each dealership (in miles):

```
CREATE TEMP TABLE customer_dealership_distance AS (
    SELECT
        customer_id,
        dealership_id,
        c.lng_lat_point <@> d.lng_lat_point AS distance
    FROM customer_points c
    CROSS JOIN dealership_points d
);
```

4. Finally, we can take the closest dealership for each customer using the following query:

```
CREATE TEMP TABLE closest_dealerships AS (
    SELECT DISTINCT ON (customer_id)
        customer_id,
        dealership_id,
        distance
    FROM customer_dealership_distance
    ORDER BY customer_id, distance
);
```

Remember that the **DISTINCT ON** clause guarantees only one record for each unique value of the column in parentheses. In this case, we will get one record for every **customer_id**, and because we sort by distance, we will get the record with the shortest distance.

5. Now that we have the data to fulfill the marketing team's request, we can now calculate the average distance from each customer to their closest dealership:

```
SELECT
    AVG(distance) AS avg_dist,
    PERCENTILE_DISC(0.5) WITHIN GROUP (ORDER BY distance) AS median_dist
FROM closest_dealerships;
```

Here is the output of the preceding query:

```
      avg_dist      |    median_dist
--------------------+-------------------
 146.778266080342 | 91.2395829323349
(1 row)
```

Figure 7.7: Average and median distances between customers and their closest dealership

The result is that the average distance is about 147 miles away, but the median distance is about 91 miles.

In this exercise, we represented the geographic points for every customer, then calculated the distance for each customer and every possible dealership, identified the closest dealership for each customer, and found the average and median distances to a dealership for our customers.

Using Array Data Types in Postgres

While the Postgres data types that we have explored so far allow us to store many different types of data, occasionally we will want to store a series of values in a table. For example, we might want to store a list of the products that a customer has purchased, or we might want to store a list of the employee ID numbers associated with a specific dealership. For this scenario, Postgres offers the **ARRAY** data type, which allows us to store just that – a list of values.

Starting with Arrays

Postgres arrays allow us to store multiple values in a field in a table. For example, consider the following first record in the **customers** table:

```
customer_id     | 1
title           | NULL
first_name      | Arlena
last_name       | Riveles
suffix          | NULL
email           | ariveles0@stumbleupon.com
gender          | F
ip_address      | 98.36.172.246
phone           | NULL
street_address  | NULL
city            | NULL
state           | NULL
postal_code     | NULL
latitude        | NULL
longitude       | NULL
date_added      | 2017-04-23 00:00:00
```

Each field contains exactly one value (the **NULL** value is still a value); however, there are some attributes that might contain multiple values with an unspecified length. For example, imagine that we wanted to have a **purchased_products** field. This could contain zero or more values within the field. For example, imagine the customer purchased the **Lemon** and **Bat Limited Edition** scooters; we can represent that as follows:

```
purchased_products | {Lemon,"Bat Limited Edition"}
```

We can define an array in a variety of ways. To get started, we can simply create an array using the following command:

```
SELECT ARRAY['Lemon', 'Bat Limited Edition'] AS example_purchased_products;
```

```
    example_purchased_products

-------------------------------

  {Lemon,"Bat Limited Edition"}
```

Postgres knows that the **'Lemon'** and **'Bat Limited Edition'** values are of the text data type, so it creates a text array to store these values.

While you can create an array for any data type, the array is limited to values for that data type only. So, you could not have an integer value followed by a text value (this would likely produce an error).

We can also create arrays using the **ARRAY_AGG** aggregate function. For example, the following query aggregates all of the vehicles for each product type:

```
SELECT product_type, ARRAY_AGG(DISTINCT model) AS models FROM products GROUP BY 1;
```

The following is the output of the preceding query:

```
 product_type |                              models
--------------+---------------------------------------------------------------------------
 automobile   | {"Model Chi","Model Epsilon","Model Gamma","Model Sigma"}
 scooter      | {Bat,"Bat Limited Edition",Blade,Lemon,"Lemon Limited Edition","Lemon Zester"}
(2 rows)
```

Figure 7.8: Output of the ARRAY_AGG function

You can also reverse this operation using the UNNEST function, which creates one row for every value in the array:

```
SELECT UNNEST(ARRAY[123, 456, 789]) AS example_ids;
```

Here is the output of the preceding query:

Figure 7.9: Output of the UNNEST command

You can also create an array by splitting a string value using the **STRING_TO_ARRAY** function. Here's an example:

```
SELECT STRING_TO_ARRAY('hello there how are you?', ' ');
```

In this example, the sentence is split using the second string (' '), and we end up with the result:

```
             string_to_array
        ----------------------------
        {hello,there,how,are,you?}
        (1 row)
```

Figure 7.10: A string value is split into an array of strings

Similarly, we can run the reverse operation, and concatenate an array of strings into a single string:

```
SELECT ARRAY_TO_STRING(ARRAY['Lemon', 'Bat Limited Edition'], ', ')  AS
example_purchased_products;
```

In this example, we can join the individual string with the second string using ', ':

```
        example_purchased_products
        --------------------------
        Lemon, Bat Limited Edition
        (1 row)
```

Figure 7.11: A new string is formed from an array of strings

There are other functions that allow you to interact with arrays. Here are a few examples of the additional array functionality that Postgres provides:

Desired Operation	Postgres Function Example	Example Output
Concatenate two arrays	array_cat(ARRAY[1, 2],ARRAY[3, 4]) or ARRAY[1, 2] || ARRAY[3, 4]	{1, 2, 3, 4}
Append a value to an array	array_append(ARRAY[1, 2], 3) or ARRAY[1, 2] || 3	{1, 2, 3}
Check if a value is contained in an array	3 = ANY(ARRAY[1, 2])	f
Check if two arrays overlap	ARRAY[1, 2, 3] && ARRAY[3, 4]	t
Check if an array contains another array	ARRAY[1, 2, 3] @> ARRAY[2, 1]	t

Figure 7.12: Examples of additional array functionality

Using JSON Data Types in Postgres

While arrays can be useful for storing a list of values in a single field, sometimes our data structures can be complex. For example, we might want to store multiple values of different types in a single field, and we might want data to be keyed with labels rather than stored sequentially. These are common issues with log-level data, as well as alternative data.

JavaScript Object Notation (JSON) is an open standard text format for storing data of varying complexity. It can be used to represent just about anything. Similar to how a database table has column names, JSON data has keys. We can represent a record from our **customers** database easily using JSON, by storing column names as keys, and row values as values. The **row_to_json** function transforms rows to JSON:

```
SELECT row_to_json(c) FROM customers c limit 1;
```

Here is the output of the preceding query:

```
{"customer_id":1,"title":null,"first_name":"Arlena","last_
name":"Riveles","suffix":null,"email":"ariveles0@stumbleupon.
com","gender":"F","ip_address":"98.36.172.246","phone":null,"street_
address":null,"city":null,"state":null,"postal_
code":null,"latitude":null,"longitude":null,"date_added":"2017-04-
23T00:00:00"}
```

This is a little hard to read, but we can add the **pretty_bool** flag to the **row_to_json** function to generate a readable version:

```
SELECT row_to_json(c, TRUE) FROM customers c limit 1;
```

Here is the output of the preceding query:

```
                         row_to_json
---------------------------------------------------
 {"customer_id":1,                                +
  "title":null,                                   +
  "first_name":"Arlena",                          +
  "last_name":"Riveles",                          +
  "suffix":null,                                  +
  "email":"ariveles0@stumbleupon.com",+
  "gender":"F",                                   +
  "ip_address":"98.36.172.246",                   +
  "phone":null,                                   +
  "street_address":null,                          +
  "city":null,                                    +
  "state":null,                                   +
  "postal_code":null,                             +
  "latitude":null,                                +
  "longitude":null,                               +
  "date_added":"2017-04-23T00:00:00"}
(1 row)
```

Figure 7.13: JSON output from row_to_json

As you can see, once we reformat the JSON, it presents a simple, readable, text representation of our row. The JSON structure contains keys and values. In this example, the keys are simply the column names, and the values come from the row values. JSON values can either be numeric values (either integers or floats), Boolean values (**true** or **false**), text values (wrapped with double quotation marks), or **null**.

JSON can also include nested data structures. For example, we can take a hypothetical scenario where we want to include purchased products in the table as well:

```
{
"customer_id":1,
"example_purchased_products":["Lemon", "Bat Limited Edition"]
}
```

Or, we can take this example one step further:

```
{
    "customer_id": 7,
    "sales": [
        {
            "product_id": 7,
            "sales_amount": 599.99,
            "sales_transaction_date": "2019-04-25T04:00:30"
        },
        {
            "product_id": 1,
            "sales_amount": 399.99,
            "sales_transaction_date": "2011-08-08T08:55:56"
        },
        {
            "product_id": 6,
            "sales_amount": 65500,
            "sales_transaction_date": "2016-09-04T12:43:12"
        }
    ],
}
```

In this example, we have a JSON object with two keys: **customer_id** and **sales**. As you can see, the **sales** key points to a JSON array of values, but each value is another JSON object representing the sale. JSON objects that exist within a JSON object are referred to as nested JSON. In this case, we have represented all of the sales transactions for a customer using a nested array that contains nested JSON objects for each sale.

While JSON is a universal format for storing data, it is inefficient, because everything is stored as one large text string. In order to retrieve a value associated with a key, you would need to first parse the text, and this has a relatively high computational cost associated with it. If you just have a few JSON objects, this performance overhead might not be a big deal; however, it might become a burden if, for example, you are trying to select the JSON object with **"customer_id": 7** from millions of other JSON objects in your database.

In the next section, we will introduce JSONB, a binary JSON format, which is optimized for Postgres and allows you to avoid a lot of the parsing overhead associated with a standard JSON text string.

JSONB: Pre-Parsed JSON

While a text JSON field needs to be parsed each time it is referenced, a JSONB value is pre-parsed, and data is stored in a decomposed binary format. This requires that the initial input be parsed up front, and the benefit is that there is a significant performance improvement when querying the keys or values in this field. This is because the keys and values do not need to be parsed – they have already been extracted and stored in an accessible binary format.

> **Note**
>
> JSONB differs from JSON in a few other ways as well. First, you cannot have more than one key with the same name. Second, the key order is not preserved. Third, semantically insignificant details, such as whitespace, are not preserved.

Accessing Data from a JSON or JSONB Field

JSON keys can be used to access the associated value using the **->** operator. Here's an example:

```
SELECT
    '{
        "a": 1,
        "b": 2,
        "c": 3
    }'::JSON -> 'b' AS data;
```

In this example, we had a three-key JSON value, and we are trying to access the value for the **b** key. The output is a single output: **2**. This is because the **-> 'b'** operation gets the value for the **b** key from the JSON, **{"a": 1, "b": 2, "c": 3}**.

Postgres also allows more complex operations to access nested JSON using the **#>** operator. Take the following example:

```
SELECT
    '{
        "a": 1,
        "b": [
            {"d": 4},
            {"d": 6},
            {"d": 4}
    ],
        "c": 3
    }'::JSON #> ARRAY['b', '1', 'd'] AS data;
```

On the right side of the **#>** operator, a text array defines the path to access the desired value. In this case, we select the **'b'** value, which is a list of nested JSON objects. Then, we select the element in the list denoted by **'1'**, which is the second element because array indexes start at 0. Finally, we select the value associated with the **'d'** key – and the output is **6**.

These functions work with JSON or JSONB fields (keep in mind it will run much faster on JSONB fields). JSONB, however, also enables additional functionality. For example, let's say you want to filter rows based on a key-value pair. You could use the **@>** operator, which checks whether the JSONB object on the left contains the key value on the right. Here's an example:

```
SELECT * FROM customer_sales WHERE customer_json @> '{"customer_
id":20}'::JSONB;
```

The preceding query outputs the corresponding JSONB record:

```
{"email": "ihughillj@nationalgeographic.com", "phone": null, "sales": [],
"last_name": "Hughill", "date_added": "2012-08-08T00:00:00", "first_name":
"Itch", "customer_id": 20}
```

With JSONB, we can also make our output look pretty using the **jsonb_pretty** function:

```
SELECT JSONB_PRETTY(customer_json) FROM customer_sales WHERE customer_json
@> '{"customer_id":20}'::JSONB;
```

Here is the output of the preceding query:

Figure 7.14: Output from the JSONB_PRETTY function

We can also select just the keys from the JSONB field, and unnest them into multiple rows using the **JSONB_OBJECT_KEYS** function. Using this function, we can also extract the value associated with each key from the original JSONB field using the **->** operator. Here's an example:

```
SELECT

    JSONB_OBJECT_KEYS(customer_json) AS keys,

    customer_json -> JSONB_OBJECT_KEYS(customer_json) AS values

FROM customer_sales

WHERE customer_json @> '{"customer_id":20}'::JSONB

;
```

The following is the output of the preceding query:

Figure 7.15: Keys and values pairs exploded into multiple rows
using the JSONB_OBJECT_KEYS function

Creating and Modifying Data in a JSONB Field

You can also add and remove elements from JSONB. For example, to add a new key-value pair, **"c": 2**, you can do the following:

```
select jsonb_insert('{"a":1,"b":"foo"}', ARRAY['c'], '2');
```

Here is the output of the preceding query:

```
{"a": 1, "b": "foo", "c": 2}
```

If you wanted to insert values into a nested JSON object, you could do that too:

```
select jsonb_insert('{"a":1,"b":"foo", "c":[1, 2, 3, 4]}', ARRAY['c', '1'],
'10');
```

This would return the following output:

```
{"a": 1, "b": "foo", "c": [1, 10, 2, 3, 4]}
```

In this example, **ARRAY['c', '1']** represents the path where the new value should be inserted. In this case, it first grabs the **'c'** key and corresponding array value, and then it inserts the value (**'10'**) at position **'1'**.

To remove a key, you can simply subtract the key that you want to remove. Here's an example:

```
SELECT '{"a": 1, "b": 2}'::JSONB - 'b';
```

In this case, we have a JSON object with two keys: **a** and **b**. When we subtract **b**, we are left with just the **a** key and its associated value:

```
{"a": 1}
```

In addition to the methodologies described here, we might want to search through multiple layers of nested objects. We will learn this in the following exercise.

Exercise 24: Searching through JSONB

We will identify the values using data stored as JSNOB. Suppose we want to identify all customers who purchased a Blade scooter; we can do this using data stored as JSNOB.

Complete the exercise by implementing the following steps:

1. First, we need to explode out each sale into its own row. We can do this using the **JSONB_ARRAY_ELEMENTS** function, which does exactly that:

```
CREATE TEMP TABLE customer_sales_single_sale_json AS (
    SELECT
        customer_json,
        JSONB_ARRAY_ELEMENTS(customer_json -> 'sales') AS sale_json
```

```
        FROM customer_sales LIMIT 10
    );
```

2. Next, we can simply filter this output, and grab the records where **product_name** is **'Blade'**:

```
SELECT DISTINCT customer_json FROM customer_sales_single_sale_json WHERE
sale_json ->> 'product_name' = 'Blade' ;
```

The **->>** operator is similar to the **->** operator, except it returns text output rather than JSONB output. This outputs the following result:

```
{"email": "nespinaye@51.la", "phone": "818-658-6748", "sales":
[{"product_id": 5, "product_name": "Blade", "sales_amount":
559.992, "sales_transaction_date": "2014-07-19T06:33:44"}],
"last_name": "Espinay", "date_added": "2014-07-05T00:00:00",
"first_name": "Nichols", "customer_id": 15}
```

Figure 7.16: Records where product_name is 'Blade'

3. We can make this result easier to read by using **JSONB_PRETTY()** to format the output:

```
SELECT DISTINCT JSONB_PRETTY(customer_json) FROM customer_sales_single_
sale_json WHERE sale_json ->> 'product_name' = 'Blade' ;
```

Here is the output of the preceding query:

```
                            jsonb_pretty
--------------------------------------------------------------------
 {                                                                 +
     "email": "nespinaye@51.la",                                  +
     "phone": "818-658-6748",                                     +
     "sales": [                                                   +
         {                                                        +
             "product_id": 5,                                     +
             "product_name": "Blade",                             +
             "sales_amount": 559.992,                             +
             "sales_transaction_date": "2014-07-19T06:33:44"      +
         }                                                        +
     ],                                                           +
     "last_name": "Espinay",                                      +
     "date_added": "2014-07-05T00:00:00",                         +
     "first_name": "Nichols",                                     +
     "customer_id": 15                                            +
 }
(1 row)
```

Figure 7.17: Format the output using JSNOB_PRETTY()

We can now easily read the formatted result after using the **JSNOB_PRETTY()** function.

In this exercise, we identified the values using data stored as JSNOB. We used **JSNOB_PRETTY()** and **JSONB_ARRAY_ELEMENTS()** to complete this exercise.

Text Analytics Using Postgres

In addition to performing analytics using complex data structures within Postgres, we can also make use of the non-numeric data available to us. Often, text contains valuable insights – you can imagine a salesperson keeping notes on prospective clients: "Very promising interaction, the customer is looking to make a purchase tomorrow" contains valuable data, as does this note: "The customer is uninterested. They no longer have a need for the product." While this text can be valuable for someone to manually read, it can also be valuable in the analysis. Keywords in these statements, such as "promising," "purchase," "tomorrow," "uninterested," and "no" can be extracted using the right techniques to try to identify top prospects in an automated fashion.

Any block of text can have keywords that can be extracted to uncover trends, for example, in customer reviews, email communications, or sales notes. In many circumstances, text data might be the most relevant data available, and we need to use it in order to create meaningful insights.

In this chapter, we will look at how we can use some Postgres functionality to extract keywords that will help us identify trends. We will also leverage text search capabilities in Postgres to enable rapid searching.

Tokenizing Text

While large blocks of text (sentences, paragraphs, and so on) can provide useful information to convey to a human reader, there are few analytical solutions that can draw insights from unprocessed text. In almost all cases, it is helpful to parse text into individual words. Often, the text is broken out into the component tokens, where each token is a sequence of characters that are grouped together to form a semantic unit. Usually, each token is simply a word in the sentence, although in certain cases (such as the word "can't"), your parsing engine might parse two tokens: "can" and "t".

> **Note**
>
> Even cutting-edge **Natural Language Processing** (**NLP**) techniques usually involve tokenization before the text can be processed. NLP can be useful to run analysis that requires a deeper understanding of the text.

Words and tokens are useful because they can be matched across documents in your data. This allows you to draw high-level conclusions at the aggregate level. For example, if we have a dataset containing sales notes, and we parse out the "interested" token, we can hypothesize that sales notes containing "interested" are associated with customers who are more likely to make a purchase.

Postgres has functionality that makes tokenization fairly easy. We can start by using the **STRING_TO_ARRAY** function, which splits a string into an array using a delimiter, for example, a space:

```
SELECT STRING_TO_ARRAY('Danny and Matt are friends.', ' ');
```

The following is the output of the preceding query:

```
{Danny,and,Matt,are,friends.}
```

In this example, the sentence **Danny and Matt are friends.** is split on the space character.

In this example, we have punctuation, which might be better off removed. We can do this easily using the **REGEXP_REPLACE** function. This function accepts four arguments: the text you want to modify, the text pattern that you want to replace, the text that should replace it, and any additional flags (most commonly, you will add the **'g'** flag, specifying that the replacement should happen globally, or as many times as the pattern is encountered). We can remove the period using a pattern that matches the punctuation defined in the **\!@#$%^&*()-=_+,.<>/?|[]** string and replaces it with space:

```
SELECT REGEXP_REPLACE('Danny and Matt are friends.', '[!,.?-]', ' ', 'g');
```

The following is the output of the preceding query:

```
Danny and Matt are friends
```

The punctuation has been removed.

Postgres also includes stemming functionality, which is useful for identifying the root stem of the token. For example, the tokens "quick" and "quickly" or "run" and "running" are not that different in terms of their meaning, and contain the same stem. The **ts_lexize** function can help us standardize our text by returning the stem of the word, for example:

```
SELECT TS_LEXIZE('english_stem', 'running');
```

The preceding code returns the following:

```
{run}
```

We can use these techniques to identify tokens in text, as we will see in the following exercise.

Exercise 25: Performing Text Analytics

In this exercise, we want to quantitatively identify keywords that correspond with higher-than-average ratings or lower-than-average ratings using text analytics. In our ZoomZoom database, we have access to some customer survey feedback, along with ratings for how likely the customer is to refer their friends to ZoomZoom. These keywords will allow us to identify key strengths and weaknesses for the executive team to consider in the future.

Follow these steps to complete the exercise:

1. Let's start by seeing what data we have:

   ```
   SELECT * FROM customer_survey limit 5;
   ```

   The following is the output of the preceding query:

   ```
   rating |                                    feedback
   --------+------------------------------------------------------------------------------------------------
         9 | I highly recommend the lemon scooter. It's so fast
        10 | I really enjoyed the sale - I was able to get the Bat for a 20% discount
         4 | Overall, the experience was ok. I don't think that the customer service rep was really understanding the issue.
         9 | The model epsilon has been a fantastic ride - one of the best cars I have ever driven.
         9 | I've been riding the scooter around town. It's been good in urban areas.
   (5 rows)
   ```

   Figure 7.18: Example customer survey responses in our database

   We can see that we have access to a numeric rating between 1 and 10, and feedback in text format.

2. In order to analyze the text, we need to parse it out into individual words and their associated ratings. We can do this using some array transformations:

   ```
   SELECT UNNEST(STRING_TO_ARRAY(feedback, ' ')) AS word, rating FROM
   customer_survey limit 10;
   ```

   The following is the output of the preceding query:

   ```
      word    | rating
   -----------+--------
    I         |      9
    highly    |      9
    recommend |      9
    the       |      9
    lemon     |      9
    scooter.  |      9
    It's      |      9
    so        |      9
    fast      |      9
    I         |     10
   (10 rows)
   ```

   Figure 7.19: Transformed text output

As we can see from this output, the tokens are not standardized, and therefore this is problematic. In particular, punctuation (for example, **It's**), capitalization (for example, **I** and **It's**), word stems, and stop words (for example, **I**, **the**, and **so**) can be addressed to make the results more relevant.

3. Standardize the text using the **ts_lexize** function and using the English stemmer **'english_stem'**. We will then remove characters that are not letters in our original text using **REGEXP_REPLACE**. Pairing these two functions together with our original query, we get the following:

```
SELECT
    (TS_LEXIZE('english_stem',
            UNNEST(STRING_TO_ARRAY(
                REGEXP_REPLACE(feedback, '[^a-zA-Z]+', ' ', 'g'),
                ' ')
            )))[1] AS token,
    rating
FROM customer_survey
LIMIT 10;
```

This returns the following:

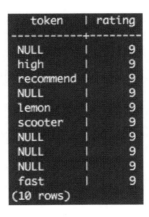

Figure 7.20: Output from TS_LEXIZE and REGEX_REPLACE

> **Note**
>
> When we apply these transformations, we call the outputs tokens rather than words. Tokens refer to each linguistic unit.

Now we have the key tokens and their associated ratings available. Note that the output of this operation produces **NULL** values, so we will need to filter out those rating pairs.

4. In the next step, we will want to find the average rating associated with each token. We can actually do this quite simply using a **GROUP BY** clause:

```
SELECT
    (TS_LEXIZE('english_stem',
                UNNEST(STRING_TO_ARRAY(
                    REGEXP_REPLACE(feedback, '[^a-zA-Z]+', ' ', 'g'),
                    ' ')
                )))[1] AS token,
    AVG(rating) AS avg_rating
FROM customer_survey
GROUP BY 1
HAVING COUNT(1) >= 3
ORDER BY 2
;
```

In this query, we group by the first expression in the **SELECT** statement where we perform the tokenization. We can now take the average rating associated with each token. We want to make sure that we only take tokens with more than a couple of occurrences so that we can filter out the noise – in this case, due to the small sample size of feedback responses, we only require that the token occurs three or more times (**HAVING COUNT(1) >= 3**). Finally, we order the results by the second expression – the average score:

word	avg_rating
pop	2.0000000000000000
batteri	2.3333333333333333
servic	2.3333333333333333
custom	2.3333333333333333
issu	2.5000000000000000
long	2.6666666666666667
ship	2.6666666666666667
email	3.5000000000000000
help	4.0000000000000000
one	4.3333333333333333
littl	4.6666666666666667
hook	5.0000000000000000
get	5.0000000000000000
work	5.0000000000000000
NULL	5.1872659176029963
realli	5.5000000000000000
scooter	5.9090909090909091
ride	6.7500000000000000
model	7.3333333333333333
lemon	7.6666666666666667
great	7.7500000000000000
fast	8.0000000000000000
dealership	9.0000000000000000
sale	9.5000000000000000
discount	9.6666666666666667
(25 rows)	

Figure 7.21: Average ratings associated with text tokens

On one end of the spectrum, we see that we have quite a few results that are negative: **pop** probably refers to popping tires, and **batteri** probably refers to issues with battery life. On the positive side, we see that customers respond favorably to **discount**, **sale**, and **dealership**.

5. Verify the assumptions by filtering survey responses that contain these tokens using an **ILIKE** expression, as follows:

```
SELECT * FROM customer_survey WHERE feedback ILIKE '%pop%';
```

This returns three relevant survey responses:

rating	feedback
1	On my second trip one of the tires popped. I would have really expected it to get repaired under the warranty.
3	I was riding to work and one my wheels popped! It was going to cost $200 to fix it - what a scam!
2	I popped a wheel, and can't seem to fix it.
(3 rows)	

Figure 7.22: Filtering survey responses using ILIKE

The **ILIKE** expression allows us to match text that contains a pattern. In this example, we are trying to find text that contains the text **pop**, and the operation is case-insensitive. By wrapping this in **%** symbols, we are specifying that the text can contain any number of characters on the left or right.

> **Note**
>
> **ILIKE** is similar to another SQL expression: **LIKE**. The **ILIKE** expression is case-insensitive, and the **LIKE** expression is case-sensitive, so typically it will make sense to use **ILIKE**. In situations where performance is critical, **LIKE** might be slightly faster.

Upon receiving the results of our analysis, we can report the key issues to our product team to review. We can also report the high-level findings that customers like discounts and also feedback have been positive following the introduction of dealerships.

Performing Text Search

While performing text analytics using aggregations, as we did earlier, in some cases, it might be helpful instead to query our database for relevant posts, similar to how you might query a search engine.

While you can do this using an **ILIKE** expression in your **WHERE** clause, this is not terribly fast or extensible. For example, what if you wanted to search the text for multiple keywords, and what if you want to be robust to misspellings, or scenarios where one of the words might be missing altogether?

For these situations, we can use the text search functionality in Postgres. This functionality is pretty powerful and scales up to millions of documents when it is fully optimized.

> **Note**
>
> "Documents" represent the individual records in a search database. Each document represents the entity that we want to search for. For example, for a blogging website, this might be a blog article, which might include the title, the author, and the article for one blog entry. For a survey, it might include the survey responses, or perhaps the survey response combined with the survey question. A document can span multiple fields or even multiple tables.

We can start with the **to_tsvector** function, which will perform a similar function to the **ts_lexize** function. Rather than produce a token from a word, this will tokenize the entire document. Here's an example:

```
SELECT
    feedback,
    to_tsvector('english', feedback) AS tsvectorized_feedback
FROM customer_survey
LIMIT 1;
```

This produces the following result:

feedback		tsvectorized_feedback
I highly recommend the lemon scooter. It's so fast		'fast':10 'high':2 'lemon':5 'recommend':3 'scooter':6

Figure 7.23: The tsvector tokenized representation of the original feedback

In this case, the feedback **I highly recommend the lemon scooter. It's so fast** was converted into a tokenized vector: **'fast':10 'high':2 'lemon':5 'recommend':3 'scooter':6**. Similar to the **ts_lexize** function, less meaningful "stop words" were removed such as "I," "the," "It's," and "so." Other words, such as **highly** were stemmed to their root (**high**). Word order was not preserved.

The **to_tsvector** function can also take in JSON or JSONB syntax and tokenize the values (no keys) as a **tsvector** object.

The output data type from this operation is a **tsvector** data type. The **tsvector** data type is specialized and specifically designed for text search operations. In addition to **tsvector**, the **tsquery** data type is useful for transforming a search query into a useful data type that Postgres can use to search. For example, suppose we want to construct a search query with the **lemon scooter** keyword – we can write it as follows:

```
SELECT to_tsquery('english', 'lemon & scooter');
```

Or, if we don't want to specify the Boolean syntax, we can write it more simply as follows:

```
SELECT plainto_tsquery('english', 'lemon scooter');
```

Both of these produce the same result:

Figure 7.24: Transformed query with Boolean syntax

> **Note**
>
> **to_tsquery** accepts Boolean syntax, such as **&** for **and** and **|** for **or**. It also accepts **!** for **not**.

You can also use Boolean operators to concatenate **tsquery** objects. For example, the **&&** operator will produce a query that requires the left query and the right query, while the **||** operator will produce a query that matches either the left or the right **tsquery** object:

```
SELECT plainto_tsquery('english', 'lemon') && plainto_tsquery('english',
'bat') || plainto_tsquery('english', 'chi');
```

This produces the following result:

```
'lemon' & 'bat' | 'chi'
```

We can query a **ts_vector** object using a **ts_query** object using the **@@** operator. For example, we can search all customer feedback for **'lemon scooter'**:

```
SELECT *
FROM customer_survey
WHERE to_tsvector('english', feedback) @@ plainto_tsquery('english', 'lemon
scooter');
```

This returns the following three results:

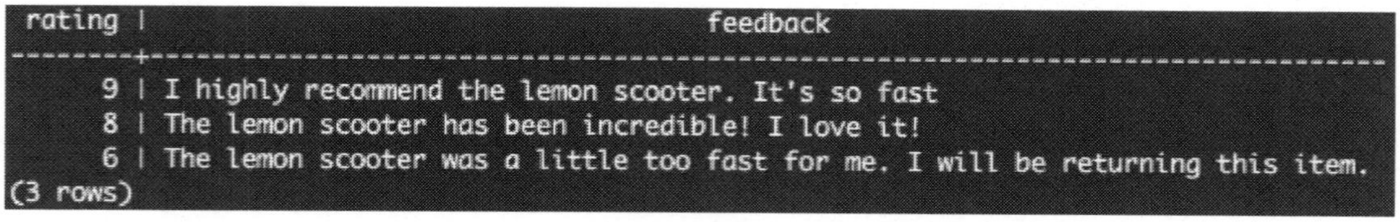

Figure 7.25: Search query output using the Postgres search functionality

Optimizing Text Search on Postgres

While the Postgres search syntax in the previous example is straightforward, it needs to convert all text documents into a **tsvector** object every time a new search is performed. Additionally, the search engine needs to check each and every document to see whether they match the query terms.

We can improve this in two ways:

- Store the **tsvector** objects so that they do not need to be recomputed.

- We can also store the tokens and their associated documents, similar to how an index in the back of a book has words or phrases and their associated page numbers so that we don't have to check each document to see whether it matches.

In order to do these two things, we will need to precompute and store the **tsvector** objects for each document and compute a **Generalized Inverted Index (GIN)**.

In order to precompute the **tsvector** objects, we will use a materialized view. A materialized view is defined as a query, but unlike a regular view, where the results are queried every time, the results for a materialized view are persisted and stored as a table.

Because a materialized view stores results in a stored table, it can get out of sync with the underlying tables that it queries.

We can create a materialized view of our survey results using the following query:

```
CREATE MATERIALIZED VIEW customer_survey_search AS (
    SELECT
        rating,
        feedback,
        to_tsvector('english', feedback)
            || to_tsvector('english', rating::text) AS searchable
    FROM customer_survey
);
```

You can see that our **searchable** column is actually composed of two columns: the **rating** and **feedback** columns. There are many scenarios where you will want to search on multiple fields, and you can easily concatenate multiple **tsvector** objects together with the **||** operator.

We can test that the view worked by querying a row:

```
SELECT * FROM customer_survey_search LIMIT 1;
```

This produces the following output:

```
rating |                    feedback                     |                        searchable
-------+-------------------------------------------------+--------------------------------------------------------
     9 | I highly recommend the lemon scooter. It's so fast | '9':11 'fast':10 'high':2 'lemon':5 'recommend':3 'scooter':6
(1 row)
```

Figure 7.26: A record from our materialized view with tsvector

Whenever we need to refresh the view (for example, after an insert or update), we can use the following syntax:

```
REFRESH MATERIALIZED VIEW CONCURRENTLY customer_survey_search;
```

This will recompute the view concurrently while the old copy of the view remains available and unlocked.

Additionally, we can add the GIN index with the following syntax:

```
CREATE INDEX idx_customer_survey_search_searchable ON customer_survey_search
USING GIN(searchable);
```

With these two operations (creating the materialized view and creating the GIN index), we can now easily query our feedback table using search terms:

```
SELECT rating, feedback FROM customer_survey_search WHERE searchable @@
plainto_tsquery('dealership');
```

The following is the output of the preceding query:

```
rating |                                  feedback
-------+---------------------------------------------------------------------------------
     8 | I really appreciated having a dealership so close to me - it made the transaction much easier!
     9 | The sales people at the dealership were so nice and helpful!
    10 | The millburn dealership is the best! Those folks are great!
(3 rows)
```

Figure 7.27: Output from the materialized view optimized for search

While the query time improvement might be small or non-existent for a small table of 32 rows, these operations greatly improve the speed for large tables (for example, with millions of rows), and enable users to quickly search their database in a matter of seconds.

Activity 9: Sales Search and Analysis

The head of sales at ZoomZoom has identified a problem: there is no easy way for the sales team to search for a customer. Thankfully, you volunteered to create a proof-of-concept internal search engine that will make all customers searchable by their contact information and the products that they have purchased in the past:

1. Using the `customer_sales` table, create a searchable materialized view with one record per customer. This view should be keyed off of the `customer_id` column and searchable on everything related to that customer: name, email, phone, and purchased products. It is OK to include other fields as well.

2. Create a searchable index on the materialized view that you created.

3. A salesperson asks you by the water cooler if you can use your new search prototype to find a customer by the name of Danny who purchased the Bat scooter. Query your new searchable view using the "Danny Bat" keywords. How many rows did you get?

4. The sales team wants to know how common it is for someone to buy a scooter and an automobile. Cross join the product table on itself to get all distinct pairs of products and remove pairs that are the same (for example, if the product name is the same). For each pair, search your view to see how many customers were found to match both products in the pair. You can assume that limited-edition releases can be grouped together with their standard model counterpart (for example, `Bat` and `Bat Limited Edition` can be considered the same scooter).

Expected Output:

```
                    query                    | count
---------------------------------------------+-------
'lemon' & 'model' & 'sigma'                  |   340
'lemon' & 'model' & 'chi'                    |   331
'bat' & 'model' & 'epsilon'                  |   241
'bat' & 'model' & 'sigma'                    |   226
'bat' & 'model' & 'chi'                      |   221
'lemon' & 'model' & 'epsilon'                |   217
'bat' & 'model' & 'gamma'                    |   153
'lemon' & 'model' & 'gamma'                  |   133
'lemon' & 'zester' & 'model' & 'chi'         |    28
'lemon' & 'zester' & 'model' & 'epsilon'     |    22
'blade' & 'model' & 'chi'                    |    21
'lemon' & 'zester' & 'model' & 'sigma'       |    17
'blade' & 'model' & 'sigma'                  |    12
'lemon' & 'zester' & 'model' & 'gamma'       |    11
'blade' & 'model' & 'epsilon'                |     4
'blade' & 'model' & 'gamma'                  |     4
(16 rows)
```

Figure 7.28: Customer counts for each scooter and automobile combination

> **Note**
>
> The solution for the activity can be found on page 336.

In this activity, we searched and analyzed the data using the materialized view. Then, we used **DISTINCT** and **JOINS** to transform the query. Lastly, we learned how to query our database using **tsquery** objects to get the final output.

Summary

In this chapter, we covered special data types including dates, timestamps, latitude and longitude, arrays, JSON and JSONB, and text data types. We learned how to transform these data types using specialized functionality for each data type, and we learned how we can perform advanced analysis using these data types and proved that this can be useful in a business context.

As our datasets grow larger and larger, these complex analyses become slower and slower. In the next chapter, we will take a deep look at how we can begin to optimize these queries using an explanation and analysis of the query plan, and using additional tools, such as indexes, that can speed up our queries.

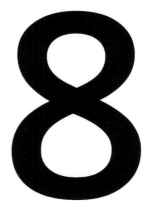

Performant SQL

Learning Objectives

By the end of this chapter, you will be able to:

- Optimize database use to allow more queries to be executed with fewer resources

- Implement index and sequential scans and understand when to most effectively use them

- Interpret the output of EXPLAIN ANALYZE

- Understand the benefits of using joins in place of other functionality

- Identify bottlenecks in queries

- Implement triggers in response to specific events

- Create and use functions to create more sophisticated and efficient queries

- Identify long-running queries and terminate them

In this chapter, we will improve the performance of some of our previous SQL queries. Now that we have a good understanding of the basics, we will build upon this foundation by making our queries more resource and time efficient. As we begin to work with larger datasets, these efficiencies become even more important, with each computational step taking longer to compute.

Introduction

In the previous chapter, we developed the skills necessary to effectively analyze data within a SQL database, and in this chapter, we will turn our attention to the efficiency of this analysis, investigating how we can increase the performance of our SQL queries. Efficiency and performance are key components of data analytics, since without considering these factors, physical constraints such as time and processing power can significantly affect the outcome of an analysis. To elaborate on these limitations, we can consider two separate scenarios.

Let's say that we are performing **post-hoc analysis** (analysis after the fact or event). In this first scenario, we have completed a study and have collected a large dataset of individual observations of a variety of different factors or features. One such example is that described within our dealership sales database – analyzing the sales data for each customer. With the data collection process, we want to analyze the data for patterns and insights as specified by our problem statement. If our dataset was sufficiently large, we could quickly encounter issues if we didn't optimize the queries first; the most common issue would simply be the time taken to execute the queries. While this doesn't sound like a significant issue, unnecessarily long processing times can cause:

- A reduction in the depth of the completed analysis. As each query takes a long time, the practicalities of project schedules may limit the number of queries, and so the depth and complexity of the analysis may be limited.

- The limiting of the selection of data for analysis. By artificially reducing the dataset using sub-sampling, we may be able to complete the analysis in a reasonable time but would have to sacrifice the number of observations being used. This may, in turn, lead to biases being accidentally included in the analysis.

- The need to use much more resources in parallel to complete the analysis in a reasonable time, thereby increasing the project cost.

Similarly, another potential issue with sub-optimal queries is an increase in the required system memory and compute power. This can result in either of the following two scenarios:

- Prevention of the analysis due to insufficient resources

- A significant increase in the cost of the project to recruit the required resources

Analysis/queries are part of a service or product. Let's think of a second scenario, where analysis is being completed as a component of a greater service or product, and so database queries may need to be completed in real time, or at least near-real time. In such cases, optimization and efficiency are key for the product to be a success. One such example is a GPS navigation system that incorporates the state of traffic as reported by other users. For such a system to be effective and provide up-to-date navigation information, the database must be analyzed at a rate that keeps up with the speed of the car and the progress of the journey. Any delays in the analysis that would prevent the navigation from being updated in response to traffic would be of significant impact to the commercial viability of the application.

After looking at these two examples, we can see that while efficiency is important in an effective and thorough post-hoc analysis, it is absolutely critical when incorporating the data analysis as a component of a separate product or service. While it is certainly not the job of a data scientist or data analyst to ensure that production and the database are working at optimal efficiency, it is critical that the queries of the underlying analysis are as effective as possible. If we do not have an efficient and current database in the first place, further refinements will not help in improving the performance of the analysis. In the next section, we will discuss methods of increasing the performance of scans for information throughout a database.

Database Scanning Methods

SQL-compliant databases provide a number of different methods for scanning, searching, and selecting data. The right scan method to use is very much dependent on the use case and the state of the database at the time of scanning. How many records are in the database? Which fields are we interested in? How many records do we expect to be returned? How often do we need to execute the query? These are just some of the questions that we may want to ask when selecting the most appropriate scanning method. Throughout this section, we will describe some of the search methods available, how they are used within SQL to execute scans, and a number of scenarios where they should/should not be used.

Query Planning

Before investigating the different methods of executing queries or scanning a database for information, it is useful to understand how the SQL server makes various decisions about the types of queries to be used. SQL-compliant databases possess a powerful tool known as a **query planner**, which implements a set of features within the server to analyze a request and decides upon the execution path. The query planner optimizes a number of different variables within the request with the aim of reducing the overall execution time. These variables are described in greater detail within the PostgreSQL documentation (https://www.postgresql.org/docs/current/runtime-config-query. html) and include parameters that correspond with the cost of sequential page fetches, CPU operations, and cache size.

In this chapter, we will not cover the details of how a query planner implements its analysis, since the technical details are quite involved. However, it is important to understand how to interpret the plan reported by the query planner. Interpreting the planner is critical if we want to get high performance from a database, as doing so allows us to modify the contents and structure of queries to optimize performance. So, before embarking on a discussion of the various scanning methods, we will gain practical experience in using and interpreting the analysis of the query planner.

Scanning and Sequential Scans

When we want to retrieve information from a database, the query planner needs to search through the available records in order to get the data we need. There are various strategies employed within the database to order and allocate the information for fast retrieval. The process that the SQL server uses to search through a database is known as scanning.

There are a number of different types of scans that can be used to retrieve information. We will start with the sequential scan, as this is the easiest to understand and is the most reliable scan available within a SQL database. If all other scans fail, you can always fall back to the reliable sequential scan to get the information you need out of a database. In some circumstances, the sequential scan isn't the fastest or most efficient; however, it will always produce a correct result. The other interesting thing to note about the sequential scan is that, at this stage in the book, while you may not be aware of it, you have already executed a number of sequential scans. Do you recall entering the following command in *Chapter 6, Importing and Exporting Data*?

```
sqlda=# SELECT * FROM customers LIMIT 5
```

The following is the output of the preceding code:

```
customer_id | title | first_name | last_name | suffix |        email         | gender |   ip_address    |    phone     |   street_address   |    city     | state | postal_code | latitude | longitude |    date_added
------------+-------+------------+-----------+--------+----------------------+--------+-----------------+--------------+--------------------+-------------+-------+-------------+----------+-----------+-------------------
          1 |       | Arlena     | Riveles   |        | ariveles0@stumbleupon.com | F |  98.36.172.246  |              |                    |             |       |             |          |           | 2017-04-23 00:00:00
          2 | Dr    | Ode        | Stovin    |        | ostovin1@npr.org     | M      |  16.97.59.186   | 314-534-4361 | 2573 Forden Parkway | Saint Louis | MO    | 63116       | 38.5814  | -90.2625  | 2014-10-02 00:00:00
          3 |       | Braden     | Jordan    |        | bjordan2@geocities.com | M    |  192.86.248.59  |              | 5651 Kennedy Park  | Pensacola   | FL    | 32598       | 30.6143  | -87.2758  | 2018-10-27 00:00:00
          4 |       | Jessika    | Nussen    |        | jnussen3@salon.com   | F      | 159.165.138.166 | 615-824-2506 | 224 Village Circle | Nashville   | TN    | 37215       | 36.0986  | -86.8219  | 2017-09-03 00:00:00
          5 |       | Lonnie     | Rembaud   |        | lrembaud4@discovery.com | F   |  18.131.58.65   | 786-499-3432 | 38 Lindbergh Way   | Miami       | FL    | 33124       | 25.5584  | -80.4582  | 2014-03-06 00:00:00
(5 rows)
```

Figure 8.1: Output of the limited SELECT statement

Extracting data using the **SELECT** command directly from the database executes a sequential scan, where the database server traverses through each record in the database and compares each record to the criteria in the sequential scan, returning those records that match the criteria. This is essentially a brute-force scan and, thus, can always be called upon to execute a search. In many situations, a sequential scan is also often the most efficient method and will be automatically selected by the **SQL** server. This is particularly the case if any of the following is true:

- The table is quite small. For instance, it may not contain a large number of records.

- The field used in searching contains a high number of duplicates.

- The planner determines that the sequential scan would be equally efficient or more efficient for the given criteria than any other scan.

In this exercise, we will introduce the **EXPLAIN** command, which displays the plan for a query before it is executed. When we use the **EXPLAIN** command in combination with a SQL statement, the SQL interpreter will not execute the statement, but rather return the steps that are going to be executed (a query plan) by the interpreter in order to return the desired results. There is a lot of information returned in a query plan and being able to comprehend the output is vital in tuning the performance of our database queries. Query planning is itself a complex topic and can require some practice in order to be comfortable in interpreting the output; even the PostgreSQL official documentation notes that plan-reading is an art that deserves significant attention in its own right. We will start with a simple plan and will work our way through more complicated queries and query plans.

Exercise 26: Interpreting the Query Planner

In this exercise, we will interpret a query planner using the **EXPLAIN** command. We will interpret the query planner of the **emails** table of the **sqlda** database. Then, we will employ a more involved query, searching for dates between two specific values in the **clicked_date** field. We will need to ensure that the **sqlda** database is loaded as described within the *Preface*.

Retrieve the **Exercise26.sql** file from the accompanying source code. This file will contain all the queries used throughout this exercise. However, we will enter them manually using the SQL interpreter to reinforce our understanding of the query planner's operation.

> **Note**
>
> All the exercises and activities in this chapter are also available on GitHub: https://github.com/TrainingByPackt/SQL-for-Data-Analytics/tree/master/Lesson08.

Observe the following steps to perform the exercise:

1. Open PostgreSQL and connect to the **sqlda** database:

   ```
   C:\> psql sqlda
   ```

   Upon successful connection, you will be presented with the interface to the PostgreSQL database:

   ```
   Type "help" for help.

   sqlda=# █
   ```

   Figure 8.2: PostgreSQL prompt

2. Enter the following command to get the query plan of the **emails** table:

   ```
   sqlda=# EXPLAIN SELECT * FROM emails;
   ```

   Information similar to the following will then be presented:

   ```
                               QUERY PLAN
   ------------------------------------------------------------------
    Seq Scan on emails  (cost=0.00..9606.58 rows=418158 width=79)
   (1 row)
   ```

   Figure 8.3: Query plan of the emails table

This information is returned by the query planner; while this is the simplest example possible, there is quite a bit to unpack in the planner information, so let's look through the output step by step:

```
                                QUERY PLAN
 ---------------------------------------------------------------
 Seq Scan on emails  (cost=0.00..9606.58 rows=418158 width=79)
 (1 row)
```

Figure 8.4: Scan type

The first aspect of the plan that is provided is the type of scan executed by the query. We will cover more of the scan types later in the chapter, but, as discussed in more detail soon, the **Seq Scan** (see *Figure 8.4*), or sequential scan, is a simple yet robust type of query:

```
                                QUERY PLAN
 ---------------------------------------------------------------
 Seq Scan on emails  (cost=0.00..9606.58 rows=418158 width=79)
 (1 row)
```

Figure 8.5: Start up cost

The first measurement reported by the planner, as shown in *Figure 8.5*, is the start up cost, which is the time expended before the scan starts. This time may be required to first sort the data or complete other pre-processing applications. It is also important to note that the time measured is actually reported in cost units (see *Figure 8.5*) as opposed to seconds or milliseconds. Often, the cost units are an indication of the number of disk requests or page fetches made, rather than this being a measure in absolute terms. The reported cost is typically more useful as a means of comparing the performance of various queries, rather than as an absolute measure of time:

```
                                QUERY PLAN
 ---------------------------------------------------------------
 Seq Scan on emails  (cost=0.00..9606.58 rows=418158 width=79)
 (1 row)
```

Figure 8.6: Total cost

The next number in the sequence (see *Figure* 8.6) indicates the total cost of executing the query if all available rows are retrieved. There are some circumstances in which all the available rows may not be retrieved, but we will cover that soon:

```
                        QUERY PLAN
----------------------------------------------------------
 Seq Scan on emails  (cost=0.00..9606.58 rows=418158 width=79)
(1 row)
```

Figure 8.7: Rows to be returned

The next figure in the plan (see *Figure* 8.7) indicates the total number of rows that are available to be returned – again, if the plan is completely executed:

```
                        QUERY PLAN
----------------------------------------------------------
 Seq Scan on emails  (cost=0.00..9606.58 rows=418158 width=79)
(1 row)
```

Figure 8.8: Width of each row

The final figure (see *Figure* 8.8), as suggested by its label, indicates the width of each row in bytes.

> **Note**
>
> When executing the **EXPLAIN** command, PostgreSQL does not actually implement the query or return the values. It does, however, return a description, along with the processing costs involved in executing each stage of the plan.

3. Query plan the **emails** table and set the limit as **5**. Enter the following statement into the PostgreSQL interpreter:

    ```
    sqlda=# EXPLAIN SELECT * FROM emails LIMIT 5;
    ```

    This repeats the previous statement, where the planner is limited to the first five records. This query will produce the following output from the planner:

```
                        QUERY PLAN
----------------------------------------------------------
 Limit  (cost=0.00..0.11 rows=5 width=79)
   ->  Seq Scan on emails  (cost=0.00..9606.58 rows=418158 width=79)
(2 rows)
```

Figure 8.9: Query plan with limited rows

Referring to *Figure* 8.9, we can see that there are two individual rows in the plan. This indicates that the plan is composed of two separate steps, with the lower line of the plan (or, in this case, the first step to be executed) being a repeat of that shown in *Figure* 8.8. The upper line of the plan is the component that limits the result to only **5** rows. The **Limit** process is an additional cost of the query; however, it is quite insignificant compared to the lower-level plan, which retrieves approximately **418158** rows at a cost of **9606** pages requests. The **Limit** stage only returns **5** rows at a cost of **0.11** page requests.

> **Note**
>
> The overall estimated cost for a request comprises the time taken to retrieve the information from the disk as well as the number of rows that need to be scanned. The internal parameters, **seq_page_cost** and **cpu_tuple_cost**, define the cost of the corresponding operations within the tablespace for the database. While not recommended at this stage, these two variables can be changed to modify the steps prepared by the planner.
>
> For more information, refer to the PostgreSQL documentation: https://www. postgresql.org/docs/current/runtime-config-query.html.

4. Now, employ a more involved query, searching for dates between two specific values in the **clicked_date** column. Enter the following statement into the PostgreSQL interpreter:

    ```
    sqlda=# EXPLAIN SELECT * FROM emails WHERE clicked_date BETWEEN '2011-01-
    01' and '2011-02-01';
    ```

    This will produce the following query plan:

    ```
    Gather  (cost=1000.00..9051.49 rows=130 width=79)
      Workers Planned: 2
      -> Parallel Seq Scan on emails  (cost=0.00..8038.49 rows=54 width=79)
            Filter: ((clicked_date >= '2011-01-01 00:00:00'::timestamp without time zone) AND
    (clicked_date <= '2011-02-01 00:00:00'::timestamp without time zone))
    (4 rows)
    ```

    Figure 8.10: Sequential scan for searching dates between two specific values

The first aspect of this query plan to note is that it comprises a few different steps. The lower-level query is similar to the previous query in that it executes a sequential scan. However, rather than limiting the output, we are filtering it on the basis of the timestamp strings provided. Notice that the sequential scan is to be completed in parallel, as indicated by the **Parallel Seq Scan**, and the fact that two workers are planned to be used. Each individual sequence scan should return approximately 54 rows, taking a cost of 8038.49 to complete. The upper level of the plan is a **Gather** state, which is executed at the start of the query. We can see here for the first time that the upfront costs are non-zero (1,000) and total **9051.49**, including the gather and search steps.

In this exercise, we worked with the query planner and the output of the EXPLAIN command. These relatively simple queries highlighted a number of the features of the SQL query planner as well as the detailed information that is provided by it. Having a good understanding of the query planner and the information it is returning to you will serve you well in your data science endeavors. Just remember that this understanding will come with time and practice; never hesitate to consult the PostgreSQL documentation: https://www.postgresql.org/docs/current/using-explain.html.

We will continue to practice reading query plans throughout this chapter as we look at different scan types and the methods, they use to improve performance.

Activity 10: Query Planning

Our aim in this activity is to query plan for reading and interpreting the information returned by the planner. Let's say that we are still dealing with our sqlda database of customer records and that our finance team would like us to implement a system to regularly generate a report of customer activity in a specific geographical region. To ensure that our report can be run in a timely manner, we need an estimate of how long the SQL queries will take. We will use the EXPLAIN command to find out how long some of the report queries will take:

1. Open PostgreSQL and connect to the sqlda database.

2. Use the EXPLAIN command to return the query plan for selecting all available records within the customers table.

3. Read the output of the plan and determine the total query cost, the setup cost, the number of rows to be returned, and the width of each row. Looking at the output, what are the units for each of the values returned from the plan after performing this step?

4. Repeat the query from *step* 2 of this activity, this time limiting the number of returned records to **15**.

Looking at the updated query plan, how many steps are involved in the query plan? What is the cost of the limiting step?

5. Generate the query plan, selecting all rows where customers live within a latitude of **30** and **40** degrees. What is the total plan cost as well as the number of rows returned by the query?

Expected output:

```
                                QUERY PLAN
---------------------------------------------------------------------------------
 Seq Scan on customers  (cost=0.00..1786.00 rows=26439 width=140)
   Filter: ((latitude > '30'::double precision) AND (latitude < '40'::double precision))
(2 rows)
```

Figure 8.11: Plan for customers living within a latitude of 30 and 40 degrees

> **Note**
>
> The solution to the activity can be found on page 340. For an additional challenge, try completing this exercise in Python using psycopg2.

In this activity, we practiced reading the plans returned by the query planner. As discussed previously, plan reading requires substantial practice to master it. This activity began this process and it is strongly recommended that you frequently use the **EXPLAIN** command to improve your plan reading.

Index Scanning

Index scans are one method of improving the performance of our database queries. Index scans differ from sequential scan in that a pre-processing step is executed before the search of database records can occur. The simplest way to think of an index scan is just like the index of a text or reference book. In writing a non-fiction book, a publisher parses through the contents of the book and writes the page numbers corresponding with each alphabetically sorted topic. Just as the publisher goes to the initial effort of creating an index for the reader's reference, so we can create a similar index within the PostgreSQL database. This index within the database creates a prepared and organized set or a subset of references to the data under specified conditions. When a query is executed and an index is present that contains information relevant to the query, the planner may elect to use the data that was pre-processed and pre-arranged within the index. Without using an index, the database needs to repeatedly scan through all records, checking each record for the information of interest.

Even if all of the desired information is at the start of the database, without indexing, the search will still scan through all available records. Clearly, this would take a significantly longer time than necessary.

There are a number of different indexing strategies that PostgreSQL can use to create more efficient searches, including **B-trees**, **hash indexes**, **Generalized Inverted Indexes** (**GINs**), and **Generalized Search Trees** (**GISTs**). Each of these different index types has its own strengths and weaknesses and, hence, is used in different situations. One of the most frequently used indexes is the B-tree, which is the default indexing strategy used by PostgreSQL and is available in almost all database software. We will first spend some time investigating the B-tree index, looking at what makes it useful as well as some of its limitations.

The B-tree Index

The B-tree index is a type of binary search tree and is characterized by the fact that it is a self-balancing structure, maintaining its own data structure for efficient searching. A generic B-tree structure can be found in *Figure 8.12*, in which we can see that each node in the tree has no more than two elements (thus providing balance) and that the first node has two children. These traits are common among B-trees, where each node is limited to **n** components, thus forcing the split into child nodes. The branches of the trees terminate at leaf nodes, which, by definition, have no children:

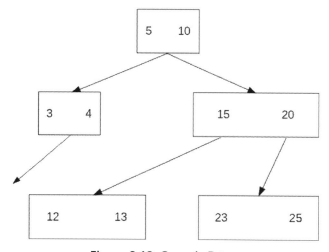

Figure 8.12: Generic B-tree

Using *Figure 8.12* as an example, say we were looking for the number **13** in the B-tree index. We would start at the first node and select whether the number was less than **5** or greater than **10**. This would lead us down the right-hand branch of the tree, where we would again choose between less than **15** and greater than **20**. We would then select less than **15** and arrive at the location of **13** in the index. We can see immediately that this operation would be much faster than looking through all available values. We can also see that for performance, the tree must be balanced to allow for an easy path for traversal. Additionally, there must be sufficient information to allow splitting. If we had a tree index with only a few possible values to split on and a large number of samples, we would simply divide the data into a few groups.

Considering B-trees in the context of database searching, we can see that we require a condition to divide the information (or split) on, and we also need sufficient information for a meaningful split. We do not need to worry about the logic of following the tree, as that will be managed by the database itself and can vary depending on the conditions for searching. Even so, it is important for us to understand the strengths and weaknesses of the method to allow us to make appropriate choices when creating the index for optimal performance.

To create an index for a set of data, we use the following syntax:

```
CREATE INDEX <index name> ON <table name>(table column);
```

We can also add additional conditions and constraints to make the index more selective:

```
CREATE INDEX <index name> ON <table name>(table column) WHERE [condition];
```

We can also specify the type of index:

```
CREATE INDEX <index name> ON <table name> USING TYPE(table column)
```

For example:

```
CREATE INDEX ix_customers ON customers USING BTREE(customer_id);
```

In the next exercise, we will start with a simple plan and work our way through more complicated queries and query plans using index scans.

Exercise 27: Creating an Index Scan

In this exercise, we will create a number of different index scans and will investigate the performance characteristics of each of the scans.

Continuing with the scenario from the previous activity, say we had completed our report service but wanted to make the queries faster. We will try to improve this performance using indexing and index scans. You will recall that we are using a table of customer information that includes contact details such as name, email address, phone number, and address information, as well as the latitude and longitude details of their address. The following are the steps to perform:

1. Ensure that the **sqlda** database is loaded as described within the *Preface*. Retrieve the **Exercise27.sql** file from the accompanying source code. This file will contain all the queries used throughout this exercise; however, we will enter them manually using the SQL interpreter to reinforce our understanding of the query planner's operation.

    > **Note**
    >
    > This file can be downloaded from the accompanying source code available at https://github.com/TrainingByPackt/SQL-for-Data-Analytics/blob/master/Lesson08/Exercise27.

2. Open PostgreSQL and connect to the **sqlda** database:

    ```
    C:\> psql sqlda
    ```

    Upon successful connection, you will be presented with the interface to the PostgreSQL database:

    ```
    Type "help" for help.

    sqlda=# █
    ```

    Figure 8.13: PostgreSQL interpreter

3. Starting with the **customers** database, use the **EXPLAIN** command to determine the cost of the query and the number of rows returned in selecting all of the entries with a **state** value of **FO**:

    ```
    sqlda=# EXPLAIN SELECT * FROM customers WHERE state='FO';
    ```

The following is the output of the preceding code:

```
                        QUERY PLAN
------------------------------------------------------------
 Seq Scan on customers  (cost=0.00..1661.00 rows=1 width=140)
   Filter: (state = 'FO'::text)
(2 rows)
```

Figure 8.14: Query plan of a sequential scan with constraint

Note that there is only **1** row returned and that the setup cost is **0**, but the total query cost is **1661**.

4. Determine how many unique **state** values there are, again using the **EXPLAIN** command:

```
sqlda=# EXPLAIN SELECT DISTINCT state FROM customers;
```

The output is as follows:

```
                       QUERY PLAN
------------------------------------------------------------------
 HashAggregate  (cost=1661.00..1661.51 rows=51 width=3)
   Group Key: state
   ->  Seq Scan on customers  (cost=0.00..1536.00 rows=50000 width=3)
```

Figure 8.15: Unique state values

So, there are **51** unique values within the **state** column.

5. Create an index called **ix_state** using the **state** column of **customers**:

```
sqlda=# CREATE INDEX ix_state ON customers(state);
```

6. Rerun the **EXPLAIN** statement from *step* 5:

```
sqlda=# EXPLAIN SELECT * FROM customers WHERE state='FO';
```

The following is the output of the preceding code:

```
                         QUERY PLAN
--------------------------------------------------------------------
 Index Scan using ix_state on customers  (cost=0.29..8.31 rows=1 width=140)
   Index Cond: (state = 'FO'::text)
```

Figure 8.16: Query plan of an index scan on the customers table

Notice that an index scan is now being used using the index we just created in *step* 5. We can also see that we have a non-zero setup cost (**0.29**), but the total cost is very much reduced, from the previous **1661** to only **8.31**! This is the power of the index scan.

Now, let's look at a slightly different example, looking at the time it takes to return a search on the **gender** column.

7. Use the **EXPLAIN** command to return the query plan for a search for all records of males within the database:

```
sqlda=# EXPLAIN SELECT * FROM customers WHERE gender='M';
```

The output is as follows:

```
                           QUERY PLAN
------------------------------------------------------------------
 Seq Scan on customers  (cost=0.00..1661.00 rows=24960 width=140)
   Filter: (gender = 'M'::text)
```

Figure 8.17: Query plan of a sequential scan on the customers table

8. Create an index called **ix_gender** using the **gender** column of **customers**:

```
sqlda=# CREATE INDEX ix_state ON customers(gender);
```

9. Confirm the presence of the index using **\d**:

```
\d customers;
```

Scrolling to the bottom, we can see the indexes using the **ix_** prefix, as well as the column from the table used to create the index:

```
    state         | text                        |         |         |
    postal_code   | text                        |         |         |
    latitude      | double precision            |         |         |
    longitude     | double precision            |         |         |
    date_added    | timestamp without time zone |         |         |
Indexes:
    "ix_gender" btree (gender)
    "ix_state" btree (state)
```

Figure 8.18: Structure of the customers table

10. Rerun the **EXPLAIN** statement from *step* 10:

```
sqlda=# EXPLAIN SELECT * FROM customers WHERE gender='M';
```

The following is the output of the preceding code:

```
                              QUERY PLAN
- - - - - - - - - - - - - - - - - - - - - - - - - - - - - - - - - - - - - - -
 Seq Scan on customers  (cost=0.00..1661.00 rows=24960 width=140)
   Filter: (gender = 'M'::text)
```

Figure 8.19: Query plan output of a sequential scan with a condition statement

Notice that the query plan has not changed at all, despite the use of the **index** scan. This is because there is insufficient information to create a useful tree within the **gender** column. There are only two possible values, **M** and **F**. The gender index essentially splits the information in two; one branch for males, and one for females. The index has not split the data into branches of the tree well enough to gain any benefit. The planner still needs to sequentially scan through at least half of the data, and so it is not worth the overhead of the index. It is for this reason that the query planner insists on not using the index.

11. Use **EXPLAIN** to return the query plan, searching for latitudes less than **38** degrees and greater than **30** degrees:

```
sqlda=# EXPLAIN SELECT * FROM customers WHERE (latitude < 38) AND
(latitude > 30);
```

The following is the output of the preceding code:

```
                              QUERY PLAN
- - - - - - - - - - - - - - - - - - - - - - - - - - - - - - - - - - - - - - - - - - - - - - - - - - - - - - -
 Seq Scan on customers  (cost=0.00..1786.00 rows=17788 width=140)
   Filter: ((latitude < '38'::double precision) AND (latitude > '30'::double precision))
(2 rows)
```

Figure 8.20: Query plan of a sequential scan on the customers table
with a multi-factor conditional statement

Notice that the query is using a sequential scan with a filter. The initial sequential scan returns **17788** before the filter and costs **1786** with **0** start up cost.

12. Create an index called **ix_latitude** using the **latitude** column of **customers**:

```
sqlda=# CREATE INDEX ix_latitude ON customers(latitude);
```

13. Rerun the query of *step 11* and observe the output of the plan:

```
                                      QUERY PLAN
--------------------------------------------------------------------------------------
 Bitmap Heap Scan on customers  (cost=382.62..1685.44 rows=17788 width=140)
   Recheck Cond: ((latitude < '38'::double precision) AND (latitude > '30'::double precision))
   ->  Bitmap Index Scan on ix_latitude  (cost=0.00..378.17 rows=17788 width=0)
         Index Cond: ((latitude < '38'::double precision) AND (latitude > '30'::double precision))
(4 rows)
```

Figure 8.21: Observe the plan after rerunning the query

We can see that the plan is a lot more involved than the previous one, with a bitmap heap scan and a bitmap index scan being used. We will cover bitmap scans soon, but first, let's get some more information by adding the **ANALYZE** command to **EXPLAIN**.

14. Use **EXPLAIN ANALYZE** to query plan the content of the **customers** table with latitude values of between **30** and **38**:

```
sqlda=# EXPLAIN ANALYZE SELECT * FROM customers WHERE (latitude < 38) AND
(latitude > 30);
```

The following output will be displayed:

```
                                      QUERY PLAN
--------------------------------------------------------------------------------------
 Bitmap Heap Scan on customers  (cost=382.62..1685.44 rows=17788 width=140) (actual time=4.064..12.818 rows=17896 loops=1)
   Recheck Cond: ((latitude < '38'::double precision) AND (latitude > '30'::double precision))
   Heap Blocks: exact=1036
   ->  Bitmap Index Scan on ix_latitude  (cost=0.00..378.17 rows=17788 width=0) (actual time=3.700..3.701 rows=17896 loops=1)
         Index Cond: ((latitude < '38'::double precision) AND (latitude > '30'::double precision))
 Planning Time: 0.301 ms
 Execution Time: 14.582 ms
(7 rows)
```

Figure 8.22: Query plan output containing additional EXPLAIN ANALYZE content

With this extra information, we can see that there is **0.3 ms** of planning time and **14.582 ms** of execution time, with the index scan taking almost the same amount of time to execute as the bitmap heat scan takes to start.

15. Now, let's create another index where latitude is between 30 and 38 on the **customers** table:

```
sqlda=# CREATE INDEX ix_latitude_less ON customers(latitude) WHERE
(latitude < 38) and (latitude > 30);
```

16. Re-execute the query of *step* 15 and compare the query plans:

```
                                      QUERY PLAN
------------------------------------------------------------------------------------------------------
Bitmap Heap Scan on customers  (cost=297.67..1600.49 rows=17788 width=140) (actual time=3.107..12.117 rows=17896 loops=1)
   Recheck Cond: ((latitude < '38'::double precision) AND (latitude > '30'::double precision))
   Heap Blocks: exact=1036
   ->  Bitmap Index Scan on ix_latitude_less  (cost=0.00..293.23 rows=17788 width=0) (actual time=2.726..2.727 rows=17896 loops=1)
Planning Time: 0.681 ms
Execution Time: 13.905 ms
(6 rows)
```

Figure 8.23: Query plan displaying the trade-off between planning and execution time

Using this more targeted index, we were able to shave **0.681 ms** off the execution time, at the cost of an additional 0.3 ms of planning time.

Thus, we have squeezed some additional performance out of our query as our indexes have made the searching process more efficient. We may have had to pay an upfront cost to create the index, but once created, repeat queries can be executed more quickly.

Activity 11: Implementing Index Scans

In this activity, we will determine whether index scans can be used to reduce query time. After creating our customer reporting system for the marketing department in *Activity 10: Query Planning*, we have received another request to allow records to be identified by their IP address or the associated customer names. We know that there are a lot of different IP addresses and we need performant searches. Plan out the queries required to search for records by IP address as well as for certain customers with the suffix **Jr** in their name.

Here are the steps to follow:

1. Use the **EXPLAIN** and **ANALYZE** commands to profile the query plan to search for all records with an IP address of **18.131.58.65**. How long does the query take to plan and execute?

2. Create a generic index based on the IP address column.

3. Rerun the query of *step* 1. How long does the query take to plan and execute?

4. Create a more detailed index based on the IP address column with the condition that the IP address is **18.131.58.65**.

5. Rerun the query of *step 1*. How long does the query take to plan and execute? What are the differences between each of these queries?

6. Use the **EXPLAIN** and **ANALYZE** commands to profile the query plan to search for all records with a suffix of **Jr**. How long does the query take to plan and execute?

7. Create a generic index based on the suffix address column.

8. Rerun the query of *step 6*. How long does the query take to plan and execute?

Expected output

```
                                      QUERY PLAN
---------------------------------------------------------------------------------------------------
 Bitmap Heap Scan on customers  (cost=5.12..318.44 rows=107 width=140) (actual time=0.146..0.440 rows=102 loops=1)
   Recheck Cond: (suffix = 'Jr'::text)
   Heap Blocks: exact=100
   ->  Bitmap Index Scan on ix_jr  (cost=0.00..5.09 rows=107 width=0) (actual time=0.092..0.092 rows=102 loops=1)
         Index Cond: (suffix = 'Jr'::text)
 Planning Time: 0.411 ms
 Execution Time: 0.511 ms
(7 rows)
```

Figure 8.24: Query plan of the scan after creating an index on the suffix column

> **Note**
>
> The solution to the activity can be found on page 341.

In this activity, we have squeezed some additional performance out of our query as our indexes have made the searching process more efficient. We will learn how the hash index works in the next section.

Hash Index

The final indexing type we will cover is the hash index. The hash index has only recently gained stability as a feature within PostgreSQL, with previous versions issuing warnings that the feature is unsafe and reporting that the method is typically not as performant as B-tree indexes. At the time of writing, the hash index feature is relatively limited in the comparative statements it can run, with equality (=) being the only one available. So, given that the feature is only just stable and somewhat limited in options for use, why would anyone use it? Well, hash indices are able to describe large datasets (in the order of tens of thousands of rows or more) using very little data, allowing more of the data to be kept in memory and reducing search times for some queries. This is particularly important for databases that are at least several gigabytes in size.

A hash index is an indexing method that utilizes a hash function to achieve its performance benefits. A hash function is a mathematical function that takes data or a series of data and returns a unique length of alphanumeric characters depending upon what information was provided and the unique hash code used. Let's say we had a customer named "Josephine Marquez." We could pass this information to a hash function, which could produce a hash result such as 01f38e. Say we also had records for Josephine's husband, Julio; the corresponding hash for Julio could be 43eb38a. A hash map uses a key-value pair relationship to find data.

We could (but are not limited to) use the values of a hash function to provide the key, using the data contained in the corresponding row of the database as the value. As long as the key is unique to the value, we can quickly access the information we require. This method can also reduce the overall size of the index in memory, if only the corresponding hashes are stored, thereby dramatically reducing the search time for a query.

The following example shows how to create a hash index:

```
sqlda=# CREATE INDEX ix_gender ON customers USING HASH(gender);
```

You will recall that the query planner is able to ignore the indices created if it deems them to be not significantly faster for the existing query or just not appropriate. As the hash scan is somewhat limited in use, it may not be uncommon for a different search to ignore the indices.

Exercise 28: Generating Several Hash Indexes to Investigate Performance

In this exercise, we will generate a number of hash indexes and investigate the potential performance increases that can be gained from using them. We will start the exercise by rerunning some of the queries of previous exercises and comparing the execution times:

1. Drop all existing indexes using the **DROP INDEX** command:

    ```
    DROP INDEX <index name>;
    ```

2. Use **EXPLAIN** and **ANALYZE** on the customer table where the gender is male, but without using a hash index:

    ```
    sqlda=# EXPLAIN ANALYZE SELECT * FROM customers WHERE gender='M';
    ```

The following output will be displayed:

```
                               QUERY PLAN
-----------------------------------------------------------------------------------
 Seq Scan on customers  (cost=0.00..1661.00 rows=24960 width=140) (actual time=0.024..26.937 rows=24956 loops=1)
   Filter: (gender = 'M'::text)
   Rows Removed by Filter: 25044
 Planning Time: 0.107 ms
 Execution Time: 29.905 ms
(5 rows)
```

Figure 8.25: Standard sequential scan

We can see here that the estimated planning time is **0.107 ms** and the execution time is **29.905 ms**.

3. Create a B-tree index on the **gender** column and repeat the query to determine the performance using the default index:

```
sqlda=# CREATE INDEX ix_gender ON customers USING btree(gender);
sqlda=#
```

The following is the output of the preceding code:

```
                               QUERY PLAN
-----------------------------------------------------------------------------------
 Seq Scan on customers  (cost=0.00..1661.00 rows=24960 width=140) (actual time=0.028..21.504 rows=24956 loops=1)
   Filter: (gender = 'M'::text)
   Rows Removed by Filter: 25044
 Planning Time: 0.444 ms
 Execution Time: 23.955 ms
(5 rows)
```

Figure 8.26: Query planner ignoring the B-tree index

We can see here that the query planner has not selected the B-tree index, but rather the sequential scan. The costs of the scans do not differ, but the planning and execution time estimates have been modified. This is not unexpected, as these measures are exactly that – estimates based on a variety of different conditions, such as data in memory and I/O constraints.

4. Repeat the following query at least five times manually and observe the time estimates after each execution:

```
sqlda=# EXPLAIN ANALYZE SELECT * FROM customers WHERE gender='M';
```

The results of the five individual queries can be seen in the following screenshot; note that the planning and execution times differ for each separate execution of the query:

```
                                    QUERY PLAN
---------------------------------------------------------------------------------------
 Seq Scan on customers  (cost=0.00..1661.00 rows=24960 width=140) (actual time=0.020..21.596 rows=24956 loops=1)
   Filter: (gender = 'M'::text)
   Rows Removed by Filter: 25044
 Planning Time: 0.521 ms
 Execution Time: 24.105 ms
(5 rows)

sqlda=# EXPLAIN ANALYZE SELECT * FROM customers WHERE gender='M';
                                    QUERY PLAN
---------------------------------------------------------------------------------------
 Seq Scan on customers  (cost=0.00..1661.00 rows=24960 width=140) (actual time=0.023..22.629 rows=24956 loops=1)
   Filter: (gender = 'M'::text)
   Rows Removed by Filter: 25044
 Planning Time: 0.158 ms
 Execution Time: 25.162 ms
(5 rows)

sqlda=# EXPLAIN ANALYZE SELECT * FROM customers WHERE gender='M';
                                    QUERY PLAN
---------------------------------------------------------------------------------------
 Seq Scan on customers  (cost=0.00..1661.00 rows=24960 width=140) (actual time=0.023..21.765 rows=24956 loops=1)
   Filter: (gender = 'M'::text)
   Rows Removed by Filter: 25044
 Planning Time: 0.153 ms
 Execution Time: 24.198 ms
(5 rows)

sqlda=# EXPLAIN ANALYZE SELECT * FROM customers WHERE gender='M';
                                    QUERY PLAN
---------------------------------------------------------------------------------------
 Seq Scan on customers  (cost=0.00..1661.00 rows=24960 width=140) (actual time=0.023..21.758 rows=24956 loops=1)
   Filter: (gender = 'M'::text)
   Rows Removed by Filter: 25044
 Planning Time: 0.158 ms
 Execution Time: 24.277 ms
(5 rows)

sqlda=# EXPLAIN ANALYZE SELECT * FROM customers WHERE gender='M';
                                    QUERY PLAN
---------------------------------------------------------------------------------------
 Seq Scan on customers  (cost=0.00..1661.00 rows=24960 width=140) (actual time=0.023..21.967 rows=24956 loops=1)
   Filter: (gender = 'M'::text)
   Rows Removed by Filter: 25044
 Planning Time: 0.163 ms
 Execution Time: 24.444 ms
(5 rows)
```

Figure 8.27: Five repetitions of the same sequential scan

5. Drop or remove the index:

   ```
   sqlda=# DROP INDEX ix_gender;
   ```

6. Create a hash index on the **gender** column:

   ```
   sqlda=# CREATE INDEX ix_gender ON customers USING HASH(gender);
   ```

7. Repeat the query from *step* 4 to see the execution time:

   ```
   sqlda=# EXPLAIN ANALYZE SELECT * FROM customers WHERE gender='M';
   ```

   The following output will be displayed:

```
                                QUERY PLAN
--------------------------------------------------------------------------------------------------
 Seq Scan on customers  (cost=0.00..1661.00 rows=24960 width=140) (actual time=0.020..22.642 rows=24956 loops=1)
   Filter: (gender = 'M'::text)
   Rows Removed by Filter: 25044
 Planning Time: 0.300 ms
 Execution Time: 25.155 ms
(5 rows)
```

Figure 8.28: Query planner ignoring the hash index

As with the B-tree index, there was no benefit to using the hash index on the **gender** column, and so it was not used by the planner.

8. Use the **EXPLAIN ANALYZE** command to profile the performance of the query that selects all customers where the state is **FO**:

   ```
   sqlda=# EXPLAIN ANALYZE SELECT * FROM customers WHERE state='FO';
   ```

   The following output will be displayed:

```
                                QUERY PLAN
-----------------------------------------------------------------------------------------------
 Seq Scan on customers  (cost=0.00..1661.00 rows=1 width=140) (actual time=22.293..22.293 rows=0 loops=1)
   Filter: (state = 'FO'::text)
   Rows Removed by Filter: 50000
 Planning Time: 0.188 ms
 Execution Time: 22.328 ms
(5 rows)
```

Figure 8.29: Sequential scan with filter by specific state

9. Create a B-tree index on the **state** column of the **customers** table and repeat the query profiling:

```
sqlda=# CREATE INDEX ix_state ON customers USING BTREE(state);
sqlda=# EXPLAIN ANALYZE SELECT * FROM customers WHERE state='FO';
```

The following is the output of the preceding code:

```
                                    QUERY PLAN
--------------------------------------------------------------------------------------------------
 Index Scan using ix_state on customers  (cost=0.29..8.31 rows=1 width=140) (actual time=0.060..0.060 rows=0 loops=1)
   Index Cond: (state = 'FO'::text)
 Planning Time: 0.374 ms
 Execution Time: 0.103 ms
(4 rows)
```

Figure 8.30: Performance benefit due to B-tree indexing

Here, we can see a significant performance increase due to the B-tree index with a slight setup cost. How does the hash scan perform? Given that the execution time has dropped from 22.3 ms to **0.103 ms**, it is reasonable to conclude that the increased planning cost has increased by approximately 50%.

10. Drop the **ix_state** B-tree index and create a hash scan:

```
sqlda=# DROP INDEX ix_state;
sqlda=# CREATE INDEX ix_state ON customers USING HASH(state);
```

11. Use **EXPLAIN** and **ANALYZE** to profile the performance of the hash scan:

```
sqlda=# EXPLAIN ANALYZE SELECT * FROM customers WHERE state='FO';
```

The following is the output of the preceding code:

```
                                    QUERY PLAN
--------------------------------------------------------------------------------------------------
 Index Scan using ix_state on customers  (cost=0.00..8.02 rows=1 width=140) (actual time=0.014..0.014 rows=0 loops=1)
   Index Cond: (state = 'FO'::text)
 Planning Time: 0.271 ms
 Execution Time: 0.048 ms
(4 rows)
```

Figure 8.31: Additional performance boost using a hash index

We can see that, for this specific query, a hash index is particularly effective, reducing both the planning/setup time and cost of the B-tree index, as well as reducing the execution time to less than 1 ms from approximately 25 ms.

In this exercise, we used hash indexes to find the effectiveness of a particular query. We saw how the execution time goes down when using a hash index in a query.

Activity 12: Implementing Hash Indexes

In this activity, we will investigate the use of hash indexes to improve performance using the **emails** table from the **sqlda** database. We have received another request from the marketing department. This time, they would like us to analyze the performance of an email marketing campaign. Given that the success rate of email campaigns is low, many different emails are sent to many customers at a time. Use the **EXPLAIN** and **ANALYZE** commands to determine the planning time and cost, as well as the execution time and cost, of selecting all rows where the email subject is **Shocking Holiday Savings On Electric Scooters**:

1. Use the **EXPLAIN** and **ANALYZE** commands to determine the planning time and cost, as well as the execution time and cost, of selecting all rows where the email subject is **Shocking Holiday Savings On Electric Scooters** in the first query and **Black Friday. Green Cars.** in the second query.

2. Create a hash scan on the **email_subject** column.

3. Repeat *step* 1. Compare the output of the query planner without the hash index to that with the hash index. What effect did the hash scan have on the performance of the two queries?

4. Create a hash scan on the **customer_id** column.

5. Use **EXPLAIN** and **ANALYZE** to estimate how long it would take to select all rows with a **customer_id** value greater than 100. What type of scan was used and why?

Expected output:

```
                            QUERY PLAN
-------------------------------------------------------------------------------------------------
 Seq Scan on emails  (cost=0.00..18651.98 rows=417309 width=79) (actual time=0.024..121.483 rows=417315 loops=1)
   Filter: (customer_id > 100)
   Rows Removed by Filter: 843
 Planning Time: 0.199 ms
 Execution Time: 152.656 ms
(5 rows)
```

Figure 8.32: Query planner ignoring the hash index due to limitations

> **Note**
>
> The solution to the activity can be found on page 343.

In this activity, a sequential scan was used in this query rather than the hash scan created due to the current limitations of hash scan usage. At the time of writing, use of the hash scan is limited to equality comparisons, which involves searching for values equal to a given value.

Effective Index Use

So far in this chapter, we have looked at a number of different scanning methods, and the use of both B-trees and hash scans as a means of reducing query times. We have also presented a number of different examples of where an index was created for a field or condition and was explicitly not selected by the query planner when executing the query as it was deemed a more inefficient choice. In this section, we will spend some time discussing the appropriate use of indexes for reducing query times, since, while indexes may seem like an obvious choice for increasing query performance, this is not always the case. Consider the following situations:

- The field you have used for your index is frequently changing: In this situation, where you are frequently inserting or deleting rows in a table, the index that you have created may quickly become inefficient as it was constructed for data that is either no longer relevant or has since had a change in value. Consider the index at the back of this book. If you move the order of the chapters around, the index is no longer valid and would need to be republished. In such a situation, you may need to periodically re-index the data to ensure the references to the data are up to date. In SQL, we can rebuild the data indices by using the **REINDEX** command, which leads to a scenario where you will need to consider the cost, means, and strategy of frequent re-indexing versus other performance considerations, such as the query benefits introduced by the index, the size of the database, or even whether changes to the database structure could avoid the problem altogether.

- The index is out of date and the existing references are either invalid or there are segments of data without an index, preventing use of the index by the query planner: In such a situation, the index is so old that it cannot be used and thus needs to be updated.

- You are frequently looking for records containing the same search criteria within a specific field: We considered an example similar to this when looking for customers within a database whose records contained latitude values of less than 38 and greater than 30, using **SELECT * FROM customers WHERE (latitude < 38) and (latitude > 30)**. In this example, it may be more efficient to create a partial index using the subset of data, as here: **CREATE INDEX ix_latitude_less ON customers(latitude) WHERE (latitude < 38) and (latitude > 30)**. In this way, the index is only created using the data we are interested in, and is thereby smaller in size, quicker to scan, easier to maintain, and can also be used in more complex queries.

- The database isn't particularly large: In such a situation, the overhead of creating and using the index may simply not be worth it. Sequential scans, particularly those using data already in RAM, are quite fast, and if you create an index on a small dataset, there is no guarantee that the query planner will use it or get any significant benefit from using it.

Performant Joins

The `JOIN` functionality in SQL-compliant databases provides a very powerful and efficient method of combining data from different sources, without the need for complicated looping structures or a series of individual SQL statements. We covered joins and join theory in detail in *Chapter 3, SQL for Data Preparation*. As suggested by the name of the command, a join takes information from two or more tables and uses the contents of the records within each table to combine the two sets of information. Because we are combining this information without the use of looping structures, this can be done very efficiently. In this section, we will consider the use of joins as a more performant alternative to looping structures. The following is the **Customer Information** table:

Customer ID	First Name	Last Name	Address
1	Meat	Hook	Melee Island
2	Captain	Blondebeard	Puerto Pollo
3	Griswold	Goodsoup	Blood Island

Figure 8.33: Customer information

The following table shows the **Order Information** table:

Order ID	Customer ID	Product Code	Qty
1618	3	GROG1	12
1619	2	POULET3	3

Figure 8.34: Order information

So, with this information, we may want to see whether there are some trends in the items that are sold based on the customer's address. We can use **JOIN** to bring these two sets of information together; we will use the **Customer ID** column to combine the two datasets and produce the information shown in the following table:

Customer ID	First Name	Last Name	Address	Order ID	Product Code	Qty
2	Captain	Blondebeard	Puerto Pollo	1619	POULET3	3
3	Griswald	Goodsoup	Blood Island	1618	GROG1	12

Figure 8.35: Join by customer ID

We can see in the preceding example that the join included all of the records where there was information available for both the customer and the order. As such, the customer **Meat Hook** was omitted from the combined information since no order information was available. In the example, we executed **INNER JOIN**; there are, however, a number of different joins available, and we will spend some time looking through each of them. The following is an example that shows the use of a performant **INNER JOIN**:

```
smalljoins=# EXPLAIN ANALYZE SELECT customers.*, order_info.order_id, order_
info.product_code, order_info.qty FROM customers INNER JOIN order_info ON
customers.customer_id=order_info.customer_id;
```

Refer to *Chapter 3, SQL for Data Preparation*, for more information on joins. In the next exercise, we will investigate the use of performant inner joins.

Exercise 29: Determining the Use of Inner Joins

In this exercise, we will investigate the use of inner joins to efficiently select multiple rows of data from two different tables. Let's say that our good friends in the marketing department gave us two separate databases: one from **SalesForce** and one from **Oracle**. We could use a **JOIN** statement to merge the corresponding information from the two sources into a single source. Here are the steps to follow:

1. Create a database called **smalljoins** on the PostgreSQL server:

   ```
   $ createdb smalljoins
   ```

2. Load the **smalljoins.dump** file provided in the accompanying source code from the GitHub repository: https://github.com/TrainingByPackt/SQL-for-Data-Analytics/blob/master/Datasets/smalljoins.dump:

   ```
   $psql smalljoins < smalljoins.dump
   ```

3. Open the database:

```
$ psql smalljoins
```

4. Inspect the information available for **customers**:

```
smalljoins=# SELECT * FROM customers;
```

The following figure shows the output of the preceding code:

```
customer_id | first_name |  last_name  |    address
------------+------------+-------------+---------------
          4 | Guybrush   | Threepwood  | Melee Island
          5 | Murray     | TheSkull    | Plunder island
          1 | Meat       | Hook        | Melee Island
          2 | Captain    | Blondebeard | Puerto Pollo
          3 | Griswold   | Goodsoup    | Blood Island
(5 rows)
```

Figure 8.36: Customer table

5. Inspect the information available for the order information:

```
smalljoins=# SELECT * FROM order_info;
```

This will display the following output:

```
order_id | customer_id | product_code | qty
---------+-------------+--------------+-----
    1620 |           4 | MON123       |   1
    1621 |           4 | MON636       |   3
    1622 |           5 | MON666       |   1
    1618 |           3 | GROG1        |  12
    1619 |           2 | POULET3      |   3
(5 rows)
```

Figure 8.37: Order information table

6. Execute an inner join where we retrieve all columns from both tables without duplicating the **customer_id** column to replicate the results from *Figure 8.35*. We will set the left table to be **customers** and the right table to be **order_info**. So, to be clear, we want all columns from **customers** and the **order_id**, **product_code**, and **qty** columns from **order_info** when a customer has placed an order. Write this as a SQL statement:

```
smalljoins=# SELECT customers.*, order_info.order_id, order_info.product_
code, order_info.qty FROM customers INNER JOIN order_info ON customers.
customer_id=order_info.customer_id;
```

The following figure shows the output of the preceding code:

```
 customer_id | first_name |  last_name  |    address     | order_id | product_code | qty
-------------+------------+-------------+----------------+----------+--------------+-----
           4 | Guybrush   | Threepwood  | Melee Island   |     1620 | MON123       |   1
           4 | Guybrush   | Threepwood  | Melee Island   |     1621 | MON636       |   3
           5 | Murray     | TheSkull    | Plunder island |     1622 | MON666       |   1
           3 | Griswold   | Goodsoup    | Blood Island   |     1618 | GROG1        |  12
           2 | Captain    | Blondebeard | Puerto Pollo   |     1619 | POULET3      |   3
(5 rows)
```

Figure 8.38 Join of customer and order information

7. Save the results of this query as a separate table by inserting the **INTO table_name** keywords:

    smalljoins=# SELECT customers.*, order_info.order_id, order_info.product_ code, order_info.qty INTO join_results FROM customers INNER JOIN order_ info ON customers.customer_id=order_info.customer_id;

    The following figure shows the output of the preceding code:

```
smalljoins=# SELECT customers.*, order_info.order_id, order_info.product_code, order_info.qty INTO join_
results FROM customers INNER JOIN order_info ON customers.customer_id=order_info.customer_id;

SELECT 5
```

Figure 8.39: Save results of join to a new table

8. Use **EXPLAIN ANALYZE** to get an estimate of the time taken to execute the join. Now, how much faster is the join?

    smalljoins=# EXPLAIN ANALYZE SELECT customers.*, order_info.order_id, order_info.product_code, order_info.qty FROM customers INNER JOIN order_ info ON customers.customer_id=order_info.customer_id;

    This will display the following output:

```
                                    QUERY PLAN
--------------------------------------------------------------------------------------------------
 Hash Join  (cost=24.18..172.89 rows=3560 width=140) (actual time=0.537..0.548 rows=10 loops=1)
   Hash Cond: (order_info.customer_id = customers.customer_id)
   ->  Seq Scan on order_info  (cost=0.00..21.30 rows=1130 width=44) (actual time=0.238..0.240 rows=10 loops=1)
   ->  Hash  (cost=16.30..16.30 rows=630 width=100) (actual time=0.225..0.226 rows=5 loops=1)
         Buckets: 1024  Batches: 1  Memory Usage: 9kB
         ->  Seq Scan on customers  (cost=0.00..16.30 rows=630 width=100) (actual time=0.199..0.202 rows=5 loops=1)
 Planning Time: 7.077 ms
 Execution Time: 1.533 ms
(8 rows)
```

Figure 8.40: Baseline reading for comparing the performance of JOIN

9. Select all of the **customer_id** values that are in **order_info** and use **EXPLAIN ANALYZE** to find out how long it takes to execute these individual queries:

```
smalljoins=# EXPLAIN ANALYZE SELECT * FROM customers WHERE customer_id IN
(SELECT customer_id FROM order_info);
```

The following screenshot shows the output of the preceding code:

```
                                        QUERY PLAN
-----------------------------------------------------------------------------------------------
Hash Join  (cost=28.62..50.08 rows=315 width=100) (actual time=0.104..0.110 rows=4 loops=1)
  Hash Cond: (customers.customer_id = order_info.customer_id)
  ->  Seq Scan on customers  (cost=0.00..16.30 rows=630 width=100) (actual time=0.015..0.017 rows=5 loops=1)
  ->  Hash  (cost=26.12..26.12 rows=200 width=4) (actual time=0.057..0.057 rows=4 loops=1)
        Buckets: 1024  Batches: 1  Memory Usage: 9kB
        ->  HashAggregate  (cost=24.12..26.12 rows=200 width=4) (actual time=0.026..0.030 rows=4 loops=1)
              Group Key: order_info.customer_id
              ->  Seq Scan on order_info  (cost=0.00..21.30 rows=1130 width=4) (actual time=0.008..0.011 rows=5 loops=1)
Planning Time: 0.199 ms
Execution Time: 0.177 ms
(10 rows)
```

Figure 8.41: Improved performance of JOIN using a hash index

Looking at the results of the two query planners, we can see that not only did the inner join take about a third of the time of the sequential query (**0.177 ms** compared with **1.533 ms**), but also that we have returned more information by the inner join, with **order_id**, **product_code**, and **qty** also being returned.

10. Execute a left join using the **customers** table as the left table and **order_info** as the right table:

```
smalljoins=# SELECT customers.*, order_info.order_id, order_info.product_
code, order_info.qty FROM customers LEFT JOIN order_info ON customers.
customer_id=order_info.customer_id;
```

The following screenshot shows the output of the preceding code:

```
 customer_id | first_name |  last_name  |    address     | order_id | product_code | qty
-------------+------------+-------------+----------------+----------+--------------+-----
           4 | Guybrush   | Threepwood  | Melee Island   |     1620 | MON123       |   1
           4 | Guybrush   | Threepwood  | Melee Island   |     1621 | MON636       |   3
           5 | Murray     | TheSkull    | Plunder island |     1622 | MON666       |   1
           3 | Griswold   | Goodsoup    | Blood Island   |     1618 | GROG1        |  12
           2 | Captain    | Blondebeard | Puerto Pollo   |     1619 | POULET3      |   3
           1 | Meat       | Hook        | Melee Island   |          |              |
(6 rows)
```

Figure 8.42: Left join of the customers and order_info tables

Notice the differences between the left join and the inner join. The left join has included the result for **customer_id 4** twice, and has included the result for **Meat Hook** once, although there is no order information available. It has included the results of the left table with blank entries for information that is not present in the right table.

11. Use **EXPLAIN ANALYZE** to determine the time and cost of executing the join:

    ```
    smalljoins=# EXPLAIN ANALYZE SELECT customers.*, order_info.order_id,
    order_info.product_code, order_info.qty FROM customers LEFT JOIN order_
    info ON customers.customer_id=order_info.customer_id;
    ```

    This will display the following output:

    ```
                                            QUERY PLAN
    -------------------------------------------------------------------------------------------
     Hash Right Join  (cost=24.18..172.89 rows=3560 width=140) (actual time=0.068..0.089 rows=6 loops=1)
       Hash Cond: (order_info.customer_id = customers.customer_id)
       ->  Seq Scan on order_info  (cost=0.00..21.30 rows=1130 width=44) (actual time=0.007..0.009 rows=5 loops=1)
       ->  Hash  (cost=16.30..16.30 rows=630 width=100) (actual time=0.034..0.034 rows=5 loops=1)
             Buckets: 1024  Batches: 1  Memory Usage: 9kB
             ->  Seq Scan on customers  (cost=0.00..16.30 rows=630 width=100) (actual time=0.020..0.024 rows=5 loops=1)
     Planning Time: 0.219 ms
     Execution Time: 0.188 ms
    (8 rows)
    ```

    Figure 8.43: Query planner for executing the left join

12. Replace the left join of *step 11* with a right join and observe the results:

    ```
    smalljoins=# EXPLAIN ANALYZE SELECT customers.*, order_info.order_id,
    order_info.product_code, order_info.qty FROM customers RIGHT JOIN order_
    info ON customers.customer_id=order_info.customer_id;
    ```

    The following screenshot shows the output of the preceding code:

    ```
     customer_id | first_name |  last_name  |    address     | order_id | product_code | qty
    -------------+------------+-------------+----------------+----------+--------------+-----
               4 | Guybrush   | Threepwood  | Melee Island   |     1620 | MON123       |   1
               4 | Guybrush   | Threepwood  | Melee Island   |     1621 | MON636       |   3
               5 | Murray     | TheSkull    | Plunder island |     1622 | MON666       |   1
               3 | Griswold   | Goodsoup    | Blood Island   |     1618 | GROG1        |  12
               2 | Captain    | Blondebeard | Puerto Pollo   |     1619 | POULET3      |   3
    (5 rows)
    ```

    Figure 8.44: Results of a right join

    Again, we have two entries for **customer_id 4**, **Guybrush Threepwood**, but we can see that the entry for **customer_id 1**, **Meat Hook**, is no longer present as we have joined on the basis of the information within the contents of the **order_id** table.

13. Use **EXPLAIN ANALYZE** to determine the time and cost of the right join:

    ```
    smalljoins=# EXPLAIN ANALYZE SELECT customers.*, order_info.order_id,
    order_info.product_code, order_info.qty FROM customers RIGHT JOIN order_
    info ON customers.customer_id=order_info.customer_id;
    ```

The following screenshot shows the output of the preceding code:

```
                                    QUERY PLAN
-------------------------------------------------------------------------------------------------
 Hash Left Join  (cost=24.18..172.89 rows=3560 width=140) (actual time=0.066..0.075 rows=5 loops=1)
   Hash Cond: (order_info.customer_id = customers.customer_id)
   ->  Seq Scan on order_info  (cost=0.00..21.30 rows=1130 width=44) (actual time=0.022..0.024 rows=5 loops=1)
   ->  Hash  (cost=16.30..16.30 rows=630 width=100) (actual time=0.021..0.022 rows=5 loops=1)
         Buckets: 1024  Batches: 1  Memory Usage: 9kB
         ->  Seq Scan on customers  (cost=0.00..16.30 rows=630 width=100) (actual time=0.007..0.012 rows=5 loops=1)
 Planning Time: 0.220 ms
 Execution Time: 0.141 ms
(8 rows)
```

Figure 8.45: Query plan of a right join

We can see that the right join was marginally faster and more cost effective, which can be attributed to one less row being returned than in the left join.

14. Insert an additional row into **order_info** with a **customer_id** value that is not present in the **customers** table:

```
smalljoins=# INSERT INTO order_info (order_id, customer_id, product_code,
qty) VALUES (1621, 6, 'MEL386', 1);
```

15. Replace the left join of *step 11* with a full outer join and observe the results:

```
smalljoins=# SELECT customers.*, order_info.order_id, order_info.
product_code, order_info.qty FROM customers FULL OUTER JOIN order_info ON
customers.customer_id=order_info.customer_id;
```

This will display the following output:

```
 customer_id | first_name |  last_name   |    address     | order_id | product_code | qty
-------------+------------+--------------+----------------+----------+--------------+-----
           4 | Guybrush   | Threepwood   | Melee Island   |     1620 | MON123       |   1
           4 | Guybrush   | Threepwood   | Melee Island   |     1621 | MON636       |   3
           5 | Murray     | TheSkull     | Plunder island |     1622 | MON666       |   1
           3 | Griswold   | Goodsoup     | Blood Island   |     1618 | GROG1        |  12
           2 | Captain    | Blondebeard  | Puerto Pollo   |     1619 | POULET3      |   3
             |            |              |                |     1621 | MEL386       |   1
           1 | Meat       | Hook         | Melee Island   |          |              |
(7 rows)
```

Figure 8.46: Results of a full outer join

Notice the line that contains **product_code MEL386**, but no information regarding the customer; there's a similar case for the line for **customer_id Meat Hook**. The full outer join has combined all available information even if some of the information is not available from either table.

16. Use the **EXPLAIN ANALYZE** command to determine the performance of the query.

    smalljoins=# EXPLAIN ANALYZE SELECT customers.*, order_info.order_id, order_info.product_code, order_info.qty FROM customers FULL OUTER JOIN order_info ON customers.customer_id=order_info.customer_id;

The following screenshot shows the output of the preceding code:

```
                                           QUERY PLAN
-------------------------------------------------------------------------------------------------
 Hash Full Join  (cost=24.18..172.89 rows=3560 width=140) (actual time=0.126..0.148 rows=7 loops=1)
   Hash Cond: (order_info.customer_id = customers.customer_id)
   ->  Seq Scan on order_info  (cost=0.00..21.30 rows=1130 width=44) (actual time=0.009..0.012 rows=6 loops=1)
   ->  Hash  (cost=16.30..16.30 rows=630 width=100) (actual time=0.064..0.065 rows=5 loops=1)
         Buckets: 1024  Batches: 1  Memory Usage: 9kB
         ->  Seq Scan on customers  (cost=0.00..16.30 rows=630 width=100) (actual time=0.021..0.026 rows=5 loops=1)
 Planning Time: 0.226 ms
 Execution Time: 0.232 ms
(8 rows)
```

Figure 8.47: Query plan of a full outer join

The performance is very similar to that of the other queries, given that an additional row is provided, which can be clearly seen in the final output.

In this exercise, we were introduced to the usage and performance benefits of joins. We observed the combination of information from two separate tables using fewer resources than individual searches require, as well as the use of **OUTER JOIN** to efficiently combine all information. In the next activity, we will build upon our understanding of joins with a much larger dataset.

Activity 13: Implementing Joins

In this activity, our goal is to implement various performant joins. In this activity, we will use joins to combine information from a table of customers as well as information from a marketing email dataset. Say we have just collated a number of different email records from a variety of different databases. We would like to distill the information down into a single table so that we can perform some more detailed analysis. Here are the steps to follow:

1. Open **PostgreSQL** and connect to the **sqlda** database.

2. Determine a list of customers (**customer_id**, **first_name**, and **last_name**) who had been sent an email, including information for the subject of the email and whether they opened and clicked on the email. The resulting table should include the **customer_id**, **first_name**, **last_name**, **email_subject**, **opened**, and **clicked** columns.

3. Save the resulting table to a new table, **customer_emails**.

4. Find those customers who opened or clicked on an email.

5. Find the customers who have a dealership in their city; customers who do not have a dealership in their city should have a blank value for the **city** columns.

6. List those customers who do not have dealerships in their city (hint: a blank field is **NULL**).

Expected output

```
customer_id |    first_name    |    last_name    | city
------------+------------------+-----------------+------
          1 | Arlena           | Riveles         |
         12 | Tyne             | Duggan          |
         21 | Pryce            | Geist           |
         24 | Barbi            | Lanegran        |
         30 | Kath             | Rivel           |
         38 | Carter           | Lagneaux        |
         44 | Waldemar         | Paroni          |
         49 | Hannah           | McGlew          |
         56 | Riva             | Cathesyed       |
         63 | Gweneth          | Maior           |
         70 | Caty             | Woolveridge     |
         72 | Jodi             | Fautly          |
```

Figure 8.48: Customers without city information

The output shows the final list of customers in the cities where we have no dealerships.

> **Note**
>
> The solution to the activity can be found on page 346.

In this activity, we used joins to combine information from a table of customers as well as information from a marketing email dataset and helped the marketing manager to solve their query.

Functions and Triggers

So far in this chapter, we have discovered how to quantify query performance via the query planner, as well as the benefits of using joins to collate and extract information from multiple database tables. In this section, we will construct reusable queries and statements via functions, as well as automatic function execution via trigger callbacks. The combination of these two SQL features can be used to not only run queries or re-index tables as data is added to/updated in/removed from the database, but also to run hypothesis tests and track the results of the tests throughout the life of the database.

Function Definitions

As in almost all other programming or scripting languages, functions in SQL are contained sections of code, which provides a lot of benefits, such as efficient code reuse and simplified troubleshooting processes. We can use functions to repeat/modify statements or queries without re-entering the statement each time or searching for its use throughout longer code segments. One of the most powerful aspects of functions is also that they allow us to break the code into smaller, testable chunks. As the popular computer science expression goes "If the code is not tested, it cannot be trusted."

So, how do we define functions in SQL? There is a relatively straightforward syntax, with the SQL syntax keywords:

```
CREATE FUNCTION some_function_name (function_arguments)
RETURNS return_type AS $return_name$
DECLARE return_name return_type;
BEGIN
  <function statements>;
RETURN <some_value>;
END; $return_name$
LANGUAGE PLPGSQL;
```

The following is a small explanation of the function used in the preceding code:

- **some_function_name** is the name issued to the function and is used to call the function at later stages.

- **function_arguments** is an optional list of function arguments. This could be empty, without any arguments provided, if we don't need any additional information to be provided to the function. To provide additional information, we can either use a list of different data types as the arguments (such as integer and numeric), or a list of arguments with parameter names (such as **min_val** integer and **max_val** numeric).

- **return_type** is the data type being returned from the function.

- **return_name** is the name of the variable to be returned (optional).

  The **DECLARE return_name return_type** statement is only required if **return_name** is provided, and a variable is to be returned from the function. If **return_name** is not required, this line can be omitted from the function definition.

- **function statements** entail the SQL statements to be executed within the function.

- **some_value** is the data to be returned from the function.

- **PLPGSQL** specifies the language to be used in the function. PostgreSQL gives the ability to use other languages; however, their use in this context lies beyond the scope of this book.

> **Note**
>
> The complete PostgreSQL documentation for functions can be found at https://www.postgresql.org/docs/current/extend.html.

Exercise 30: Creating Functions without Arguments

In this exercise, we will create the most basic function – one that simply returns a constant value – so we can build up a familiarity with the syntax. We will construct our first SQL function that does not take any arguments as additional information. This function may be used to repeat SQL query statements that provide basic statistics about the data within the tables of the **sqlda** database. These are the steps to follow:

1. Connect to the **sqlda** database:

   ```
   $ psql sqlda
   ```

2. Create a function called **fixed_val** that does not accept any arguments and returns an integer. This is a multi-line process. Enter the following line first:

   ```
   sqlda=# CREATE FUNCTION fixed_val() RETURNS integer AS $$
   ```

   This line starts the function declaration for **fixed_val**, and we can see that there are no arguments to the function, as indicated by the open/closed brackets, (), nor any returned variables.

3. In the next line, notice that the characters within the command prompt have adjusted to indicate that it is awaiting input for the next line of the function:

   ```
   sqlda$#
   ```

4. Enter the **BEGIN** keyword (notice that as we are not returning a variable, the line containing the **DECLARE** statement has been omitted):

   ```
   sqlda$# BEGIN
   ```

5. We want to return the value **1** from this function, so enter the statement **RETURN 1**:

   ```
   sqlda$# RETURN 1;
   ```

6. End the function definition:

   ```
   sqlda$# END; $$
   ```

7. Finally, add the **LANGUAGE** statement, as shown in the following function definition:

```
sqlda-# LANGUAGE PLPGSQL;
```

This will complete the function definition.

8. Now that the function is defined, we can use it. As with almost all other SQL statements we have completed to date, we simply use a **SELECT** command:

```
sqlda=# SELECT * FROM fixed_val();
```

This will display the following output:

```
 fixed_val
-----------
         1
(1 row)
```

Figure 8.49: Output of the function call

Notice that the function is called using the open and closed brackets in the **SELECT** statement.

9. Use **EXPLAIN** and **ANALYZE** in combination with this statement to characterize the performance of the function:

```
sqlda=# EXPLAIN ANALYZE SELECT * FROM fixed_val();
```

The following screenshot shows the output of the preceding code:

```
                                QUERY PLAN
-------------------------------------------------------------------------------------
 Function Scan on fixed_val  (cost=0.25..0.26 rows=1 width=4) (actual time=0.031..0.032 rows=1 loops=1)
 Planning Time: 0.060 ms
 Execution Time: 0.060 ms
(3 rows)
```

Figure 8.50: Performance of the function call

So far, we have seen how to create a simple function, but simply returning a fixed value is not particularly useful. We will now create a function that determines the number of samples in the **sales** table. Notice that the three rows being referenced in the preceding screensnhot refer not to the result of **SELECT * FROM fixed_val();** but rather the result of the query planner. Looking at the first line of the information returned by the query planner, we can see that only one row of information is returned from the **SELECT** statement.

10. Create a function called **num_samples** that does not take any arguments but returns an integer called **total** that represents the number of samples in the **sales** table:

```
sqlda=# CREATE FUNCTION num_samples() RETURNS integer AS $total$
```

11. We want to return a variable called **total**, and thus we need to declare it. Declare the **total** variable as an integer:

```
sqlda$# DECLARE total integer;
```

12. Enter the **BEGIN** keyword:

```
sqlda$# BEGIN
```

13. Enter the statement that determines the number of samples in the table and assigns the result to the **total** variable:

```
sqlda$# SELECT COUNT(*) INTO total FROM sales;
```

14. Return the value for **total**:

```
sqlda$# RETURN total;
```

15. End the function with the variable name:

```
sqlda$# END; $total$
```

16. Add the **LANGUAGE** statement as shown in the following function definition:

```
sqlda-# LANGUAGE PLPGSQL;
```

This will complete the function definition, and upon successful creation, the **CREATE_FUNCTION** statement will be shown.

17. Use the function to determine how many rows or samples there are in the **sales** table:

```
sqlda=# SELECT num_samples();
```

The following figure shows the output of the preceding code:

```
num_samples
- - - - - - - - - - - - -
        37711
(1 row)
```

Figure 8.51: Output of the num_samples function call

We can see that by using the **SELECT** statement in combination with our SQL function, there are 37,711 records within the **sales** database.

In this exercise, we have created our first user-defined SQL function and discovered how to create and return information from variables within the function.

Activity 14: Defining a Maximum Sale Function

Our aim here is to create a user-defined function so we can calculate the largest sale amount in a single function call. In this activity, we will reinforce our knowledge of functions as we create a function that determines the highest sale amount in a database. At this stage, our marketing department is starting to make a lot of data analysis requests and we need to be more efficient in fulfilling them, as they are currently just taking too long. Perform the following steps:

1. Connect to the **sqlda** database.

2. Create a function called **max_sale** that does not take any input arguments but returns a numeric value called **big_sale**.

3. Declare the **big_sale** variable and begin the function.

4. Insert the maximum sale amount into the **big_sale** variable.

5. Return the value for **big_sale**.

6. End the function with the **LANGUAGE** statement.

7. Call the function to find what the biggest sale amount in the database is?

Expected output

```
      max
--------
  115000
(1 row)
```

Figure 8.52: Output of the maximum sales function call

> **Note**
>
> The solution to the activity can be found on page 348.

In this activity, we created a user-defined function to calculate the largest sale amount from a single function call using the **MAX** function.

Exercise 31: Creating Functions with Arguments Using a Single Function

Our goal is now to create a function that will allow us to calculate information from multiple tables using a single function. In this exercise, we will create a function that determines the average value from the sales **amount** column, with respect to the value of the corresponding channel. After creating our previous user-defined function to determine the biggest sale in the database, we have observed a significant increase in the efficiency with which we fulfill our marketing department's requests.

Perform the following steps to complete the exercise:

1. Connect to the **sqlda** database:

    ```
    $ psql sqlda
    ```

2. Create a function called **avg_sales** that takes a text argument input, **channel_type**, and returns a numeric output:

    ```
    sqlda=# CREATE FUNCTION avg_sales(channel_type TEXT) RETURNS numeric AS
    $channel_avg$
    ```

3. Declare the numeric **channel_avg** variable and begin the function:

    ```
    sqlda$# DECLARE channel_avg numeric;
    sqlda$# BEGIN
    ```

4. Determine the average **sales_amount** only when the channel value is equal to **channel_type**:

    ```
    sqlda$# SELECT AVG(sales_amount) INTO channel_avg FROM sales WHERE
    channel=channel_type;
    ```

5. Return **channel_avg**:

    ```
    sqlda$# RETURN channel_avg;
    ```

6. End the function and specify the **LANGUAGE** statement:

    ```
    sqlda$# END; $channel_avg$
    sqlda-# LANGUAGE PLPGSQL;
    ```

7. Determine the average sales amount for the **internet** channel:

    ```
    sqlda=# SELECT avg_sales('internet');
    ```

The following figure shows the output of the preceding code:

```
          avg_sales
    -------------------
     6413.11540412024
    (1 row)
```

Figure 8.53: Output of the average sales function call with the internet parameter

Now do the same for the **dealership** channel:

```
sqlda=# SELECT avg_sales('dealership');
```

The following figure shows the output of the preceding code:

```
          avg_sales
    -------------------
     7939.33132075954
    (1 row)
```

Figure 8.54: Output of the average sales function call with the dealership parameter

This output shows the average sales for a dealership, which is **7939.331**.

In this exercise, we were introduced to using function arguments to further modify the behavior of functions and the outputs they return.

The \df and \sf commands

You can use the **\df** command in PostgreSQL to get a list of functions available in memory, including the variables and data types passed as arguments:

```
                            List of functions
 Schema |      Name       | Result data type | Argument data types | Type
--------+-----------------+------------------+---------------------+------
 public | avg_sales       | numeric          | channel_type text   | func
 public | avg_sales_since | numeric          | since_date date     | func
 public | fixed_val       | integer          |                     | func
 public | max_sale        | numeric          |                     | func
 public | num_samples     | integer          |                     | func
(5 rows)
```

Figure 8.55: Result of the \df command on the sqlda database

The **\sf function_name** command in PostgreSQL can be used to review the function definition for already-defined functions:

```
CREATE OR REPLACE FUNCTION public.num_samples()
 RETURNS integer
 LANGUAGE plpgsql
AS $function$
DECLARE total integer;
BEGIN
SELECT COUNT(*) INTO total FROM sales;
RETURN total;
END; $function$
```

Figure 8.56: Contents of the function using \sf

Activity 15: Creating Functions with Arguments

In this activity, our goal is to create a function with arguments and compute the output. In this activity, we will construct a function that computes the average sales amount for transaction sales within a specific date range. Each date is to be provided to the function as a text string. These are the steps to follow:

1. Create the function definition for a function called **avg_sales_window** that returns a numeric value and takes two **DATE** values to specify the from and to dates in the form **YYYY-MM-DD**.

2. Declare the return variable as a numeric data type and begin the function.

3. Select the average sales amount as the return variable where the sales transaction date is within the specified date.

4. Return the function variable, end the function, and specify the **LANGUAGE** statement.

5. Use the function to determine the average sales values between 2013-04-12 and 2014-04-12.

Expected output

```
avg_sales_window
------------------
 477.686246311006
(1 row)
```

Figure 8.57: Output of average sales since the function call

> **Note**
>
> The solution to the activity can be found on page 349.

In this activity, we constructed a function that computes the average sales amount for transaction sales within a specific date range from the database.

Triggers

Triggers, known as events or callbacks in other programming languages, are useful features that, as the name suggests, trigger the execution of SQL statements or functions in response to a specific event. Triggers can be initiated when one of the following happens:

- A row is inserted into a table

- A field within a row is updated

- A row within a table is deleted

- A table is truncated – that is, all rows are quickly removed from a table

The timing of the trigger can also be specified to occur:

- Before an insert, update, delete, or truncate operation

- After an insert, update, delete, or truncate operation

- Instead of an insert, update, delete, or truncate operation

Depending upon the context and the purpose of the database, triggers can have a wide variety of different use cases and applications. In a production environment where a database is being used to store business information and make process decisions (such as for a ride-sharing application or an e-commerce store), triggers can be used before any operation to create access logs to the database. These logs can then be used to determine who has accessed or modified the data within the database. Alternatively, triggers could be used to re-map database operations to a different database or table using the **INSTEAD OF** trigger.

In the context of a data analysis application, triggers can be used to either create datasets of specific features in real time (such as for determining the average of data over time or a sample-to-sample difference), test hypotheses concerning the data, or flag outliers being inserted/modified in a dataset.

Given that triggers are used frequently to execute SQL statements in response to events or actions, we can also see why functions are often written specifically for or paired with triggers. Self-contained, repeatable function blocks can be used for both trialing/debugging the logic within the function as well as inserting the actual code within the trigger. So, how do we create a trigger? Similarly, to the case with function definitions, there is a standard syntax; again, the SQL keywords:

```
CREATE TRIGGER some_trigger_name { BEFORE | AFTER | INSTEAD OF } { INSERT |
DELETE | UPDATE | TRUNCATE } ON table_name

FOR EACH { ROW | STATEMENT }

EXECUTE PROCEDURE function_name ( function_arguments)
```

Looking at this generic trigger definition, we can see that there are a few individual components:

- We need to provide a name for the trigger in place of **some_trigger_name**.

- We need to select when the trigger is going to occur; either **BEFORE**, **AFTER**, or **INSTEAD OF** an event.

- We need to select what type of event we want to trigger on; either **INSERT**, **DELETE**, **UPDATE**, or **TRUNCATE**.

- We need to provide the table we want to monitor for events in **table_name**.

- The **FOR EACH** statement is used to specify how the trigger is to be fired. We can fire the trigger for each **ROW** that is within the scope of the trigger, or just once per **STATEMENT** despite the number of rows being inserted into the table.

- Finally, we just need to provide **function_name** and any relevant/required **function_arguments** to provide the functionality that we want to use on each trigger.

Some other functions that we will use are these:

- The **get_stock** function takes a product code as a **TEXT** input and returns the currently available stock for the specific product code.

- The **insert_order** function is used to add a new order to the **order_info** table and takes **customer_id INTEGER**, **product_code TEXT**, and **qty INTEGER** as inputs; it will return the **order_id** instance generated for the new record.

- The **update_stock** function will extract the information from the most recent order and will update the corresponding stock information from the **products** table for the corresponding **product_code**.

There are a number of different options available for SQL triggers that lie outside the scope of this book. For the complete trigger documentation, you can refer to https://www.postgresql.org/docs/current/sql-createtrigger.html.

Exercise 32: Creating Triggers to Update Fields

In this exercise, we will create a trigger that updates the fields whenever data is added. For this exercise, we will use the **smalljoins** database from the section of this chapter on joins and will create a trigger that updates the stock value within products for a product each time that an order is inserted into the **order_info** table. Using such a trigger, we can update our analysis in real time as end users interact with the database. These triggers will remove the need for us to run the analysis for the marketing department manually; instead, they will generate the results for us.

For this scenario, we will create a trigger to update the records for the available stock within the database for each of our products. As items are bought, the triggers will be fired, and the quantity of available stock will be updated. Here are the steps to perform:

1. Load the prepared functions into the **smalljoins** database using the **Functions.sql** file which can be found in the accompanying source code, it is also available on GitHub: https://github.com/TrainingByPackt/SQL-for-Data-Analytics/tree/master/Lesson08/Exercise32:

   ```
   $ psql smalljoins < Functions.sql
   ```

2. Connect to the **smalljoins** database:

   ```
   $ psql smalljoins
   ```

3. Get a list of the functions using the **\df** command after loading the function definitions:

   ```
   smalljoins=# \df
   ```

   This will display the following output:

   ```
                             List of functions
    Schema |     Name     | Result data type | Argument data types | Type
   --------+--------------+------------------+---------------------+------
    public | get_stock    | integer          | text                | func
    public | insert_order | integer          | integer, text, integer | func
    public | update_stock | integer          |                     | func
   (3 rows)
   ```

   Figure 8.58: List of functions

4. First, let's look at the current state of the **products** table:

```
smalljoins=# SELECT * FROM products;
```

The following figure shows the output of the preceding code:

```
 product_code |            name            | stock
--------------+----------------------------+-------
 MON636       | Red Herring                |    99
 GROG1        | Grog                       |    65
 POULET3      | El Pollo Diablo            |     2
 MON123       | Rubber Chicken + Pulley    |     7
 MON666       | Murray"s Arm               |     0
(5 rows)
```

Figure 8.59: List of products

For the **order_info** table, we can write the following query:

```
smalljoins=# SELECT * FROM order_info;
```

The following figure shows the output of the preceding code:

```
 order_id | customer_id | product_code | qty
----------+-------------+--------------+-----
     1618 |           3 | GROG1        |  12
     1619 |           2 | POULET3      |   3
     1620 |           4 | MON123       |   1
     1621 |           4 | MON636       |   3
     1622 |           5 | MON666       |   1
(5 rows)
```

Figure 8.60: List of order information

5. Insert a new order using the **insert_order** function with **customer_id 4**, **product_code MON636**, and **qty 10**:

```
smalljoins=# SELECT insert_order(4, 'MON636', 10);
```

The following figure shows the output of the preceding code:

```
 insert_order
--------------
         1623
(1 row)
```

Figure 8.61: Creating a new order

6. Review the entries for the **order_info** table:

```
smalljoins=# SELECT * FROM order_info;
```

This will display the following output:

```
 order_id | customer_id | product_code | qty
----------+-------------+--------------+-----
     1618 |           3 | GROG1        |  12
     1619 |           2 | POULET3      |   3
     1620 |           4 | MON123       |   1
     1621 |           4 | MON636       |   3
     1622 |           5 | MON666       |   1
     1623 |           4 | MON636       |  10
(6 rows)
```

Figure 8.62: List of updated order information

Notice the additional row with **order_id 1623**.

7. Update the **products** table to account for the newly sold 10 Red Herrings using the **update_stock** function:

```
smalljoins=# SELECT update_stock();
```

The following figure shows the output of the preceding code:

```
 update_stock
--------------
           89
(1 row)
```

Figure 8.63: Call updated_stock function to update

This function call will determine how many Red Herrings are left in inventory (after the sales of the 10 additional herrings) and will update the table accordingly.

8. Review the **products** table and notice the updated stock value for **Red Herring**:

```
smalljoins=# SELECT * FROM products;
```

The following figure shows the output of the preceding code:

```
 product_code |          name          | stock
--------------+------------------------+-------
 GROG1        | Grog                   |    65
 POULET3      | El Pollo Diablo        |     2
 MON123       | Rubber Chicken + Pulley |    7
 MON666       | Murray"s Arm           |     0
 MON636       | Red Herring            |    89
(5 rows)
```

Figure 8.64: List of updated product values

Updating the stock values manually will quickly become tedious. Let's create a trigger to do this automatically whenever a new order is placed.

9. Delete (**DROP**) the previous **update_stock** function. Before we can create a trigger, we must first adjust the **update_stock** function to return a trigger, which has the benefit of allowing for some simplified code:

```
smalljoins=# DROP FUNCTION update_stock;
```

10. Create a new **update_stock** function that returns a trigger. Note that the function definition is also contained within the **Trigger.sql** file for reference or direct loading into the database:

```
smalljoins=# CREATE FUNCTION update_stock() RETURNS TRIGGER AS $stock_
trigger$
smalljoins$# DECLARE stock_qty integer;
smalljoins$# BEGIN
smalljoins$# stock_qty := get_stock(NEW.product_code) - NEW.qty;
smalljoins$# UPDATE products SET stock=stock_qty WHERE product_code=NEW.
product_code;
smalljoins$# RETURN NEW;
smalljoins$# END; $stock_trigger$
smalljoins-# LANGUAGE PLPGSQL;
```

Note that in this function definition, we are using the **NEW** keyword followed by the dot operator (**.**) and the **product_code** (**NEW.product_code**) and **qty** (**NEW.qty**) field names from the **order_info** table. The **NEW** keyword refers to the record that was recently inserted, updated, or deleted and provides a reference to the information within the record.

In this exercise, we want the trigger to fire after the record is inserted into **order_info** and thus the **NEW** reference will contain this information. So, we can use the **get_stock** function with **NEW.product_code** to get the currently available stock for the record and simply subtract the **NEW.qty** value from the order record.

11. Finally, let's create the trigger. We want the trigger to occur **AFTER** an **INSERT** operation on the **order_info** table. For each row, we want to execute the newly modified **update_stock** function to update the stock values in the product table:

```
smalljoins=# CREATE TRIGGER update_trigger
smalljoins-# AFTER INSERT ON order_info
smalljoins-# FOR EACH ROW
smalljoins-# EXECUTE PROCEDURE update_stock();
```

12. Now that we have created a new trigger, let's test it. Call the **insert_order** function to insert a new record into the **order_info** table:

```
smalljoins=# SELECT insert_order(4, 'MON123', 2);
```

The following figure shows the output of the preceding code:

```
    insert_order
   ---------------
             1624
(1 row)
```

Figure 8.65: Insert a new order to use the trigger

13. Look at the records from the **order_info** table:

```
smalljoins=# SELECT * FROM order_info;
```

This will display the following output:

```
 order_id | customer_id | product_code | qty
----------+-------------+--------------+-----
     1618 |           3 | GROG1        |  12
     1619 |           2 | POULET3      |   3
     1620 |           4 | MON123       |   1
     1621 |           4 | MON636       |   3
     1622 |           5 | MON666       |   1
     1623 |           3 | MON636       |  10
     1624 |           4 | MON123       |   2
(7 rows)
```

Figure 8.66: Order information with an update from the trigger

14. Look at the records for the **products** table:

```
smalljoins=# SELECT * FROM products;
```

The following figure shows the output of the preceding code:

```
 product_code |             name            | stock
--------------+-----------------------------+-------
 MON666       | Murray"s Arm                |     0
 GROG1        | Grog                        |    65
 POULET3      | El Pollo Diablo             |     2
 MON636       | Red Herring                 |    89
 MON123       | Rubber Chicken + Pulley     |     5
(5 rows)
```

Figure 8.67: Updated product information from the trigger

Our trigger worked! We can see that the available stock for the **Rubber Chicken + Pulley MON123** has been reduced from **7** to **5**, in accordance with the quantity of the inserted order.

In this exercise, we have successfully constructed a trigger to execute a secondary function following the insertion of a new record into the database.

Activity 16: Creating a Trigger to Track Average Purchases

Our goal here is to create a trigger for keeping track of the data that is updated. Let's say you are working as a data scientist for Monkey Islands, finest distributor of questionable and obscure items. The business is looking at trying a few different strategies to increase the number of items in each sale. To simplify your analysis, you decide to add a simple trigger that for each new order computes the average quantity in all the orders and puts the result in a new table along with the corresponding **order_id**. Here are the steps to follow:

1. Connect to the **smalljoins** database.

2. Create a new table called **avg_qty_log** that is composed of an **order_id integer** field and an **avg_qty numeric** field.

3. Create a function called **avg_qty** that does not take any arguments but returns a trigger. The function computes the average value for all order quantities (**order_info.qty**) and inserts the average value, along with the most recent **order_id**, into **avg_qty**.

4. Create a trigger called **avg_trigger** that calls the **avg_qty** function **AFTER** each row is inserted into the **order_info** table.

5. Insert some new rows into the **order_info** table with quantities of **6**, **7**, and **8**.

6. Look at the entries in **avg_qty_log**. Is the average quantity of each order increasing?

Expected output

```
order_id |       avg_qty
---------+--------------------
    1625 | 4.7500000000000000
    1626 | 5.0000000000000000
    1627 | 5.3000000000000000
(3 rows)
```

Figure 8.68: Average order quantity over time

> **Note**
>
> The solution to the activity can be found on page 350.

In this activity, we created a trigger for continuously keeping track of the data that is updated to analyze a product in the database.

Killing Queries

Sometimes, you have a lot of data, or perhaps insufficient hardware resources, and a query just runs for a very long time. In such a situation, you may need to stop the query, perhaps so you can implement an alternative query to get the information you need, but without the delayed response. In this section of the chapter, we are going to investigate how we can stop hanging, or, at least, hanging extremely long queries through the use of a secondary PostgreSQL interpreter. The following are some of the commands that we will use to kill queries:

- **pg_sleep** is a command that allows you to tell the SQL interpreter to essentially do nothing for the next period of time as defined by the input to the function in seconds.

- The **pg_cancel_backend** command causes the interpreter to end the query specified by the process ID (**pid**). The process will be terminated cleanly, allowing for appropriate resource cleanup. Clean termination should also be the first preference as it reduces the possibility of data corruption and damage to the database.

- The **pg_terminate_background** command stops an existing process but, as opposed to **pg_cancel_background**, forces the process to terminate without cleaning up any resources being used by the query. The query is immediately terminated, and data corruption may occur as a result.

Exercise 33: Canceling a Long Query

Our goal here is to learn how to cancel a long query to save time when we are stuck at query execution. You have been lucky enough to receive a large data store and you decided to run what you originally thought was a simple enough query to get some basic descriptive statistics of the data. For some reason, however, the query is taking an extremely long time and you are not even sure that it is running. You decide it is time to cancel the query, which means you would like to send a stop signal to the query but allow it sufficient time to clean up its resources gracefully. As there may be a wide variety of hardware available to us and the data required to induce a long query could be quite a lot to download, we will simulate a long query using the **pg_sleep** command. Here are the steps to follow.

For this exercise, you will require two separate SQL interpreter sessions running in separate windows, as shown in the following figure:

1. Launch two separate interpreters by running **psql sqlda**:

   ```
   C:\> psql sqlda
   ```

   This will display the following output in two separate windows:

```
ben@hillvalley:~$ psql sqlda              ben@hillvalley:~$ psql sqlda
psql (11.4 (Ubuntu 11.4-0ubuntu0.19.04.1))  psql (11.4 (Ubuntu 11.4-0ubuntu0.19.04.1))
Type "help" for help.                     Type "help" for help.

sqlda=#                                   sqlda=#
```

Figure 8.69: Running multiple terminals

2. In the first terminal, execute the sleep command with a parameter of **1000** seconds:

   ```
   sqlda=# SELECT pg_sleep(1000);
   ```

   After pressing *Enter*, you should notice that the cursor of the interpreter does not return:

```
sqlda=# SELECT pg_sleep(1000);
```

Figure 8.70: Sleeping interpreter

3. In the second terminal, select the **pid** and **query** columns from the **pg_stat_activity** table where **state** is **active**:

   ```
   sqlda=# SELECT pid, query FROM pg_stat_activity WHERE state = 'active';
   ```

   The following figure shows the output of the preceding code:

```
 pid   |                              query
-------+-------------------------------------------------------------------
 14117 | SELECT pid, query FROM pg_stat_activity WHERE state = 'active';
 14131 | SELECT pg_sleep(1000);
(2 rows)
```

Figure 8.71: Active queries

4. In the second terminal, pass the process ID of the **pg_sleep** query to the **pg_cancel_backend** command to terminate the **pg_sleep** query with a graceful cleanup:

```
sqlda=# SELECT pg_cancel_backend(14131);
```

The following figure shows the output of the preceding code:

```
pg_cancel_backend
-------------------
t
(1 row)
```

Figure 8.72: Successful cancelation of the query

5. Observe the first terminal and notice that the sleep command is no longer executing, as indicated by the return message:

```
ERROR:  canceling statement due to user request
sqlda=# █
```

Figure 8.73: Message indicating the cancelation of the query

This output screenshot shows an error as the query was canceled after the user's request.

In this exercise, we learned how to cancel a query that has taken a long time to execute.

Activity 17: Terminating a Long Query

Now our aim is to terminate a long query using the **pg_terminate_background** command just as we used **pg_cancel_backend** to stop the process. In this activity, we will consider the scenario as being one in which the cancelation of the query was not enough to stop the excessively long process. In such a situation, we require something a little heavier handed that, rather than requesting a clean termination of the process, forces a process to be terminated. Launch two separate SQL interpreters. Here are the steps to follow:

1. In the first terminal, execute the **sleep** command with a parameter of **1000** seconds.

2. In the second terminal, identify the process ID of the sleep query.

3. Using the **pid** value, force the **sleep** command to terminate using the **pg_terminate_background** command.

4. Verify in the first terminal that the **sleep** command has been terminated. Notice the message returned by the interpreter.

Expected output

```
sqlda=# SELECT pg_sleep(1000);
FATAL:  terminating connection due to administrator command
server closed the connection unexpectedly
        This probably means the server terminated abnormally
        before or while processing the request.
The connection to the server was lost. Attempting reset: Succeeded.
sqlda=# █
```

Figure 8.74: Terminated pg_sleep process

> **Note**
>
> The solution to the activity can be found on page 352.

In this activity, we terminated a long-running query using the **pg_terminate_background** command.

Summary

In this chapter, we have covered a wide variety of topics all designed to help us understand and improve the performance of our SQL queries. The chapter began with a thorough discussion of the query planner, including the **EXPLAIN** and **ANALYZE** statements, as well as various indexing methods. We discussed a number of different compromises and considerations that can be made to reduce the time taken to execute queries. We considered a number of scenarios where indexing methods would be of benefit and others where the query planner may disregard the index, thus reducing the efficiency of the query. We then moved on to the use of joins to efficiently combine information from a number of different tables and ended with an in-depth look at functions and automatic function calls through the use of triggers.

In the next chapter, we will combine all of the topics we have covered thus far in a final case study, applying our SQL knowledge and the scientific method in general, as we solve a real-world problem.

Using SQL to Uncover the Truth – a Case Study

Learning Objectives

By the end of this chapter, you will be able to:

- Use the scientific method and critical thinking to glean insights about your data
- Solve real-world problems outside of those described within this book by using the skills that you have acquired
- Convert data and hypotheses into actionable tasks and insights
- Use the skills developed in this book to solve problems in your specific problem domain

In this chapter, we will examine an extensive and detailed real-world case study of sales data. This case study will not only demonstrate the processes used in SQL analysis to find solutions for actual problems but will also provide you with confidence and experience in solving such problems.

Introduction

Throughout *SQL for Data Analytics*, you have learned a range of new skills, including basic descriptive statistics, SQL commands and importing and exporting data in PostgreSQL, as well as more advanced methods, such as functions and triggers. In this final chapter of the book, we will combine these new skills with the scientific method and critical thinking to solve the real-world problem of understanding the cause of an unexpected drop in sales. This chapter provides a case study and will help you to develop confidence in applying your new SQL skillset to your own problem domains. To solve the problem presented in this use case, we will use the complete range of your newly developed skills, from using basic SQL searches to filter out the available information to aggregating and joining multiple sets of information and using windowing methods to group the data in a logical manner. By completing case studies such as this, you will refine one of the key tools in your data analysis toolkit, providing a boost to your data science career.

Case Study

Throughout this chapter, we will cover the following case study. The new ZoomZoom Bat Scooter is now available for sale exclusively through its website. Sales are looking good, but suddenly, pre-orders start plunging by 20% after a couple of weeks. What's going on? As the best data analyst at ZoomZoom, it's been assigned to you to figure it out.

Scientific Method

In this case study, we will be following the scientific method to help solve our problem, which, at its heart, is about testing guesses (or hypotheses) using objectively collected data. We can decompose the scientific method into the following key steps:

1. Define the question to answer what caused the drop-in sales of the Bat Scooter after approximately 2 weeks.

2. Complete background research to gather sufficient information to propose an initial hypothesis for the event or phenomenon.

3. Construct a hypothesis to explain the event or answer the question.

4. Define and execute an objective experiment to test the hypothesis. In an ideal scenario, all aspects of the experiment should be controlled and fixed, except for the phenomenon that is being tested under the hypothesis.

5. Analyze the data collected during the experiment.

6. Report the result of the analysis, which will hopefully explain why there was a drop in the sale of Bat Scooters.

It is to be noted that in this chapter, we are completing a post-hoc analysis of the data, that is, the event has happened, and all available data has been collected. Post-hoc data analysis is particularly useful when events have been recorded that cannot be repeated or when certain external factors cannot be controlled. It is with this data that we are able to perform our analysis, and, as such, we will extract information to support or refute our hypothesis. We will, however, be unable to definitively confirm or reject the hypothesis without practical experimentation. The question that will be the subject of this chapter and that we need to answer is this: why did the sales of the ZoomZoom Bat Scooter drop by approximately 20% after about 2 weeks?

So, let's start with the absolute basics.

Exercise 34: Preliminary Data Collection Using SQL Techniques

In this exercise, we will collect preliminary data using SQL techniques. We have been told that the pre-orders for the ZoomZoom Bat Scooter were good, but the orders suddenly dropped by 20%. So, when was production started on the scooter, and how much was it selling for? How does the Bat Scooter compare with other types of scooters in terms of price? The goal of this exercise is to answer these questions:

1. Load the **sqlda** database from the accompanying source code located at https://github.com/TrainingByPackt/SQL-for-Data-Analytics/tree/master/Datasets:

   ```
   $ psql sqlda
   ```

2. List the model, **base_msrp** (MSRP: manufacturer's suggested retail price) and **production_start_date** fields within the product table for product types matching **scooter**:

   ```
   sqlda=# SELECT model, base_msrp, production_start_date FROM products WHERE
   product_type='scooter';
   ```

   The following table shows the details of all the products for the **scooter** product type:

model	base_msrp	production_start_date
Lemon	399.99	2010-03-03 00:00:00
Lemon Limited Edition	799.99	2011-01-03 00:00:00
Lemon	499.99	2013-05-01 00:00:00
Blade	699.99	2014-06-23 00:00:00
Bat	599.99	2016-10-10 00:00:00
Bat Limited Edition	699.99	2017-02-15 00:00:00
Lemon Zester	349.99	2019-02-04 00:00:00

   (7 rows)

   Figure 9.1: Basic list of scooters with a base manufacturer suggesting
   a retail price and production date

Looking at the results from the search, we can see that we have two scooter products with **Bat** in the name; **Bat** and **Bat Limited Edition**. The **Bat** Scooter, which started production on October 10, 2016, with a suggested retail price of $599.99; and the **Bat Limited Edition** Scooter, which started production approximately 4 months later, on February 15, 2017, at a price of $699.99.

Looking at the product information supplied, we can see that the Bat Scooter is somewhat unique from a price perspective, being the only scooter with a suggested retail price of $599.99. There are two others at $699.99 and one at $499.99.

Similarly, if we consider the production start date in isolation, the original Bat Scooter is again unique in that it is the only scooter starting production in the last quarter or even half of the year (date format: YYYY-MM-DD). All other scooters start production in the first half of the year, with only the Blade scooter starting production in June.

In order to use the sales information in conjunction with the product information available, we also need to get the product ID for each of the scooters.

3. Extract the model name and product IDs for the scooters available within the database. We will need this information to reconcile the product information with the available sales information:

    ```
    sqlda=# SELECT model, product_id FROM products WHERE product_
    type='scooter';
    ```

    The query yields the product IDs shown in the following table:

    ```
                   model          | product_id
    --------------------------+------------
        Lemon                 |          1
        Lemon Limited Edition |          2
        Lemon                 |          3
        Blade                 |          5
        Bat                   |          7
        Bat Limited Edition   |          8
        Lemon Zester          |         12
    (7 rows)
    ```

    Figure 9.2: Scooter product ID codes

4. Insert the results of this query into a new table called **product_names**:

    ```
    sqlda=# SELECT model, product_id INTO product_names FROM products WHERE
    product_type='scooter';
    ```

Inspect the contents of the **product_names** table shown in the following figure:

```
            model          | product_id
---------------------------+------------
 Lemon                     |          1
 Lemon Limited Edition     |          2
 Lemon                     |          3
 Blade                     |          5
 Bat                       |          7
 Bat Limited Edition       |          8
 Lemon Zester              |         12
(7 rows)
```

Figure 9.3: Contents of the new product_names table

As described in the output, we can see that the Bat Scooter lies between the price points of some of the other scooters and that it was also manufactured a lot later in the year compared to the others.

By completing this very preliminary data collection step, we have the information required to collect sales data on the Bat Scooter as well as other scooter products for comparison. While this exercise involved using the simplest SQL commands, it has already yielded some useful information.

This exercise has also demonstrated that even the simplest SQL commands can reveal useful information and that they should not be underestimated. In the next exercise, we will try to extract the sales information related to the reduction in sales of the Bat Scooter.

Exercise 35: Extracting the Sales Information

In this exercise, we will use a combination of simple **SELECT** statements, as well as aggregate and window functions, to examine the sales data. With the preliminary information at hand, we can use it to extract the Bat Scooter sales records and discover what is actually going on. We have a table, **product_names**, that contains both the model names and product IDs. We will need to combine this information with the sales records and extract only those for the Bat Scooter:

1. Load the **sqlda** database:

   ```
   $ psql sqlda
   ```

2. List the available fields in the **sqlda** database:

   ```
   sqlda=# \d
   ```

The preceding query yields the following fields present in the database:

```
                                    Table "public.sales"
         Column          |              Type               | Collation | Nullable | Default
-------------------------+---------------------------------+-----------+----------+---------
 customer_id             | bigint                          |           |          |
 product_id              | bigint                          |           |          |
 sales_transaction_date  | timestamp without time zone     |           |          |
 sales_amount            | double precision                |           |          |
 channel                 | text                            |           |          |
 dealership_id           | double precision                |           |          |
```

Figure 9.4: Structure of the sales table

We can see that we have references to customer and product IDs, as well as the transaction date, sales information, the sales channel, and the dealership ID.

3. Use an inner join on the **product_id** columns of both the **product_names** table and the sales table. From the result of the inner join, select the model, **customer_id**, **sales_transaction_date**, **sales_amount**, channel, and **dealership_id**, and store the values in a separate table called **product_sales**:

```
sqlda=# SELECT model, customer_id, sales_transaction_date, sales_amount,
channel, dealership_id INTO products_sales FROM sales INNER JOIN product_
names ON sales.product_id=product_names.product_id;
```

The output of the preceding code can be seen in the next step.

> **Note**
>
> Throughout this chapter, we will be storing the results of queries and calculations in separate tables as this will allow you to look at the results of the individual steps in the analysis at any time. In a commercial/production setting, we would typically only store the end result in a separate table, depending upon the context of the problem being solved.

4. Look at the first five rows of this new table by using the following query:

```
sqlda=# SELECT * FROM products_sales LIMIT 5;
```

The following table lists the top five customers who made a purchase. It shows the sale amount and the transaction details, such as the date and time:

```
model | customer_id | sales_transaction_date | sales_amount | channel  | dealership_id
------+-------------+------------------------+--------------+----------+--------------
Lemon |       41604 | 2012-03-30 22:45:29    |       399.99 | internet |
Lemon |       41531 | 2010-09-07 22:53:16    |       399.99 | internet |
Lemon |       41443 | 2011-05-24 02:19:11    |       399.99 | internet |
Lemon |       41291 | 2010-08-08 14:12:52    |      319.992 | internet |
Lemon |       41084 | 2012-01-09 03:34:52    |      319.992 | internet |
(5 rows)
```

Figure 9.5: The combined product sales table

5. Select all the information from the **product_sales** table that is available for the Bat Scooter and order the sales information by **sales_transaction_date** in ascending order. By selecting the data in this way, we can look at the first few days of the sales records in detail:

```
sqlda=# SELECT * FROM products_sales WHERE model='Bat' ORDER BY sales_
transaction_date;
```

The preceding query generates the following output:

```
model | customer_id | sales_transaction_date | sales_amount |   channel   | dealership_id
------+-------------+------------------------+--------------+-------------+--------------
Bat   |        4319 | 2016-10-10 00:41:57    |       599.99 | internet    |
Bat   |       40250 | 2016-10-10 02:47:28    |       599.99 | dealership  |      4
Bat   |       35497 | 2016-10-10 04:21:08    |       599.99 | dealership  |      2
Bat   |        4553 | 2016-10-10 07:42:59    |       599.99 | dealership  |     11
Bat   |       11678 | 2016-10-10 09:21:08    |       599.99 | internet    |
Bat   |       45868 | 2016-10-10 10:29:29    |       599.99 | internet    |
Bat   |       24125 | 2016-10-10 18:57:25    |       599.99 | dealership  |      1
Bat   |       31307 | 2016-10-10 21:22:38    |       599.99 | internet    |
Bat   |       42213 | 2016-10-10 21:27:36    |       599.99 | internet    |
Bat   |       47790 | 2016-10-11 01:28:58    |       599.99 | dealership  |     20
Bat   |        6342 | 2016-10-11 03:04:57    |       599.99 | internet    |
Bat   |       45880 | 2016-10-11 04:09:19    |       599.99 | dealership  |      7
Bat   |       43477 | 2016-10-11 05:24:50    |       599.99 | internet    |
Bat   |        6322 | 2016-10-11 08:48:07    |       599.99 | internet    |
Bat   |       46653 | 2016-10-11 15:47:01    |       599.99 | dealership  |      6
Bat   |        9045 | 2016-10-12 00:15:20    |       599.99 | dealership  |     19
Bat   |       23679 | 2016-10-12 00:17:53    |      539.991 | internet    |
Bat   |       49856 | 2016-10-12 00:26:15    |       599.99 | dealership  |     10
Bat   |       45256 | 2016-10-12 02:08:01    |      539.991 | dealership  |      7
Bat   |       48809 | 2016-10-12 05:08:43    |       599.99 | internet    |
Bat   |       42625 | 2016-10-12 06:17:55    |       599.99 | internet    |
Bat   |       39653 | 2016-10-12 06:28:25    |       599.99 | dealership  |      7
Bat   |       49226 | 2016-10-12 10:26:13    |      539.991 | internet    |
Bat   |       18602 | 2016-10-12 15:09:53    |       599.99 | internet    |
```

Figure 9.6: Ordered sales records

6. Count the number of records available by using the following query:

```
sqlda=# SELECT COUNT(model) FROM products_sales WHERE model='Bat';
```

The model count for the **'Bat'** model is as shown here:

```
count
-------
 7328
(1 row)
```

Figure 9.7: Count of the number of sales records

So, we have **7328** sales, beginning October 10, 2016. Check the date of the final sales record by performing the next step.

7. Determine the last sale date for the Bat Scooter by selecting the maximum (using the **MAX** function) for **sales_transaction_date**:

```
sqlda=# SELECT MAX(sales_transaction_date) FROM products_sales WHERE
model='Bat';
```

The last sale date is shown here:

```
         max
---------------------
 2019-05-31 22:15:30
(1 row)
```

Figure 9.8: Last sale date

The last sale in the database occurred on May 31, 2019.

8. Collect the daily sales volume for the Bat Scooter and place it in a new table called **bat_sales** to confirm the information provided by the sales team stating that sales dropped by 20% after the first 2 weeks:

```
sqlda=# SELECT * INTO bat_sales FROM products_sales WHERE model='Bat'
ORDER BY sales_transaction_date;
```

9. Remove the time information to allow tracking of sales by date, since, at this stage, we are not interested in the time at which each sale occurred. To do so, run the following query:

```
sqlda=# UPDATE bat_sales SET sales_transaction_date=DATE(sales_
transaction_date);
```

10. Display the first five records of **bat_sales** ordered by **sales_transaction_date**:

```
sqlda=# SELECT * FROM bat_sales ORDER BY sales_transaction_date LIMIT 5;
```

The following is the output of the preceding code:

```
model | customer_id | sales_transaction_date | sales_amount |   channel    | dealership_id
------+-------------+------------------------+--------------+--------------+--------------
Bat   |        4553 | 2016-10-10 00:00:00    |       599.99 | dealership   |           11
Bat   |       35497 | 2016-10-10 00:00:00    |       599.99 | dealership   |            2
Bat   |       40250 | 2016-10-10 00:00:00    |       599.99 | dealership   |            4
Bat   |        4319 | 2016-10-10 00:00:00    |       599.99 | internet     |
Bat   |       11678 | 2016-10-10 00:00:00    |       599.99 | internet     |
(5 rows)
```

Figure 9.9: First five records of Bat Scooter sales

11. Create a new table (**bat_sales_daily**) containing the sales transaction dates and a daily count of total sales:

```
sqlda=# SELECT sales_transaction_date, COUNT(sales_transaction_date) INTO
bat_sales_daily FROM bat_sales GROUP BY sales_transaction_date ORDER BY
sales_transaction_date;
```

12. Examine the first **22** records (a little over 3 weeks), as sales were reported to have dropped after approximately the first 2 weeks:

```
sqlda=# SELECT * FROM bat_sales_daily LIMIT 22;
```

This will display the following output:

```
sales_transaction_date | count
-----------------------+-------
2016-10-10 00:00:00    |     9
2016-10-11 00:00:00    |     6
2016-10-12 00:00:00    |    10
2016-10-13 00:00:00    |    10
2016-10-14 00:00:00    |     5
2016-10-15 00:00:00    |    10
2016-10-16 00:00:00    |    14
2016-10-17 00:00:00    |     9
2016-10-18 00:00:00    |    11
2016-10-19 00:00:00    |    12
2016-10-20 00:00:00    |    10
2016-10-21 00:00:00    |     6
2016-10-22 00:00:00    |     2
2016-10-23 00:00:00    |     5
2016-10-24 00:00:00    |     6
2016-10-25 00:00:00    |     9
2016-10-26 00:00:00    |     2
2016-10-27 00:00:00    |     4
2016-10-28 00:00:00    |     7
2016-10-29 00:00:00    |     5
2016-10-30 00:00:00    |     5
2016-10-31 00:00:00    |     3
(22 rows)
```

Figure 9.10: First 3 weeks of sales

We can see a drop-in sales after October 20, as there are 7 days in the first 11 rows that record double-digit sales, and none over the next 11 days.

At this stage, we can confirm that there has been a drop off in sales, although we are yet to quantify precisely the extent of the reduction or the reason for the drop off in sales.

Activity 18: Quantifying the Sales Drop

In this activity, we will use our knowledge of the windowing methods that we learned in *Chapter 5, Window Functions for Data Analysis.* In the previous exercise, we identified the occurrence of the sales drop as being approximately 10 days after launch. Here, we will try to quantify the drop off in sales for the Bat Scooter.

Perform the following steps to complete the activity:

1. Load the **sqlda** database from the accompanying source code located at https://github.com/TrainingByPackt/SQL-for-Data-Analytics/tree/master/Datasets.

2. Using the **OVER** and **ORDER BY** statements, compute the daily cumulative sum of sales. This provides us with a discrete count of sales over time on a daily basis. Insert the results into a new table called **bat_sales_growth**.

3. Compute a 7-day **lag** of the **sum** column, and then insert all the columns of **bat_sales_daily** and the new **lag** column into a new table, **bat_sales_daily_delay**. This **lag** column indicates what sales were like 1 week prior to the given record, allowing us to compare sales with the previous week.

4. Inspect the first 15 rows of **bat_sales_growth**.

5. Compute the sales growth as a percentage, comparing the current sales volume to that of 1 week prior. Insert the resulting table into a new table called **bat_sales_delay_vol**.

6. Compare the first 22 values of the **bat_sales_delay_vol** table to ascertain a sales drop.

Expected Output

```
sales_transaction_date | count |  sum | lag  |          volume
-----------------------+-------+------+------+--------------------------
 2016-10-10 00:00:00   |    9  |   9  |      |
 2016-10-11 00:00:00   |    6  |  15  |      |
 2016-10-12 00:00:00   |   10  |  25  |      |
 2016-10-13 00:00:00   |   10  |  35  |      |
 2016-10-14 00:00:00   |    5  |  40  |      |
 2016-10-15 00:00:00   |   10  |  50  |      |
 2016-10-16 00:00:00   |   14  |  64  |      |
 2016-10-17 00:00:00   |    9  |  73  |   9  |  7.1111111111111111
 2016-10-18 00:00:00   |   11  |  84  |  15  |  4.6000000000000000
 2016-10-19 00:00:00   |   12  |  96  |  25  |  2.8400000000000000
 2016-10-20 00:00:00   |   10  | 106  |  35  |  2.0285714285714286
 2016-10-21 00:00:00   |    6  | 112  |  40  |  1.8000000000000000
 2016-10-22 00:00:00   |    2  | 114  |  50  |  1.2800000000000000
 2016-10-23 00:00:00   |    5  | 119  |  64  | 0.85937500000000000000
 2016-10-24 00:00:00   |    6  | 125  |  73  | 0.71232876712328767123
 2016-10-25 00:00:00   |    9  | 134  |  84  | 0.59523809523809523810
 2016-10-26 00:00:00   |    2  | 136  |  96  | 0.41666666666666666667
 2016-10-27 00:00:00   |    4  | 140  | 106  | 0.32075471698113207547
 2016-10-28 00:00:00   |    7  | 147  | 112  | 0.31250000000000000000
 2016-10-29 00:00:00   |    5  | 152  | 114  | 0.33333333333333333333
 2016-10-30 00:00:00   |    5  | 157  | 119  | 0.31932773109243697479
 2016-10-31 00:00:00   |    3  | 160  | 125  | 0.28000000000000000000
(22 rows)
```

Figure 9.11: Relative sales volume of the Bat Scooter over 3 weeks

> **Note**
>
> The solution to the activity can be found on page 354.

While the count and cumulative **sum** columns are reasonably straightforward, why do we need the **lag** and **volume** columns? This is because we are looking for drops in sales growth over the first couple of weeks, hence, we compare the daily sum of sales to the same values 7 days earlier (the lag). By subtracting the sum and lag values and dividing by the lag, we obtain the volume value and can determine sales growth compared to the previous week.

Notice that the sales volume on October 17 is 700% above that of the launch date of October 10. By October 22, the volume is over double that of the week prior. As time passes, this relative difference begins to decrease dramatically. By the end of October, the volume is 28% higher than the week prior. At this stage, we have observed and confirmed the presence of a reduction in sales growth after the first 2 weeks. The next stage is to attempt to explain the causes of the reduction.

Exercise 36: Launch Timing Analysis

In this exercise, we will try to identify the causes of a sales drop. Now that we have confirmed the presence of the sales growth drop, we will try to explain the cause of the event. We will test the hypothesis that the timing of the scooter launch attributed to the reduction in sales. Remember, in *Exercise 34, Preliminary Data Collection Using SQL Techniques*, that the ZoomZoom Bat Scooter launched on October 10, 2016. Observe the following steps to complete the exercise:

1. Load the **sqlda** database:

   ```
   $ psql sqlda
   ```

2. Examine the other products in the database. In order to determine whether the launch date attributed to the sales drop, we need to compare the ZoomZoom Bat Scooter to other scooter products according to the launch date. Execute the following query to check the launch dates:

   ```
   sqlda=# SELECT * FROM products;
   ```

   The following figure shows the launch dates for all the products:

```
product_id |         model          | year | product_type | base_msrp  | production_start_date | production_end_date
-----------+------------------------+------+--------------+------------+-----------------------+--------------------
         1 | Lemon                  | 2010 | scooter      |    399.99  | 2010-03-03 00:00:00   | 2012-06-08 00:00:00
         2 | Lemon Limited Edition  | 2011 | scooter      |    799.99  | 2011-01-03 00:00:00   | 2011-03-30 00:00:00
         3 | Lemon                  | 2013 | scooter      |    499.99  | 2013-05-01 00:00:00   | 2018-12-28 00:00:00
         4 | Model Chi              | 2014 | automobile   | 115,000.00 | 2014-06-23 00:00:00   | 2018-12-28 00:00:00
         5 | Blade                  | 2014 | scooter      |    699.99  | 2014-06-23 00:00:00   | 2015-01-27 00:00:00
         6 | Model Sigma            | 2015 | automobile   |  65,500.00 | 2015-04-15 00:00:00   | 2018-10-01 00:00:00
         7 | Bat                    | 2016 | scooter      |    599.99  | 2016-10-10 00:00:00   |
         8 | Bat Limited Edition    | 2017 | scooter      |    699.99  | 2017-02-15 00:00:00   |
         9 | Model Epsilon          | 2017 | automobile   |  35,000.00 | 2017-02-15 00:00:00   |
        10 | Model Gamma            | 2017 | automobile   |  85,750.00 | 2017-02-15 00:00:00   |
        11 | Model Chi              | 2019 | automobile   |  95,000.00 | 2019-02-04 00:00:00   |
        12 | Lemon Zester           | 2019 | scooter      |    349.99  | 2019-02-04 00:00:00   |
(12 rows)
```

Figure 9.12: Products with launch dates

All the other products launched before July, compared to the Bat Scooter, which launched in October.

3. List all scooters from the **products** table, as we are only interested in comparing scooters:

```
sqlda=# SELECT * FROM products WHERE product_type='scooter';
```

The following table shows all the information for products with the product type of **scooter**:

```
product_id |        model          | year | product_type | base_msrp | production_start_date | production_end_date
-----------+----------------------+------+--------------+-----------+-----------------------+---------------------
         1 | Lemon                | 2010 | scooter      |    399.99 | 2010-03-03 00:00:00   | 2012-06-08 00:00:00
         2 | Lemon Limited Edition| 2011 | scooter      |    799.99 | 2011-01-03 00:00:00   | 2011-03-30 00:00:00
         3 | Lemon                | 2013 | scooter      |    499.99 | 2013-05-01 00:00:00   | 2018-12-28 00:00:00
         5 | Blade                | 2014 | scooter      |    699.99 | 2014-06-23 00:00:00   | 2015-01-27 00:00:00
         7 | Bat                  | 2016 | scooter      |    599.99 | 2016-10-10 00:00:00   |
         8 | Bat Limited Edition  | 2017 | scooter      |    699.99 | 2017-02-15 00:00:00   |
        12 | Lemon Zester         | 2019 | scooter      |    349.99 | 2019-02-04 00:00:00   |
(7 rows)
```

Figure 9.13: Scooter product launch dates

To test the hypothesis that the time of year had an impact on sales performance, we require a scooter model to use as the control or reference group. In an ideal world, we could launch the ZoomZoom Bat Scooter in a different location or region, for example, but just at a different time, and then compare the two. However, we cannot do this here. Instead, we will choose a similar scooter launched at a different time. There are several different options in the product database, each with its own similarities and differences to the experimental group (ZoomZoom Bat Scooter). In our opinion, the Bat Limited Edition Scooter is suitable for comparison (the control group). It is slightly more expensive, but it was launched only 4 months after the Bat Scooter. Looking at its name, the Bat Limited Edition Scooter seems to share most of the same features, with a number of extras given that it's a "limited edition."

4. Select the first five rows of the **sales** database:

```
sqlda=# SELECT * FROM sales LIMIT 5;
```

The sales information for the first five customers is as follows:

```
customer_id | product_id | sales_transaction_date | sales_amount |  channel    | dealership_id
------------+------------+------------------------+--------------+-------------+--------------
          1 |          7 | 2017-07-19 08:38:41    |      479.992 | internet    |
         22 |          7 | 2017-08-14 09:59:02    |       599.99 | dealership  |           20
        145 |          7 | 2019-01-20 10:40:11    |      479.992 | internet    |
        289 |          7 | 2017-05-09 14:20:04    |      539.991 | dealership  |            7
        331 |          7 | 2019-05-21 20:03:21    |      539.991 | dealership  |            4
(5 rows)
```

Figure 9.14: First five rows of sales data

5. Select the **model** and **sales_transaction_date** columns from both the products and sales tables for the Bat Limited Edition Scooter. Store the results in a table, **bat_ltd_sales**, ordered by the **sales_transaction_date** column, from the earliest date to the latest:

```
sqlda=# SELECT products.model, sales.sales_transaction_date INTO bat_ltd_
sales FROM sales INNER JOIN products ON sales.product_id=products.product_
id WHERE sales.product_id=8 ORDER BY sales.sales_transaction_date;
```

6. Select the first five lines of **bat_ltd_sales**, using the following query:

```
sqlda=# SELECT * FROM bat_ltd_sales LIMIT 5;
```

The following table shows the transaction details for the first five entries of **Bat Limited Edition**:

```
        model         | sales_transaction_date
----------------------+------------------------
 Bat Limited Edition  | 2017-02-15 01:49:02
 Bat Limited Edition  | 2017-02-15 09:42:37
 Bat Limited Edition  | 2017-02-15 10:48:31
 Bat Limited Edition  | 2017-02-15 12:22:41
 Bat Limited Edition  | 2017-02-15 13:51:34
(5 rows)
```

Figure 9.15: First five sales of the Bat Limited Edition Scooter

7. Calculate the total number of sales for **Bat Limited Edition**. We can check this by using the **COUNT** function:

```
sqlda=# SELECT COUNT(model) FROM bat_ltd_sales;
```

The total sales count can be seen in the following figure:

```
 count
-------
 5803
(1 row)
```

Figure 9.16: Count of Bat Limited Edition sales

This is compared to the original Bat Scooter, which sold 7,328 items.

8. Check the transaction details of the last Bat Limited Edition sale. We can check this by using the **MAX** function:

```
sqlda=# SELECT MAX(sales_transaction_date) FROM bat_ltd_sales;
```

The transaction details of the last **Bat Limited Edition** product are as follows:

```
            max
---------------------
2019-05-31 15:08:03
(1 row)
```

Figure 9.17: Last date (MAX) of the Bat Limited Edition sale

9. Adjust the table to cast the transaction date column as a date, discarding the time information. As with the original Bat Scooter, we are only interested in the date of the sale, not the date and time of the sale. Write the following query:

    ```
    sqlda=# ALTER TABLE bat_ltd_sales ALTER COLUMN sales_transaction_date TYPE date;
    ```

10. Again, select the first five records of **bat_ltd_sales**:

    ```
    sqlda=# SELECT * FROM bat_ltd_sales LIMIT 5;
    ```

    The following table shows the first five records of **bat_ltd_sales**:

    ```
             model        | sales_transaction_date
    ---------------------+------------------------
    Bat Limited Edition | 2017-02-15
    Bat Limited Edition | 2017-02-15
    Bat Limited Edition | 2017-02-15
    Bat Limited Edition | 2017-02-15
    Bat Limited Edition | 2017-02-15
    (5 rows)
    ```

Figure 9.18: Select the first five Bat Limited Edition sales by date

11. In a similar manner to the standard Bat Scooter, create a count of sales on a daily basis. Insert the results into the **bat_ltd_sales_count** table by using the following query:

    ```
    sqlda=# SELECT sales_transaction_date, count(sales_transaction_date) INTO bat_ltd_sales_count FROM bat_ltd_sales GROUP BY sales_transaction_date ORDER BY sales_transaction_date;
    ```

12. List the sales count of all the **Bat Limited** products using the following query:

    ```
    sqlda=# SELECT * FROM bat_ltd_sales_count;
    ```

The sales count is shown in the following figure:

```
sales_transaction_date | count
-----------------------+------
    2017-02-15         |   6
    2017-02-16         |   2
    2017-02-17         |   1
    2017-02-18         |   4
    2017-02-19         |   5
    2017-02-20         |   6
    2017-02-21         |   5
    2017-02-22         |   4
    2017-02-23         |   6
    2017-02-24         |   2
    2017-02-25         |   2
    2017-02-26         |   2
    2017-02-27         |   4
    2017-02-28         |   4
    2017-03-01         |   5
    2017-03-02         |   1
```

Figure 9.19: Bat Limited Edition daily sales

13. Compute the cumulative sum of the daily sales figures and insert the resulting table into **bat_ltd_sales_growth**:

```
sqlda=# SELECT *, sum(count) OVER (ORDER BY sales_transaction_date) INTO
bat_ltd_sales_growth FROM bat_ltd_sales_count;
```

14. Select the first 22 days of sales records from **bat_ltd_sales_growth**:

```
sqlda=# SELECT * FROM bat_ltd_sales_growth LIMIT 22;
```

The following table displays the first 22 records of sales growth:

```
sales_transaction_date | count | sum
-----------------------+-------+-----
    2017-02-15         |   6   |   6
    2017-02-16         |   2   |   8
    2017-02-17         |   1   |   9
    2017-02-18         |   4   |  13
    2017-02-19         |   5   |  18
    2017-02-20         |   6   |  24
    2017-02-21         |   5   |  29
    2017-02-22         |   4   |  33
    2017-02-23         |   6   |  39
    2017-02-24         |   2   |  41
    2017-02-25         |   2   |  43
    2017-02-26         |   2   |  45
    2017-02-27         |   4   |  49
    2017-02-28         |   4   |  53
    2017-03-01         |   5   |  58
    2017-03-02         |   1   |  59
    2017-03-03         |   3   |  62
    2017-03-04         |   8   |  70
    2017-03-05         |   4   |  74
    2017-03-06         |   7   |  81
    2017-03-07         |   7   |  88
    2017-03-08         |   8   |  96
(22 rows)
```

Figure 9.20: Bat Limited Edition sales – cumulative sum

15. Compare this sales record with the one for the original Bat Scooter sales, as shown in the following code:

```
sqlda=# SELECT * FROM bat_sales_growth LIMIT 22;
```

The following table shows the sales details for the first 22 records of the **bat_sales_growth** table:

```
 sales_transaction_date | count | sum
------------------------+-------+-----
 2016-10-10 00:00:00    |     9 |   9
 2016-10-11 00:00:00    |     6 |  15
 2016-10-12 00:00:00    |    10 |  25
 2016-10-13 00:00:00    |    10 |  35
 2016-10-14 00:00:00    |     5 |  40
 2016-10-15 00:00:00    |    10 |  50
 2016-10-16 00:00:00    |    14 |  64
 2016-10-17 00:00:00    |     9 |  73
 2016-10-18 00:00:00    |    11 |  84
 2016-10-19 00:00:00    |    12 |  96
 2016-10-20 00:00:00    |    10 | 106
 2016-10-21 00:00:00    |     6 | 112
 2016-10-22 00:00:00    |     2 | 114
 2016-10-23 00:00:00    |     5 | 119
 2016-10-24 00:00:00    |     6 | 125
 2016-10-25 00:00:00    |     9 | 134
 2016-10-26 00:00:00    |     2 | 136
 2016-10-27 00:00:00    |     4 | 140
 2016-10-28 00:00:00    |     7 | 147
 2016-10-29 00:00:00    |     5 | 152
 2016-10-30 00:00:00    |     5 | 157
 2016-10-31 00:00:00    |     3 | 160
(22 rows)
```

Figure 9.21: Bat Scooter cumulative sales for 22 rows

Sales of the limited-edition scooter did not reach double digits during the first 22 days, nor did the daily volume of sales fluctuate as much. In keeping with the overall sales figure, the limited edition sold 64 fewer units over the first 22 days.

16. Compute the 7-day **lag** function for the **sum** column and insert the results into the **bat_ltd_sales_delay** table:

```
sqlda=# SELECT *, lag(sum , 7) OVER (ORDER BY sales_transaction_date) INTO
bat_ltd_sales_delay FROM bat_ltd_sales_growth;
```

17. Compute the sales growth for **bat_ltd_sales_delay** in a similar manner to the exercise completed in *Activity 18, Quantifying the Sales Drop*. Label the column for the results of this calculation as **volume** and store the resulting table in **bat_ltd_sales_vol**:

```
sqlda=# SELECT *, (sum-lag)/lag AS volume INTO bat_ltd_sales_vol FROM bat_ltd_sales_delay;
```

18. Look at the first 22 records of sales in **bat_ltd_sales_vol**:

```
sqlda=# SELECT * FROM bat-ltd_sales_vol LIMIT 22;
```

The sales volume can be seen in the following figure:

```
sales_transaction_date | count | sum | lag |          volume
-----------------------+-------+-----+-----+---------------------------
 2017-02-15            |   6   |  6  |     |
 2017-02-16            |   2   |  8  |     |
 2017-02-17            |   1   |  9  |     |
 2017-02-18            |   4   | 13  |     |
 2017-02-19            |   5   | 18  |     |
 2017-02-20            |   6   | 24  |     |
 2017-02-21            |   5   | 29  |     |
 2017-02-22            |   4   | 33  |  6  |     4.5000000000000000
 2017-02-23            |   6   | 39  |  8  |     3.8750000000000000
 2017-02-24            |   2   | 41  |  9  |     3.5555555555555556
 2017-02-25            |   2   | 43  | 13  |     2.3076923076923077
 2017-02-26            |   2   | 45  | 18  |     1.5000000000000000
 2017-02-27            |   4   | 49  | 24  |     1.0416666666666667
 2017-02-28            |   4   | 53  | 29  | 0.82758620689655172414
 2017-03-01            |   5   | 58  | 33  | 0.75757575757575757576
 2017-03-02            |   1   | 59  | 39  | 0.51282051282051282051
 2017-03-03            |   3   | 62  | 41  | 0.51219512195121951220
 2017-03-04            |   8   | 70  | 43  | 0.62790697674418604651
 2017-03-05            |   4   | 74  | 45  | 0.64444444444444444444
 2017-03-06            |   7   | 81  | 49  | 0.65306122448979591837
 2017-03-07            |   7   | 88  | 53  | 0.66037735849056603774
 2017-03-08            |   8   | 96  | 58  | 0.65517241379310344828
(22 rows)
```

Figure 9.22: Bat Scooter cumulative sales showing volume

Looking at the **volume** column in the preceding diagram, we can again see that the sales growth is more consistent than the original Bat Scooter. The growth within the first week is less than that of the original model, but it is sustained over a longer period. After 22 days of sales, the sales growth of the limited-edition scooter is 65% compared to the previous week, as compared with the 28% growth identified in the second activity of the chapter.

At this stage, we have collected data from two similar products launched at different time periods and found some differences in the trajectory of the sales growth over the first 3 weeks of sales. In a professional setting, we may also consider employing more sophisticated statistical comparison methods, such as tests for differences of mean, variance, survival analysis, or other techniques. These methods lie outside the scope of this book and, as such, limited comparative methods will be used.

While we have shown there to be a difference in sales between the two Bat Scooters, we also cannot rule out the fact that the sales differences can be attributed to the difference in the sales price of the two scooters, with the limited-edition scooter being $100 more expensive. In the next activity, we will compare the sales of the Bat Scooter to the 2013 Lemon, which is $100 cheaper, was launched 3 years prior, is no longer in production, and started production in the first half of the calendar year.

Activity 19: Analyzing the Difference in the Sales Price Hypothesis

In this activity, we are going to investigate the hypothesis that the reduction in sales growth can be attributed to the price point of the Bat Scooter. Previously, we considered the launch date. However, there could be another factor – the sales price included. If we consider the product list of scooters shown in *Figure 9.23*, and exclude the Bat model scooter, we can see that there are two price categories, $699.99 and above, or $499.99 and below. The Bat Scooter sits exactly between these two groups; perhaps the reduction in sales growth can be attributed to the different pricing model. In this activity, we will test this hypothesis by comparing Bat sales to the 2013 Lemon:

```
 product_id |        model        | year | product_type | base_msrp | production_start_date | production_end_date
------------+---------------------+------+--------------+-----------+-----------------------+---------------------
         12 | Lemon Zester        | 2019 | scooter      |    349.99 | 2019-02-04 00:00:00   |
          1 | Lemon               | 2010 | scooter      |    399.99 | 2010-03-03 00:00:00   | 2012-06-08 00:00:00
          3 | Lemon               | 2013 | scooter      |    499.99 | 2013-05-01 00:00:00   | 2018-12-28 00:00:00
          7 | Bat                 | 2016 | scooter      |    599.99 | 2016-10-10 00:00:00   |
          5 | Blade               | 2014 | scooter      |    699.99 | 2014-06-23 00:00:00   | 2015-01-27 00:00:00
          8 | Bat Limited Edition | 2017 | scooter      |    699.99 | 2017-02-15 00:00:00   |
          2 | Lemon Limited Edition | 2011 | scooter    |    799.99 | 2011-01-03 00:00:00   | 2011-03-30 00:00:00
(7 rows)
```

Figure 9.23: List of scooter models

The following are the steps to perform:

1. Load the **sqlda** database from the accompanying source code located at https://github.com/TrainingByPackt/SQL-for-Data-Analytics/tree/master/Datasets.

2. Select the **sales_transaction_date** column from the year 2013 for **Lemon** model sales and insert the column into a table called **lemon_sales**.

3. Count the sales records available for 2013 for the **Lemon** model.

4. Display the latest **sales_transaction_date** column.

5. Convert the **sales_transaction_date** column to a date type.

6. Count the number of sales per day within the **lemon_sales** table and insert the data into a table called **lemon_sales_count**.

7. Calculate the cumulative sum of sales and insert the corresponding table into a new table labeled **lemon_sales_sum**.

8. Compute the 7-day **lag** function on the **sum** column and save the result to **lemon_sales_delay**.

9. Calculate the growth rate using the data from **lemon_sales_delay** and store the resulting table in **lemon_sales_growth**.

10. Inspect the first 22 records of the **lemon_sales_growth** table by examining the **volume** data.

Expected Output

```
sales_transaction_date | count | sum | lag |          volume
-----------------------+-------+-----+-----+--------------------------
2013-05-01             |     6 |   6 |     |
2013-05-02             |     8 |  14 |     |
2013-05-03             |     4 |  18 |     |
2013-05-04             |     9 |  27 |     |
2013-05-05             |     9 |  36 |     |
2013-05-06             |     6 |  42 |     |
2013-05-07             |     8 |  50 |     |
2013-05-08             |     6 |  56 |   6 |      8.3333333333333333
2013-05-09             |     6 |  62 |  14 |      3.4285714285714286
2013-05-10             |     9 |  71 |  18 |      2.9444444444444444
2013-05-11             |     3 |  74 |  27 |      1.7407407407407407
2013-05-12             |     4 |  78 |  36 |      1.1666666666666667
2013-05-13             |     7 |  85 |  42 |      1.0238095238095238
2013-05-14             |     3 |  88 |  50 | 0.76000000000000000000
2013-05-15             |     3 |  91 |  56 | 0.62500000000000000000
2013-05-16             |     4 |  95 |  62 | 0.53225806451612903226
2013-05-17             |     6 | 101 |  71 | 0.42253521126760563380
2013-05-18             |     9 | 110 |  74 | 0.48648648648648648649
2013-05-19             |     6 | 116 |  78 | 0.48717948717948717949
2013-05-20             |     6 | 122 |  85 | 0.43529411764705882353
2013-05-21             |    11 | 133 |  88 | 0.51136363636363636364
2013-05-22             |     8 | 141 |  91 | 0.54945054945054945055
(22 rows)
```

Figure 9.24: Sales growth of the Lemon Scooter

Note

The solution to the activity can be found on page 356.

Now that we have collected data to test the two hypotheses of timing and cost, what observations can we make and what conclusions can we draw? The first observation that we can make is regarding the total volume of sales for the three different scooter products. The Lemon Scooter, over its production life cycle of 4.5 years, sold 16,558 units, while the two Bat Scooters, the Original and Limited Edition models, sold 7,328 and 5,803 units, respectively, and are still currently in production, with the Bat Scooter launching about 4 months earlier and with approximately 2.5 years of sales data available. Looking at the sales growth of the three different scooters, we can also make a few different observations:

- The original Bat Scooter, which launched in October at a price of $599.99, experienced a 700% sales growth in its second week of production and finished the first 22 days with 28% growth and a sales figure of 160 units.

- The Bat Limited Edition Scooter, which launched in February at a price of $699.99, experienced 450% growth at the start of its second week of production and finished with 96 sales and 66% growth over the first 22 days.

- The 2013 Lemon Scooter, which launched in May at a price of $499.99, experienced 830% growth in the second week of production and ended its first 22 days with 141 sales and 55% growth.

Based on this information, we can make a number of different conclusions:

- The initial growth rate starting in the second week of sales correlates to the cost of the scooter. As the cost increased to $699.99, the initial growth rate dropped from 830% to 450%.

- The number of units sold in the first 22 days does not directly correlate to the cost. The $599.99 Bat Scooter sold more than the 2013 Lemon Scooter in that first period despite the price difference.

- There is some evidence to suggest that the reduction in sales can be attributed to seasonal variations given the significant reduction in growth and the fact that the original Bat Scooter is the only one released in October. So far, the evidence suggests that the drop can be attributed to the difference in launch timing.

Before we draw the conclusion that the difference can be attributed to seasonal variations and launch timing, let's ensure that we have extensively tested a range of possibilities. Perhaps marketing work, such as email campaigns, that is, when the emails were sent, and the frequency with which the emails were opened, made a difference.

Now that we have considered both the launch timing and the suggested retail price of the scooter as a possible cause of the reduction in sales, we will direct our efforts to other potential causes, such as the rate of opening of marketing emails. Does the marketing email opening rate have an effect on sales growth throughout the first 3 weeks? We will find this out in our next exercise.

Exercise 37: Analyzing Sales Growth by Email Opening Rate

In this exercise, we will analyze the sales growth using the email opening rate. To investigate the hypothesis that a decrease in the rate of opening emails impacted the Bat Scooter sales rate, we will again select the Bat and Lemon Scooters and will compare the email opening rate.

Perform the following steps to complete the exercise:

1. Load the **sqlda** database:

   ```
   $ psql sqlda
   ```

2. Firstly, look at the **emails** table to see what information is available. Select the first five rows of the **emails** table:

   ```
   sqlda=# SELECT * FROM emails LIMIT 5;
   ```

   The following table displays the email information for the first five rows:

```
email_id | customer_id |        email_subject        | opened | clicked | bounced |      sent_date      |    opened_date      | clicked_date
---------+-------------+-----------------------------+--------+---------+---------+---------------------+---------------------+-------------
       1 |          18 | Introducing A Limited Edition | f      | f       | f       | 2011-01-03 15:00:00 |                     |
       2 |          36 | Introducing A Limited Edition | f      | f       | f       | 2011-01-03 15:00:00 |                     |
       3 |          41 | Introducing A Limited Edition | t      | f       | f       | 2011-01-03 15:00:00 | 2011-01-04 10:41:11 |
       4 |          52 | Introducing A Limited Edition | f      | f       | f       | 2011-01-03 15:00:00 |                     |
       5 |          59 | Introducing A Limited Edition | f      | f       | f       | 2011-01-03 15:00:00 |                     |
(5 rows)
```

Figure 9.25: Sales growth of the Lemon Scooter

To investigate our hypothesis, we need to know whether an email was opened, and when it was opened, as well as who the customer was who opened the email and whether that customer purchased a scooter. If the email marketing campaign was successful in maintaining the sales growth rate, we would expect a customer to open an email soon before a scooter was purchased.

The period in which the emails were sent, as well as the ID of customers who received and opened an email, can help us to determine whether a customer who made a sale may have been encouraged to do so following the receipt of an email.

3. To determine the hypothesis, we need to collect the **customer_id** column from both the **emails** table and the **bat_sales** table for the Bat Scooter, the **opened**, **sent_date**, **opened_date**, and **email_subject** columns from **emails** table, as well as the **sales_transaction_date** column from the **bat_sales** table. As we only want the email records of customers who purchased a Bat Scooter, we will join the **customer_id** column in both tables. Then, insert the results into a new table – **bat_emails**:

```
sqlda=# SELECT emails.email_subject, emails.customer_id, emails.opened,
emails.sent_date, emails.opened_date, bat_sales.sales_transaction_date
INTO bat_emails FROM emails INNER JOIN bat_sales ON bat_sales.customer_
id=emails.customer_id ORDER BY bat_sales.sales_transaction_date;
```

4. Select the first 10 rows of the **bat_emails** table, ordering the results by **sales_transaction_date**:

```
sqlda=# SELECT * FROM bat_emails LIMIT 10;
```

The following table shows the first 10 rows of the **bat_emails** table ordered by **sales_transaction_date**:

```
            email_subject            | customer_id | opened |     sent_date      |    opened_date     | sales_transaction_date
-------------------------------------+-------------+--------+--------------------+--------------------+------------------------
A New Year, And Some New EVs         |       11678 | f      | 2019-01-07 15:00:00 |                    | 2016-10-10 00:00:00
A Brand New Scooter...and Car        |       46250 | f      | 2014-05-06 15:00:00 |                    | 2016-10-10 00:00:00
We Really Outdid Ourselves this Year |       24125 | f      | 2017-01-15 15:00:00 |                    | 2016-10-10 00:00:00
Tis' the Season for Savings          |       31307 | t      | 2015-11-26 15:00:00 | 2015-11-27 04:55:07 | 2016-10-10 00:00:00
25% off all EVs. It's a Christmas Miracle! | 42213 | f    | 2016-11-25 15:00:00 |                    | 2016-10-10 00:00:00
Zoom Zoom Black Friday Sale          |       46250 | f      | 2014-11-28 15:00:00 |                    | 2016-10-10 00:00:00
Save the Planet with some Holiday Savings. | 4553 | f     | 2018-11-23 15:00:00 |                    | 2016-10-10 00:00:00
The 2013 Lemon Scooter is Here       |       24125 | t      | 2013-03-01 15:00:00 | 2013-03-02 14:43:34 | 2016-10-10 00:00:00
The 2013 Lemon Scooter is Here       |       46250 | f      | 2013-03-01 15:00:00 |                    | 2016-10-10 00:00:00
Save the Planet with some Holiday Savings. | 46250 | f    | 2018-11-23 15:00:00 |                    | 2016-10-10 00:00:00
(10 rows)
```

Figure 9.26: Email and sales information joined on customer_id

We can see here that there are several emails unopened, over a range of sent dates, and that some customers have received multiple emails. Looking at the subjects of the emails, some of them don't seem related to the Zoom scooters at all.

5. Select all rows where the **sent_date** email predates the **sales_transaction_date** column, order by **customer_id**, and limit the output to the first 22 rows. This will help us to know which emails were sent to each customer before they purchased their scooter. Write the following query to do so:

```
sqlda=# SELECT * FROM bat_emails WHERE sent_date < sales_transaction_date
ORDER BY customer_id LIMIT 22;
```

The following table lists the emails sent to the customers before the **sales_transaction_date** column:

```
        email_subject            | customer_id | opened |      sent_date      |      opened_date      | sales_transaction_date
---------------------------------+-------------+--------+---------------------+-----------------------+------------------------
 An Electric Car for a New Age   |           7 | t      | 2015-04-01 15:00:00 | 2015-04-02 15:10:55   | 2019-04-25 00:00:00
 The 2013 Lemon Scooter is Here  |           7 | f      | 2013-03-01 15:00:00 |                       | 2019-04-25 00:00:00
 Tis' the Season for Savings     |           7 | f      | 2015-11-26 15:00:00 |                       | 2019-04-25 00:00:00
 Black Friday. Green Cars.       |           7 | f      | 2017-11-24 15:00:00 |                       | 2019-04-25 00:00:00
 We cut you a deal: 20%% off a Blade |       7 | t      | 2014-09-18 15:00:00 | 2014-09-19 15:11:17   | 2019-04-25 00:00:00
 Zoom Zoom Black Friday Sale     |           7 | f      | 2014-11-28 15:00:00 |                       | 2019-04-25 00:00:00
 Like a Bat out of Heaven        |           7 | f      | 2016-09-21 15:00:00 |                       | 2019-04-25 00:00:00
 Save the Planet with some Holiday Savings. | 7 | f    | 2018-11-23 15:00:00 |                       | 2019-04-25 00:00:00
 Shocking Holiday Savings On Electric Scooters | 7 | f | 2013-11-29 15:00:00 |                       | 2019-04-25 00:00:00
 25% off all EVs. It's a Christmas Miracle! |  7 | t   | 2016-11-25 15:00:00 | 2016-11-26 03:55:30   | 2019-04-25 00:00:00
 We Really Outdid Ourselves this Year |      7 | f      | 2017-01-15 15:00:00 |                       | 2019-04-25 00:00:00
 A Brand New Scooter...and Car   |           7 | f      | 2014-05-06 15:00:00 |                       | 2019-04-25 00:00:00
 A New Year, And Some New EVs    |           7 | f      | 2019-01-07 15:00:00 |                       | 2019-04-25 00:00:00
 Tis' the Season for Savings     |          22 | f      | 2015-11-26 15:00:00 |                       | 2017-08-14 00:00:00
 Like a Bat out of Heaven        |          22 | f      | 2016-09-21 15:00:00 |                       | 2017-08-14 00:00:00
 Zoom Zoom Black Friday Sale     |          22 | t      | 2014-11-28 15:00:00 | 2014-11-29 11:31:03   | 2017-08-14 00:00:00
 The 2013 Lemon Scooter is Here  |          22 | f      | 2013-03-01 15:00:00 |                       | 2017-08-14 00:00:00
 25% off all EVs. It's a Christmas Miracle! | 22 | f   | 2016-11-25 15:00:00 |                       | 2017-08-14 00:00:00
 We Really Outdid Ourselves this Year |     22 | f      | 2017-01-15 15:00:00 |                       | 2017-08-14 00:00:00
 Shocking Holiday Savings On Electric Scooters | 22 | f | 2013-11-29 15:00:00 |                      | 2017-08-14 00:00:00
 We cut you a deal: 20%% off a Blade |     22 | f      | 2014-09-18 15:00:00 |                       | 2017-08-14 00:00:00
 An Electric Car for a New Age   |          22 | f      | 2015-04-01 15:00:00 |                       | 2017-08-14 00:00:00
(22 rows)
```

Figure 9.27: Emails sent to customers before the sale transaction date

6. Delete the rows of the **bat_emails** table where emails were sent more than 6 months prior to production. As we can see, there are some emails that were sent years before the transaction date. We can easily remove some of the unwanted emails by removing those sent before the Bat Scooter was in production. From the products table, the production start date for the Bat Scooter is October 10, 2016:

```
sqlda=# DELETE FROM bat_emails WHERE sent_date < '2016-04-10';
```

> **Note**
>
> In this exercise, we are removing information that we no longer require from an existing table. This differs from the previous exercises, where we created multiple tables each with slightly different information from other. The technique you apply will differ depending upon the requirements of the problem being solved; do you require a traceable record of analysis, or is efficiency and reduced storage key?

7. Delete the rows where the sent date is after the purchase date, as they are not relevant to the sale:

```
sqlda=# DELETE FROM bat_emails WHERE sent_date > sales_transaction_date;
```

8. Delete those rows where the difference between the transaction date and the sent date exceeds 30, as we also only want those emails that were sent shortly before the scooter purchase. An email 1 year beforehand is probably unlikely to influence a purchasing decision, but one closer to the purchase date may have influenced the sales decision. We will set a limit of 1 month (30 days) before the purchase. Write the following query to do so:

```
sqlda=# DELETE FROM bat_emails WHERE (sales_transaction_date-sent_date) >
'30 days';
```

9. Examine the first 22 rows again ordered by **customer_id** by running the following query:

```
sqlda=# SELECT * FROM bat_emails ORDER BY customer_id LIMIT 22;
```

The following table shows the emails where the difference between the transaction date and the sent date is less than 30:

email_subject	customer_id	opened	sent_date	opened_date	sales_transaction_date
25% off all EVs. It's a Christmas Miracle!	129	t	2016-11-25 15:00:00	2016-11-26 06:31:37	2016-11-28 00:00:00
A New Year, And Some New EVs	145	f	2019-01-07 15:00:00		2019-01-20 00:00:00
Black Friday. Green Cars.	150	f	2017-11-24 15:00:00		2017-12-19 00:00:00
Black Friday. Green Cars.	173	f	2017-11-24 15:00:00		2017-12-05 00:00:00
We Really Outdid Ourselves this Year	196	f	2017-01-15 15:00:00		2017-01-23 00:00:00
We Really Outdid Ourselves this Year	319	f	2017-01-15 15:00:00		2017-01-29 00:00:00
Like a Bat out of Heaven	369	f	2016-09-21 15:00:00		2016-10-13 00:00:00
Like a Bat out of Heaven	414	f	2016-09-21 15:00:00		2016-10-20 00:00:00
25% off all EVs. It's a Christmas Miracle!	418	f	2016-11-25 15:00:00		2016-12-21 00:00:00
A New Year, And Some New EVs	560	t	2019-01-07 15:00:00	2019-01-08 15:56:14	2019-01-29 00:00:00
We Really Outdid Ourselves this Year	600	f	2017-01-15 15:00:00		2017-01-18 00:00:00
A New Year, And Some New EVs	660	t	2019-01-07 15:00:00	2019-01-08 23:37:03	2019-01-08 00:00:00
A New Year, And Some New EVs	681	f	2019-01-07 15:00:00		2019-01-13 00:00:00
Black Friday. Green Cars.	806	t	2017-11-24 15:00:00	2017-11-25 16:59:40	2017-11-29 00:00:00
A New Year, And Some New EVs	881	t	2019-01-07 15:00:00	2019-01-08 21:07:28	2019-01-22 00:00:00
25% off all EVs. It's a Christmas Miracle!	934	t	2016-11-25 15:00:00	2016-11-26 09:22:45	2016-12-24 00:00:00
25% off all EVs. It's a Christmas Miracle!	983	f	2016-11-25 15:00:00		2016-11-29 00:00:00
A New Year, And Some New EVs	1060	f	2019-01-07 15:00:00		2019-01-27 00:00:00
25% off all EVs. It's a Christmas Miracle!	1288	f	2016-11-25 15:00:00		2016-12-11 00:00:00
25% off all EVs. It's a Christmas Miracle!	1317	f	2016-11-25 15:00:00		2016-12-13 00:00:00
A New Year, And Some New EVs	1400	t	2019-01-07 15:00:00	2019-01-08 15:01:00	2019-01-10 00:00:00
Save the Planet with some Holiday Savings.	1417	f	2018-11-23 15:00:00		2018-11-26 00:00:00

(22 rows)

Figure 9.28: Emails sent close to the date of sale

At this stage, we have reasonably filtered the available data based on the dates the email was sent and opened. Looking at the preceding **email_subject** column, it also appears that there are a few emails unrelated to the Bat Scooter, for example, **25% of all EVs. It's a Christmas Miracle!** and **Black Friday. Green Cars**. These emails seem more related to electric car production instead of scooters, and so we can remove them from our analysis.

10. Select the distinct value from the **email_subject** column to get a list of the different emails sent to the customers:

```
sqlda=# SELECT DISTINCT(email_subject) FROM bat_emails;
```

The following table shows a list of distinct email subjects:

```
                        email_subject
--------------------------------------------------
Black Friday. Green Cars.
25% off all EVs. It's a Christmas Miracle!
A New Year, And Some New EVs
Like a Bat out of Heaven
Save the Planet with some Holiday Savings.
We Really Outdid Ourselves this Year
(6 rows)
```

Figure 9.29: Unique email subjects sent to potential customers of the Bat Scooter

11. Delete all records that have **Black Friday** in the email subject. These emails do not appear relevant to the sale of the Bat Scooter:

```
sqlda=# DELETE FROM bat_emails WHERE position('Black Friday' in email_
subject)>0;
```

> **Note**
>
> The **position** function in the preceding example is used to find any records where the **Black Friday** string is at the first character in the mail or more in **email_structure**. Thus, we are deleting any rows where **Black Friday** is in the email subject. For more information on PostgreSQL, refer to the documentation regarding string functions: https://www.postgresql.org/docs/current/functions-string.html.

12. Delete all rows where **25% off all EVs. It's a Christmas Miracle!** and **A New Year, And Some New EVs** can be found in the **email_subject**:

```
sqlda=# DELETE FROM bat_emails WHERE position('25% off all EV' in email_
subject)>0;
sqlda=# DELETE FROM bat_emails WHERE position('Some New EV' in email_
subject)>0;
```

13. At this stage, we have our final dataset of emails sent to customers. Count the number of rows that are left in the sample by writing the following query:

```
sqlda=# SELECT count(sales_transaction_date) FROM bat_emails;
```

We can see that **401** rows are left in the sample:

```
       count
      -------
        401
      (1 row)
```

Figure 9.30: Count of the final Bat Scooter email dataset

14. We will now compute the percentage of emails that were opened relative to sales. Count the emails that were opened by writing the following query:

```
sqlda=# SELECT count(opened) FROM bat_emails WHERE opened='t'
```

We can see that **98** emails were opened:

```
       count
      -------
         98
      (1 row)
```

Figure 9.31: Count of opened Bat Scooter campaign emails

15. Count the customers who received emails and made a purchase. We will determine this by counting the number of unique (or distinct) customers that are in the **bat_emails** table:

```
sqlda=# SELECT COUNT(DISTINCT(customer_id)) FROM bat_emails;
```

We can see that **396** customers who received an email made a purchase:

```
       count
      -------
        396
      (1 row)
```

Figure 9.32: Count of unique customers who received a Bat Scooter campaign email

16. Count the unique (or distinct) customers who made a purchase by writing the following query:

```
sqlda=# SELECT COUNT(DISTINCT(customer_id)) FROM bat_sales;
```

Following is the output of the preceding code:

```
       count
      -------
        6659
      (1 row)
```

Figure 9.33: Count of unique customers

17. Calculate the percentage of customers who purchased a Bat Scooter after receiving an email:

```
sqlda=# SELECT 396.0/6659.0 AS email_rate;
```

The output of the preceding query is displayed as follows:

```
        email_rate
-------------------------
    0.05946838864694398558
(1 row)
```

Figure 9.34: Percentage of customers who received an email

> **Note**
>
> In the preceding calculation, you can see that we included a decimal place in the figures, for example, 396.0 instead of a simple integer value (396). This is because the resulting value will be represented as less than 1 percentage point. If we excluded these decimal places, the SQL server would have completed the division operation as integers and the result would be 0.

Just under 6% of customers who made a purchase received an email regarding the Bat Scooter. Since 18% of customers who received an email made a purchase, there is a strong argument to be made that actively increasing the size of the customer base who receive marketing emails could increase Bat Scooter sales.

18. Limit the scope of our data to be all sales prior to November 1, 2016 and put the data in a new table called **bat_emails_threewks**. So far, we have examined the email opening rate throughout all available data for the Bat Scooter. Check the rate throughout for the first 3 weeks, where we saw a reduction in sales:

```
sqlda=# SELECT * INTO bat_emails_threewks FROM bat_emails WHERE sales_
transaction_date < '2016-11-01';
```

19. Now, count the number of emails opened during this period:

```
sqlda=# SELECT COUNT(opened) FROM bat_emails_threewks;
```

We can see that we have sent **82** emails during this period:

```
    count
    -------
      82
    (1 row)
```

Figure 9.35: Count of emails opened in the first 3 weeks

20. Now, count the number of emails opened in the first 3 weeks:

```
sqlda=# SELECT COUNT(opened) FROM bat_emails_threewks WHERE opened='t';
```

The following is the output of the preceding code:

```
 count
-------
    15
(1 row)
```

Figure 9.36: Count of emails opened

We can see that **15** emails were opened in the first 3 weeks.

21. Count the number of customers who received emails during the first 3 weeks of sales and who then made a purchase by using the following query:

```
sqlda=# SELECT COUNT(DISTINCT(customer_id)) FROM bat_emails_threewks;
```

We can see that **82** customers received emails during the first 3 weeks:

```
 count
-------
    82
(1 row)
```

Figure 9.37: Customers who made a purchase in the first 3 weeks

22. Calculate the percentage of customers who opened emails pertaining to the Bat Scooter and then made a purchase in the first 3 weeks by using the following query:

```
sqlda=# SELECT 15.0/82.0 AS sale_rate;
```

The following table shows the calculated percentage:

```
       sale_rate
------------------------
 0.18292682926829268293
(1 row)
```

Figure 9.38: Percentage of customers in the first 3 weeks who opened emails

Approximately 18% of customers who received an email about the Bat Scooter made a purchase in the first 3 weeks. This is consistent with the rate for all available data for the Bat Scooter.

23. Calculate how many unique customers we have in total throughout the first 3 weeks. This information is useful context when considering the percentages, we just calculated. 3 sales out of 4 equate to 75% but, in this situation, we would prefer a lower rate of the opening but for a much larger customer base. Information on larger customer bases is generally more useful as it is typically more representative of the entire customer base, rather than a small sample of it. We already know that 82 customers received emails:

```
sqlda=# SELECT COUNT(DISTINCT(customer_id)) FROM bat_sales WHERE sales_
transaction_date < '2016-11-01';
```

The following output reflects **160** customers where the transaction took place before November 1, 2016:

```
    count
  -------
     160
  (1 row)
```

Figure 9.39: Number of distinct customers from bat_sales

There were 160 customers in the first 3 weeks, 82 of whom received emails, which is slightly over 50% of customers. This is much more than 6% of customers over the entire period of availability of the scooter.

Now that we have examined the performance of the email marketing campaign for the Bat Scooter, we need a control or comparison group to establish whether the results were consistent with that of other products. Without a group to compare against, we simply do not know whether the email campaign of the Bat Scooter was good, bad, or neither. We will perform the next exercise to investigate performance.

Exercise 38: Analyzing the Performance of the Email Marketing Campaign

In this exercise, we will investigate the performance of the email marketing campaign for the Lemon Scooter to allow for a comparison with the Bat Scooter. Our hypothesis is that if the email marketing campaign performance of the Bat Scooter is consistent with another, such as the 2013 Lemon, then the reduction in sales cannot be attributed to differences in the email campaigns.

Perform the following steps to complete the exercise:

1. Load the **sqlda** database:

   ```
   $ psql sqlda
   ```

2. Drop the existing **lemon_sales** table:

   ```
   sqlda=# DROP TABLE lemon_sales;
   ```

3. The 2013 Lemon Scooter is **product_id = 3**. Select **customer_id** and **sales_transaction_date** from the sales table for the 2013 Lemon Scooter. Insert the information into a table called **lemon_sales**:

   ```
   sqlda=# SELECT customer_id, sales_transaction_date INTO lemon_sales FROM sales WHERE product_id=3;
   ```

4. Select all information from the **emails** database for customers who purchased a 2013 Lemon Scooter. Place the information in a new table called **lemon_emails**:

   ```
   sqlda=# SELECT emails.customer_id, emails.email_subject, emails.opened, emails.sent_date, emails.opened_date, lemon_sales.sales_transaction_date INTO lemon_emails FROM emails INNER JOIN lemon_sales ON emails.customer_id=lemon_sales.customer_id;
   ```

5. Remove all emails sent before the start of production of the 2013 Lemon Scooter. For this, we first require the date when production started:

   ```
   sqlda=# SELECT production_start_date FROM products Where product_id=3;
   ```

The following table shows the **production_start_date** column:

```
      production_start_date
   -----------------------
    2013-05-01 00:00:00
   (1 row)
```

Figure 9.40: Production start date of the Lemon Scooter

Now, delete the emails that were sent before the start of production of the 2013 Lemon Scooter:

```
sqlda=# DELETE FROM lemon_emails WHERE sent_date < '2013-05-01';
```

6. Remove all rows where the sent date occurred after the **sales_transaction_date** column:

```
sqlda=# DELETE FROM lemon_emails WHERE sent_date > sales_transaction_date;
```

7. Remove all rows where the sent date occurred more than 30 days before the **sales_transaction_date** column:

```
sqlda=# DELETE FROM lemon_emails WHERE (sales_transaction_date - sent_
date) > '30 days';
```

8. Remove all rows from **lemon_emails** where the email subject is not related to a Lemon Scooter. Before doing this, we will search for all distinct emails:

```
sqlda=# SELECT DISTINCT(email_subject) FROM lemon_emails;
```

The following table shows the distinct email subjects:

```
                          email_subject
------------------------------------------------
    Tis' the Season for Savings
    25% off all EVs. It's a Christmas Miracle!
    A Brand New Scooter...and Car
    Like a Bat out of Heaven
    Save the Planet with some Holiday Savings.
    Shocking Holiday Savings On Electric Scooters
    We Really Outdid Ourselves this Year
    An Electric Car for a New Age
    We cut you a deal: 20%% off a Blade
    Black Friday. Green Cars.
    Zoom Zoom Black Friday Sale
(11 rows)
```

Figure 9.41: Lemon Scooter campaign emails sent

Now, delete the email subject not related to the Lemon Scooter using the **DELETE** command:

```
sqlda=# DELETE FROM lemon_emails WHERE POSITION('25% off all EVs.' in
email_subject)>0;
sqlda=# DELETE FROM lemon_emails WHERE POSITION('Like a Bat out of Heaven'
in email_subject)>0;
sqlda=# DELETE FROM lemon_emails WHERE POSITION('Save the Planet' in
email_subject)>0;
sqlda=# DELETE FROM lemon_emails WHERE POSITION('An Electric Car' in
email_subject)>0;
```

```
sqlda=# DELETE FROM lemon_emails WHERE POSITION('We cut you a deal' in
email_subject)>0;
sqlda=# DELETE FROM lemon_emails WHERE POSITION('Black Friday. Green
Cars.' in email_subject)>0;
sqlda=# DELETE FROM lemon_emails WHERE POSITION('Zoom' in email_
subject)>0;
```

9. Now, check how many emails of **lemon_scooter** customers were opened:

```
sqlda=# SELECT COUNT(opened) FROM lemon_emails WHERE opened='t';
```

We can see that **128** emails were opened:

```
         count
        -------
           128
        (1 row)
```

Figure 9.42: Lemon Scooter campaign emails opened

10. List the number of customers who received emails and made a purchase:

```
sqlda=# SELECT COUNT(DISTINCT(customer_id)) FROM lemon_emails;
```

The following figure shows that **506** customers made a purchase after receiving emails:

```
         count
        -------
           506
        (1 row)
```

Figure 9.43: Unique customers who purchased a Lemon Scooter

11. Calculate the percentage of customers who opened the received emails and made a purchase:

```
sqlda=# SELECT 128.0/506.0 AS email_rate;
```

We can see that 25% of customers opened the emails and made a purchase:

```
            email_rate
        ------------------------
         0.25296442687747035573
        (1 row)
```

Figure 9.44: Lemon Scooter customer email rate

12. Calculate the number of unique customers who made a purchase:

    ```
    sqlda=# SELECT COUNT(DISTINCT(customer_id)) FROM lemon_sales;
    ```

    We can see that **13854** customers made a purchase:

    ```
              count
           -------
            13854
           (1 row)
    ```

    Figure 9.45: Count of unique Lemon Scooter customers

13. Calculate the percentage of customers who made a purchase having received an email. This will enable a comparison with the corresponding figure for the Bat Scooter:

    ```
    sqlda=# SELECT 506.0/13854.0 AS email_sales;
    ```

    The preceding calculation generates a 36% output:

    ```
             email_sales
        ------------------------
         0.03652374765410711708
        (1 row)
    ```

    Figure 9.46: Lemon Scooter customers who received an email

14. Select all records from **lemon_emails** where a sale occurred within the first 3 weeks of the start of production. Store the results in a new table – **lemon_emails_ threewks**:

    ```
    sqlda=# SELECT * INTO lemon_emails_threewks FROM lemon_emails WHERE sales_
    transaction_date < '2013-06-01';
    ```

15. Count the number of emails that were made for Lemon Scooters in the first 3 weeks:

    ```
    sqlda=# SELECT COUNT(sales_transaction_date) FROM lemon_emails_threewks;
    ```

    The following is the output of the preceding code:

    ```
             count
          -------
              0
          (1 row)
    ```

    Figure 9.47: Unique sales of the Lemon Scooter in the first 3 weeks

There is a lot of interesting information here. We can see that 25% of customers who opened an email made a purchase, which is a lot higher than the 18% figure for the Bat Scooter. We have also calculated that just over 3.6% of customers who purchased a Lemon Scooter were sent an email, which is much lower than the almost 6% of Bat Scooter customers. The final interesting piece of information we can see is that none of the Lemon Scooter customers received an email during the first 3 weeks of product launch compared with the 82 Bat Scooter customers, which is approximately 50% of all customers in the first 3 weeks!

In this exercise, we investigated the performance of an email marketing campaign for the Lemon Scooter to allow for a comparison with the Bat Scooter using various SQL techniques.

Conclusions

Now that we have collected a range of information about the timing of the product launches, the sales prices of the products, and the marketing campaigns, we can make some conclusions regarding our hypotheses:

- In *Exercise 36, Launch Timing Analysis*, we gathered some evidence to suggest that launch timing could be related to the reduction in sales after the first 2 weeks, although this cannot be proven.

- There is a correlation between the initial sales rate and the sales price of the scooter, with a reduced-sales price trending with a high sales rate (*Activity 19, Analyzing the Difference in the Sales Price Hypothesis*).

- The number of units sold in the first 3 weeks does not directly correlate to the sale price of the product (*Activity 19, Analyzing the Difference in the Sales Price Hypothesis*).

- There is evidence to suggest that a successful marketing campaign could increase the initial sales rate, with an increased email opening rate trending with an increased sales rate (*Exercise 37, Analyzing Sales Growth by Email Opening Rate*). Similarly, an increase in the number of customers receiving email trends with increased sales (*Exercise 38, Analyzing the Performance of the Email Marketing Campaign*).

- The Bat Scooter sold more units in the first 3 weeks than the Lemon or Bat Limited Scooters (*Activity 19, Analyzing the Difference in the Sales Price Hypothesis*).

In-Field Testing

At this stage, we have completed our post-hoc analysis (that is, data analysis completed after an event) and have evidence to support a couple of theories as to why the sales of the Bat Scooter dropped after the first 2 weeks. However, we cannot confirm these hypotheses to be true as we cannot isolate one from the other. This is where we need to turn to another tool in our toolkit: in-field testing. Precisely as the name suggests, in-field testing is testing hypotheses in the field, for instance, while a new product is being launched or existing sales are being made. One of the most common examples of in-field testing is A/B testing, whereby we randomly divide our users or customers into two groups, A and B, and provide them with a slightly modified experience or environment and observe the result. As an example, let's say we randomly assigned customers in group A to a new marketing campaign and customers in group B to the existing marketing campaign. We could then monitor sales and interactions to see whether one campaign was better than the other. Similarly, if we wanted to test the launch timing, we could launch in Northern California, for example, in early November, and Southern California in early December, and observe the differences.

The essence of in-field testing is that unless we test our post-hoc data analysis hypotheses, we will never know whether our hypothesis is true and, in order to test the hypothesis, we must only alter the conditions to be tested, for example, the launch date. To confirm our post-hoc analysis, we could recommend that the sales teams apply one or more of the following scenarios and monitor the sales records in real time to determine the cause of the reduction in sales:

- Release the next scooter product at different times of the year in two regions that have a similar climate and equivalent current sales record. This would help to determine whether launch timing had an effect.

- Release the next scooter product at the same time in regions with equivalent existing sales records at different price points and observe for differences in sales.

- Release the next scooter product at the same time and same price point in regions with equivalent existing sales records and apply two different email marketing campaigns. Track the customers who participated in each campaign and monitor the sales.

Summary

Congratulations! You have just completed your first real-world data analysis problem using SQL. In this chapter, you developed the skills necessary to develop hypotheses for problems and systematically gather the data required to support or reject your hypothesis. You started this case study with a reasonably difficult problem of explaining an observed discrepancy in sales data and discovered two possible sources (launch timing and marketing campaign) for the difference while rejecting one alternative explanation (sales price). While being a required skill for any data analyst, being able to understand and apply the scientific method in our exploration of problems will allow you to be more effective and find interesting threads of investigation. In this chapter, you used the SQL skills developed throughout this book; from simple **SELECT** statements to aggregating complex datatypes as well as windowing methods. After completing this chapter, you will be able to continue and repeat this type of analysis in your own data analysis projects to help find actionable insights.

Appendix

> **About**
>
> This section is included to assist the readers to perform the activities in the book. It includes detailed steps that are to be performed by the readers to achieve the objectives of the activities.

Chapter 1: Understanding and Describing Data

Activity 1: Classifying a New Dataset

Solution

1. The unit of observation is a car purchase.

2. **Date** and **Sales Amount** are quantitative, while **Make** is qualitative.

3. While there could be many ways to convert **Make** into quantitative data, one commonly accepted method would be to map each of the **Make** types to a number. For instance, Ford could map to 1, Honda could map to 2, Mazda could map to 3, Toyota could map to 4, Mercedes could map to 5, and Chevy could map to 6.

Activity 2: Exploring Dealership Sales Data

Solution

1. Open Microsoft Excel to a blank workbook.

2. Go to the **Data** tab and click on **From Text**.

3. Find the path to the `dealerships.csv` file and click on **OK**.

4. Choose the **Delimited** option in the **Text Import Wizard** dialog box, and make sure to start the import at row **1**. Now, click on **Next**.

5. Select the delimiter for your file. As this file is only one column, it has no delimiters, although CSVs traditionally use commas as delimiters (in future, use whatever is appropriate for your dataset). Now, click on **Next**.

6. Select **General** for the **Column Data Format**. Now, click on **Finish**.

7. For the dialog box asking **Where you want to put the data?**, select **Existing Sheet**, and leave what is in the textbox next to it as is. Now, click on **OK**. You should see something similar to the following diagram:

Location	Net Annual Sales	Number of Female Employees
Millburn, NJ	150803012	27
Los Angeles, CA	110872084	17
Houston, TX	183945873	22
Miami, FL	156355396	18
San Mateo, CA	143108603	17
Seattle, WA	142755480	33
Arlington VA	144772604	28
Portland, OR	179608438	32
Reno, NV	145101244	19
Chicago, IL	171491596	24
Atlanta, GA	198386988	27
Orlando, FL	180188054	24
Jacksonville, FL	158479693	32
Round Rock, TX	181820474	27
Phoenix, AZ	95512810.7	18
Charlotte, NC	199653776	32
Philadelphia, PA	193111679	31
Kansas City, MO	176816637	35
Dallas, TX	168769837	33
Boston, MA	350520724	20

Figure 1.33: The dealerships.csv file loaded

8. Histograms may vary a little bit depending on what parameters are chosen, but it should look similar to the following:

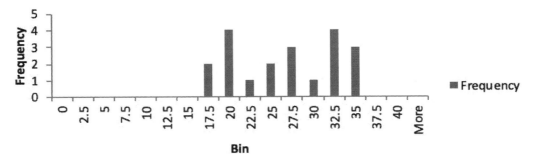

Figure 1.34: A histogram showing the number of female employees

9. Here, the mean sales are $171,603,750.13, and the median sales are $184,939,292.

10. The standard deviation of sales is $50,152,290.42.

11. The Boston, MA dealership is an outlier. This can be shown graphically or by using the IQR method.

12. You should get the following four quintiles:

n-Quintile	Value
1	144439803.80
2	157629974.20
3	177933357.40
4	185779034.20

Figure 1.35: Quintiles and their values

14. Removing the outlier of Boston, you should get a correlation coefficient of 0.55. This value implies that there is a strong correlation between the number of female employees and the sales of a dealership. While this may be evidence that more female employees lead to more revenue, it may also be a simple consequence of a third effect. In this case, larger dealerships have a larger number of employees in general, which also means that women will be at these locations as well. There may be other correlational interpretations as well.

Chapter 2: The Basics of SQL for Analytics

Activity 3: Querying the customers Table Using Basic Keywords in a SELECT Query

Solution

1. Open your favorite SQL client and connect to the **sqlda** database. Examine the schema for the **customers** table from the schema dropdown. Notice the names of the columns, the same as we did in *Exercise 6, Querying Salespeople,* for the **salespeople** table.

2. Execute the following query to fetch customers in the state of Florida in alphabetical order:

```
SELECT email
FROM customers
WHERE state='FL'
ORDER BY email
```

The following is the output of the preceding code:

	email text
1	aachrameevu44@goo.gl
2	aambresinlnt@walmart.com
3	aanstiss12af@eepurl.com
4	aantonove9l@last.fm
5	aarnaudet1v3@cisco.com
6	aarsmithxoe@dion.ne.jp
7	aastle11rg@slate.com
8	aaxelbey77x@cocolog-nifty.com
9	aazemary2f@washingtonpost.com
10	ababarm8m@ow.ly
11	abarkessi6f@wikimedia.org

Figure 2.13: Emails of customers from Florida in alphabetical order

3. Execute the following query to pull all the first names, last names, and email addresses for ZoomZoom customers in New York City in the state of New York. The customers would be ordered alphabetically by the last name followed by the first name:

```
SELECT first_name, last_name, email
FROM customers
WHERE city='New York City'
and state='NY'
ORDER BY last_name, first_name
```

The following is the output of the preceding code:

	first_name text	last_name text	email text
1	Nell	Abdy	nabdyec4@fema.gov
2	Thomasine	Absolon	tabsolonomk@forbes.com
3	Ram	Acheson	racheson1ai@bloglovin.com
4	Pru	Achrameev	pachrameev2sr@example.com
5	Jandy	Adamowicz	jadamowiczb1w@clickbank.net
6	Kati	Adrian	kadrianeem@51.la
7	Orly	Aers	oaersx61@redcross.org
8	Bradney	Aglione	baglionee5n@usgs.gov
9	Mellicent	Ainslee	mainsleeir0@abc.net.au
10	Fergus	Aireton	fairetonq16@yellowpages.com
11	Ugo	Aldam	ualdamhnc@wikimedia.org

Figure 2.14: Details of customers from New York City in alphabetical order

4. Execute the following query to fetch all customers that have a phone number ordered by the date the customer was added to the database:

```
SELECT *
FROM customers
WHERE phone IS NOT NULL
ORDER BY date_added
```

The following is the output of the preceding code:

customer_id bigint	title text	first_name text	last_name text	suffix text	email text	gender text	ip_address text	phone text	street_address text	city text	state text	postal_code text	latitude double precision	longitude double precision	date_added timestamp without time zone
2625	[null]	Binky	Dawtrey	[null]	bdewtr...	M	15.75.236.78	804-990...	0353 Iowa Road	Rich...	VA	23208	37.5593	-77.4471	2010-03-15 00:00:00
6173	[null]	Danila	Gristwood	[null]	dgrist...	F	254.239.58.1...	832-157...	79865 Hagan Terr...	Katy	TX	77493	29.8678	-95.8298	2010-03-15 00:00:00
13390	[null]	Danika	Lough	[null]	dlough...	F	188.19.7.207	212-769...	38463 Forest Dal...	New ...	NY	10019	40.7651	-73.9858	2010-03-15 00:00:00
7486	[null]	Ciro	Ferencowicz	[null]	cferen...	M	8.151.167.184	786-458...	61 Village Crossing	Miami	FL	33111	25.5564	-80.4582	2010-03-15 00:00:00
17099	[null]	Pearla	Halksworth	[null]	phalks...	F	114.138.82.24	541-196...	130 Marcy Crossi...	Euge...	OR	97405	44.0165	-123.0998	2010-03-15 00:00:00
18685	[null]	Ingram	Crossman	[null]	icross...	M	207.145.1.202	503-352...	86 Michigan Junc...	Salem	OR	97306	44.8685	-123.0438	2010-03-15 00:00:00
30046	[null]	Nanete	Hassur	[null]	nhassu...	F	232.115.170...	209-364...	13961 Steensland...	Stoc...	CA	95205	37.9625	-121.2624	2010-03-15 00:00:00
35683	[null]	Betteanne	Ruif	[null]	bruifrj6...	F	52.208.248.90	503-396...	1 Cordelia Crossing	Salem	OR	97306	44.8685	-123.0438	2010-03-15 00:00:00
22640	[null]	Shana	Nugent	[null]	snuge...	F	207.239.127...	202-378...	96725 Cordelia La...	Was...	DC	20010	38.9327	-77.0322	2010-03-16 00:00:00
34189	[null]	Devlin	Barhems	[null]	dbarhe...	M	180.175.21.2...	240-895...	0 Park Meadow St...	Rock...	MD	20851	39.0763	-77.1234	2010-03-16 00:00:00
46277	Mr	Salomon	Rillatt	[null]	srillatt...	M	33.205.88.187	504-700...	5799 Thackeray C...	New ...	LA	70179	30.033	-89.8826	2010-03-16 00:00:00

Figure 2.15: Customers with a phone number ordered by the date
the customer was added to the database

Activity 4: Marketing Operations

Solution

1. Open your favorite SQL client and connect to the **sqlda** database.

2. Run the following query to create the table with New York City customers:

```
CREATE TABLE customers_nyc AS (
SELECT * FROM
customers
where city='New York City'
and state='NY');
```

customer_id bigint	title text	first_name text	last_name text	suffix text	email text	gender text	ip_address text	phone text	street_address text	city text	state text	postal_code text	latitude double precision	longitude double precision	date_added timestamp wit
52	[null]	Giusto	Backe	[null]	gbacke1f@digg.com	M	26.56.68.189	212-959...	6 Onsgard Terrace	New ...	NY	10131	40.7808	-73.9772	2010-07-06 00:
162	[null]	Artair	Betchley	[null]	abetchley4h@dagondesign.com	M	108.147.128...	[null]	7 Boyd Road	New ...	NY	10099	40.7808	-73.9772	2014-06-25 00:
374	[null]	Verge	Esel	[null]	vesel4d@vistaprint.com	M	58.238.20.156	917-653...	6 Algoma Park	New ...	NY	10014	40.7339	-74.0054	2016-02-17 00:
406	[null]	Rozine	Jeal	[null]	rjealh9@howstuffworks.com	F	50.235.92.29	917-610...	64653 Homewoo...	New ...	NY	10105	40.7628	-73.9785	2010-09-15 00:
456	Rev	Cybil	Noke	[null]	cnokecn@digsy.com	F	5.31.139.106	212-306...	86 Sycamore Park...	New ...	NY	10260	40.7808	-73.9772	2017-01-21 00:
472	[null]	Rawley	Yegorov	[null]	ryegorovd3@google.es	M	183.199.243...	212-560...	872 Old Shore Par...	New ...	NY	10034	40.8662	-73.9221	2014-11-24 00:
496	[null]	Layton	Spolton	[null]	lspoltondr@free.fr	M	108.112.8.165	646-900...	7 Old Gate Drive	New ...	NY	10024	40.7864	-73.9764	2010-12-20 00:
1028	[null]	Issy	Andrieux	[null]	iandrieuxsj@dell.com	F	199.50.5.37	212-206...	33337 Dahle Way	New ...	NY	10115	40.8111	-73.9642	2017-11-27 00:
1037	[null]	Magdalene	Veryard	[null]	mveryardss@behance.net	F	98.201.129.2...	[null]	41028 Katie Juncl...	New ...	NY	10039	40.8265	-73.9383	2014-08-04 00:
1063	[null]	Joliet	Beadles	[null]	jbeadlesti@time.com	F	47.96.88.226	212-645...	34984 Goodland ...	New ...	NY	10120	40.7506	-73.9894	2014-08-17 00:

Figure 2.16: Table showing customers from New York City

3. Then, run the following query statement to delete users with the postal code **10014**:

```
DELETE FROM customers_nyc WHERE postal_code='10014';
```

4. Execute the following query to add the new **event** column:

```
ALTER TABLE customers_nyc ADD COLUMN event text;
```

5. Update the **customers_nyc** table and set the event to **thank-you party** using the following query:

```
UPDATE customers_nyc
SET event = 'thank-you party';
```

customer_id bigint	title text	first_name text	last_name text	suffix text	email text	gender text	ip_address text	phone text	street_address text	city text	state text	postal_code text	latitude double precision	longitude double precision	date_added timestamp without time zone	event text
52	[null]	Giusto	Backs	[null]	gbacks...	M	26.56.68.189	212-959...	6 Onsgard Terrace	New ...	NY	10131	40.7808	-73.9772	2010-07-06 00:00:00	thank-you party
406	[null]	Rozina	Jaal	[null]	rjealb9...	F	50.235.32.29	917-610...	64653 Hornewoo...	New ...	NY	10105	40.7628	-73.9785	2010-09-15 00:00:00	thank-you party
456	Rev	Cybil	Noke	[null]	cnokec...	F	5.31.139.106	212-306...	88 Sycamore Park...	New ...	NY	10260	40.7808	-73.9772	2017-01-21 00:00:00	thank-you party
472	[null]	Rawley	Yagorov	[null]	ryngor...	M	183.199.243...	212-556...	872 Old Shore Par...	New ...	NY	10034	40.8662	-73.9221	2014-11-24 00:00:00	thank-you party
496	[null]	Layton	Spolton	[null]	lspolto...	M	108.112.8.165	646-900...	7 Old Gate Drive	New ...	NY	10024	40.7864	-73.9764	2010-12-20 00:00:00	thank-you party
1029	[null]	Issy	Andreux	[null]	iandrie...	F	199.90.5.37	212-206...	33337 Dahle Way	New ...	NY	10115	40.8111	-73.9642	2017-11-27 00:00:00	thank-you party
1037	[null]	Magdalene	Veryard	[null]	mverys...	F	93.201.129 2...	[null]	41028 Katie Junct...	New ...	NY	10039	40.8265	-73.9383	2014-03-04 00:00:00	thank-you party
1063	[null]	Juliet	Beadles	[null]	jbeadle...	F	47.96.88.226	212-645...	34984 Goodland ...	New ...	NY	10120	40.7506	-73.9894	2014-08-17 00:00:00	thank-you party
1211	[null]	Gwyneth	McCobb	[null]	gmcco...	F	38.182.151.2...	[null]	4 Jana Park	New ...	NY	10160	40.7808	-73.9772	2014-01-08 00:00:00	thank-you party
1262	[null]	Conrado	Escoffier	[null]	cescoff...	M	23.120.12.44	646-523...	2 Atwood Court	New ...	NY	10060	40.7808	-73.9772	2015-02-17 00:00:00	thank-you party

Figure 2.17: The customers_nyc table with event set as 'thank-you party'

6. Now, we will delete the **customers_nyc** table as asked by the manager using **DROP TABLE**:

```
DROP TABLE customers_nyc;
```

This will delete the **customers_nyc** table from the database.

Chapter 3: SQL for Data Preparation

Activity 5: Building a Sales Model Using SQL Techniques

Solution

1. Open your favorite SQL client and connect to the **sqlda** database.

2. Follow the steps mentioned with the scenario and write the query for it. There are many approaches to this query, but one of these approaches could be:

```
SELECT
c.*,
p.*,
COALESCE(s.dealership_id, -1),
CASE WHEN p.base_msrp - s.sales_amount >500 THEN 1 ELSE 0 END AS high_
savings
FROM sales s
INNER JOIN customers c ON c.customer_id=s.customer_id
INNER JOIN products p ON p.product_id=s.product_id
LEFT JOIN dealerships d ON s.dealership_id = d.dealership_id;
```

3. The following is the output of the preceding code:

customer_id bigint	title text	first_name text	last_name text	suffix text	email text	gender text	ip_address text	phone text	street_address text	city text	state text	postal_code text	latitude double precision	longitude double precision	date_added timestamp without time zone
1	[null]	Ariena	Riveles	[null]	arivele...	F	98.36.172.246	[null]	[null]	[null]	[null]	[null]	[null]	[null]	2017-04-23 00:00:00
4	[null]	Jessika	Nussen	[null]	jnusse...	F	159.165.138...	615-824...	224 Village Circle	Nash...	TN	37215	36.0986	-86.8219	2017-09-03 00:00:00
5	[null]	Lonnie	Rembaud	[null]	lremba...	F	18.131.58.65	786-499...	38 Lindbergh Way	Miami	FL	33124	25.5584	-80.4582	2014-03-06 00:00:00
6	[null]	Cortie	Locksley	[null]	clocksl...	M	140.194.59.82	[null]	6537 Delladonne ...	Miami	FL	33158	25.6364	-80.3187	2013-03-31 00:00:00
7	[null]	Wood	Kennham	[null]	wkenn...	M	191.190.135...	407-552...	001 Onsgard Park	Orla...	FL	32891	28.5663	-81.2608	2011-08-25 00:00:00
7	[null]	Wood	Kennham	[null]	wkenn...	M	191.190.135...	407-552...	001 Onsgard Park	Orla...	FL	32891	28.5663	-81.2608	2011-08-25 00:00:00
7	[null]	Wood	Kennham	[null]	wkenn...	M	191.190.135...	407-552...	001 Onsgard Park	Orla...	FL	32891	28.5663	-81.2608	2011-08-25 00:00:00
11	Mrs	Urbano	Middlehurst	[null]	umiddl...	M	185.118.6.23	918-339...	5203 7th Trail	Tulsa	OK	74156	36.3024	-95.9605	2011-10-22 00:00:00
12	Mr	Tyne	Duggan	[null]	tdugga...	F	13.29.231.228	[null]	[null]	[null]	[null]	[null]	[null]	[null]	2017-10-25 00:00:00

Figure 3.21: Building a sales model query

Thus, have the data to build a new model that will help the data science team to predict which customers are the best prospects for remarketing from the output generated.

Chapter 4: Aggregate Functions for Data Analysis

Activity 6: Analyzing Sales Data Using Aggregate Functions

Solution

1. Open your favorite SQL client and connect to the **sqlda** database.

2. Calculate the number of unit sales the company has achieved by using the **COUNT** function:

    ```
    SELECT COUNT(*)
    FROM sales;
    ```

    You should get **37,711** sales.

3. Determine the total sales amount in dollars for each state; we can use the **SUM** aggregate function here:

    ```
    SELECT c.state, SUM(sales_amount) as total_sales_amount
    FROM sales s
    INNER JOIN customers c ON c.customer_id=s.customer_id
    GROUP BY 1
    ORDER BY 1;
    ```

    You will get the following output:

state text	sales_amount double precision
AK	1124268.776
AL	4820333.791
AR	1487923.589
AZ	4109364.447
CA	27942722.0350006
CO	5377388.30800006
CT	3038361.316
DC	7211615.1750001
DE	957264.298

Figure 4.23: Total sales in dollars by US state

4. Determine the top five dealerships in terms of most units sold, using the **GROUP BY** clause and set **LIMIT** as **5**:

```
SELECT s.dealership_id, COUNT(*)
FROM sales s
WHERE channel='dealership'
GROUP BY 1
ORDER BY 2 DESC
LIMIT 5
```

You should get the following output:

dealership_id double precision	count bigint
10	1781
7	1583
18	1465
11	1312
1	1297

Figure 4.24: Top five dealerships by units sold

5. Calculate the average sales amount for each channel, as seen in the **sales** table, and look at the average sales amount first by **channel** sales, then by **product_id**, and then by both together. This can be done using **GROUPING SETS** as follows:

```
SELECT s.channel, s.product_id, AVG(sales_amount) as avg_sales_amount
FROM sales s
GROUP BY
GROUPING SETS(
(s.channel), (s.product_id),
(s.channel, s.product_id)
)
ORDER BY 1, 2
```

You should get the following output:

channel text	product_id bigint	avg_sales_amount double precision
dealership	3	477.253737607644
dealership	4	109822.274881517
dealership	5	664.330132075472
dealership	6	62563.3763837638
dealership	7	573.744146637002
dealership	8	668.850500463391
dealership	9	33402.6845637584
dealership	10	81270.1121794872
dealership	11	91589.7435897436

Figure 4.25: Sales after the GROUPING SETS channel and product_id

From the preceding figure, we can see the channel and product ID of all the products as well as the sales amount generated by each product.

Using aggregates, you have unlocked patterns that will help your company understand how to make more revenue and make the company better overall.

Chapter 5: Window Functions for Data Analysis

Activity 7: Analyzing Sales Using Window Frames and Window Functions

Solution

1. Open your favorite SQL client and connect to the **sqlda** database.

2. Calculate the total sales amount for all individual months in 2018 using the **SUM** function:

```
SELECT sales_transaction_date::DATE,
SUM(sales_amount) as total_sales_amount
FROM sales
WHERE sales_transaction_date>='2018-01-01'
AND sales_transaction_date<'2019-01-01'
GROUP BY 1
ORDER BY 1;
```

The following is the output of the preceding code:

sales_transaction_date date	total_sales_amount double precision
2018-01-01	123689.951
2018-01-02	183859.79
2018-01-03	40029.854
2018-01-04	187119.878
2018-01-05	186459.904
2018-01-06	100479.888
2018-01-07	42989.864
2018-01-08	11089.815
2018-01-09	98119.878
2018-01-10	10449.823
2018-01-11	6449.891
2018-01-12	160659.838
2018-01-13	77789.869
2018-01-14	234429.898
2018-01-15	74429.847
2018-01-16	129189.854
2018-01-17	153839.873
2018-01-18	255529.864

Figure 5.15: Total sales amount by month

3. Now, calculate the rolling 30-day average for the daily number of sales deals, using a window frame:

```
WITH daily_deals as (
SELECT sales_transaction_date::DATE,
COUNT(*) as total_deals
FROM sales
GROUP BY 1
),

moving_average_calculation_30 AS (
SELECT sales_transaction_date, total_deals,
AVG(total_deals) OVER (ORDER BY sales_transaction_date ROWS BETWEEN 30
PRECEDING and CURRENT ROW) AS deals_moving_average,
ROW_NUMBER() OVER (ORDER BY sales_transaction_date) as row_number
FROM daily_deals
ORDER BY 1)

SELECT sales_transaction_date,
CASE WHEN row_number>=30 THEN deals_moving_average ELSE NULL END
    AS deals_moving_average_30
FROM moving_average_calculation_30
WHERE sales_transaction_date>='2018-01-01'
AND sales_transaction_date<'2019-01-01';
```

The following is the output of the preceding code:

sales_transaction_date date	deals_moving_average_30 numeric
2018-01-01	17.9354838709677419
2018-01-02	18.3548387096774194
2018-01-03	18.3548387096774194
2018-01-04	18.1290322580645161
2018-01-05	17.9354838709677419
2018-01-06	17.5806451612903226
2018-01-07	17.5161290322580645
2018-01-08	17.8064516129032258
2018-01-09	17.8709677419354839
2018-01-10	17.8387096774193548
2018-01-11	17.4193548387096774
2018-01-12	17.1935483870967742

Figure 5.16: Rolling 30-day average of sales

4. Next, calculate what decile each dealership would be in compared to other dealerships based on the total sales amount, using window functions:

```
WITH total_dealership_sales AS
(
SELECT dealership_id,
SUM(sales_amount) AS total_sales_amount
FROM sales
WHERE sales_transaction_date>='2018-01-01'
AND sales_transaction_date<'2019-01-01'
AND channel='dealership'
GROUP BY 1
)

SELECT *,
NTILE(10) OVER (ORDER BY total_sales_amount)
FROM total_dealership_sales;
```

The following is the output of the preceding code:

dealership_id double precision	total_sales_amount double precision	ntile integer
13	538079.414	1
9	618263.995	1
8	671619.251	2
4	905158.609	2
17	907058.842	3
20	949849.053	3
12	1086033.376	4
15	1197118.234	4
6	1316253.465	5
14	1551108.481	5
3	1622872.801	6
16	1981062.341	6

Figure 5.17: Decile for dealership sales amount

Chapter 6: Importing and Exporting Data

Activity 8: Using an External Dataset to Discover Sales Trends

Solution

1. The dataset can be downloaded from GitHub using the link provided. Once you go to the web page, you should be able to **Save Page As...** using the menus on your browser:

Figure 6.24: Saving the public transportation .csv file

2. The simplest way to transfer the data in a CSV file to pandas is to create a new Jupyter notebook. At the command line, type **jupyter notebook** (if you do not have a notebook server running already). In the browser window that pops up, create a new Python 3 notebook. In the first cell, you can type in the standard **import** statements and the connection information (replacing **your_X** with the appropriate parameter for your database connection):

```
from sqlalchemy import create_engine
import pandas as pd
% matplotlib inline

cnxn_string = ("postgresql+psycopg2://{username}:{pswd}"
               "@{host}:{port}/{database}")

engine = create_engine(cnxn_string.format(
    username="your_username",
    pswd="your_password",
    host="your_host",
    port=5432,
    database="your_db"))
```

3. We can read in the data using a command such as the following (replacing the path specified with the path to the file on your local computer):

```
data = pd.read_csv("~/Downloads/public_transportation'_statistics_by_zip_
code.csv", dtype={'zip_code':str})
```

Check that the data looks correct by creating a new cell, entering **data**, and then hitting *Shift* + *Enter* to see the contents of **data**. You can also use **data.head()** to see just the first few rows:

```
Out[11]:
```

	zip_code	public_transportation_pct	public_transportation_population
0	01379	3.3	13
1	01440	0.4	34
2	01505	0.9	23
3	01524	0.5	20
4	01529	1.8	32

Figure 6.25: Reading the public transportation data into pandas

4. Now, we can transfer data to our database using **data.to_sql()**:

```
import csv
from io import StringIO

def psql_insert_copy(table, conn, keys, data_iter):
    # gets a DBAPI connection that can provide a cursor
    dbapi_conn = conn.connection
    with dbapi_conn.cursor() as cur:
        s_buf = StringIO()
        writer = csv.writer(s_buf)
        writer.writerows(data_iter)
        s_buf.seek(0)

        columns = ', '.join('"{}"'.format(k) for k in keys)
        if table.schema:
            table_name = '{}.{}'.format(table.schema, table.name)
        else:
            table_name = table.name
```

```
        sql = 'COPY {} ({}) FROM STDIN WITH CSV'.format(
            table_name, columns)
        cur.copy_expert(sql=sql, file=s_buf)

    data.to_sql('public_transportation_by_zip', engine, if_exists='replace',
    method=psql_insert_copy)
```

5. Looking at the maximum and minimum values, we do see something strange: the minimum value is -666666666. We can assume that these values are missing, and we can remove them from the dataset:

```
SELECT
    MAX(public_transportation_pct) AS max_pct,
    MIN(public_transportation_pct) AS min_pct
FROM public_transportation_by_zip;
```

max_pct	min_pct
100	-666666666

Figure 6.26: Screenshot showing minimum and maximum values

6. In order to calculate the requested sales amounts, we can run a query in our database. Note that we will have to filter out the erroneous percentages below 0 based on our analysis in step 6. There are several ways to do this, but this single statement would work:

```
SELECT
    (public_transportation_pct > 10) AS is_high_public_transport,
    COUNT(s.customer_id) * 1.0 / COUNT(DISTINCT c.customer_id) AS sales_
per_customer
FROM customers c
INNER JOIN public_transportation_by_zip t ON t.zip_code = c.postal_code
LEFT JOIN sales s ON s.customer_id = c.customer_id
WHERE public_transportation_pct >= 0
GROUP BY 1
;
```

Here's an explanation of this query:

We can identify customers living in an area with public transportation by looking at the public transportation data associated with their postal code. If **public_transportation_pct > 10**, then the customer is in a high public transportation area. We can group by this expression to identify the population that is or is not in a high public transportation area.

We can look at sales per customer by counting the sales (for example, using the **COUNT(s.customer_id)** aggregate) and dividing by the unique number of customers (for example, using the **COUNT(DISTINCT c.customer_id)** aggregate). We want to make sure that we retain fractional values, so we can multiply by 1.0 to cast the entire expression to a float: **COUNT(s.customer_id) * 1.0 / COUNT(DISTINCT c.customer_id)**.

In order to do this, we need to join our customer data to the public transportation data, and finally to the sales data. We need to exclude all zip codes where **public_transportation_pct** is greater than, or equal to, 0 so that we exclude the missing data (denoted by -666666666).

Finally, we end with the following query:

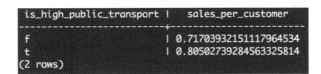

Figure 6.27: Calculating the requested sales amount

From this, we see that customers in high public transportation areas have 12% more product purchases than customers in low public transportation areas.

7. If we try to plot our data, we will get a strange distribution with two bars. This is because of the outlier values that we discovered in step 5. Instead, we can read this data from our database, and add a **WHERE** clause to remove the outlier values:

```
data = pd.read_sql_query('SELECT * FROM public_transportation_by_zip WHERE
public_transportation_pct > 0 AND public_transportation_pct < 50', engine)
data.plot.hist(y='public_transportation_pct')
```

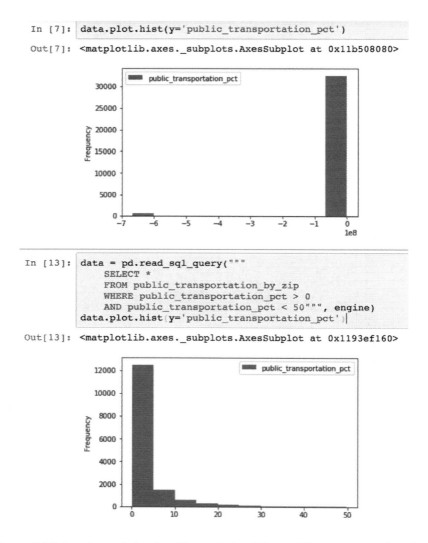

Figure 6.28: Jupyter notebook with analysis of the public transportation data

8. We can then rerun our command from step 5 to get the timing of the standard **to_sql()** function:

```
data.to_sql('public_transportation_by_zip', engine, if_exists='replace')
```

```
In [4]: import csv
        from io import StringIO

        def psql_insert_copy(table, conn, keys, data_iter):
            # gets a DBAPI connection that can provide a cursor
            dbapi_conn = conn.connection
            with dbapi_conn.cursor() as cur:
                s_buf = StringIO()
                writer = csv.writer(s_buf)
                writer.writerows(data_iter)
                s_buf.seek(0)

                columns = ', '.join('"{}"'.format(k) for k in keys)
                if table.schema:
                    table_name = '{}.{}'.format(table.schema, table.name)
                else:
                    table_name = table.name

                sql = 'COPY {} ({}) FROM STDIN WITH CSV'.format(
                    table_name, columns)
                cur.copy_expert(sql=sql, file=s_buf)
```

```
%time data.to_sql('public_transportation_by_zip', engine, method=psql_insert_copy, if_exists='replace')
CPU times: user 102 ms, sys: 21.1 ms, total: 123 ms         With COPY: ~1 Second
Wall time: 1.2 s
```

```
In [5]: %time data.to_sql('public_transportation_by_zip', engine, if_exists='replace')
CPU times: user 4.58 s, sys: 4.16 s, total: 8.75 s          Without COPY: ~9 minutes
Wall time: 9min 15s
```

Figure 6.29: Inserting records with COPY and without COPY is much faster

9. For this analysis, we can actually tweak the query from step 7:

```
CREATE TEMP VIEW public_transport_statistics AS (
    SELECT
        10 * ROUND(public_transportation_pct/10) AS public_transport,
        COUNT(s.customer_id) * 1.0 / COUNT(DISTINCT c.customer_id) AS
sales_per_customer
    FROM customers c
    INNER JOIN public_transportation_by_zip t ON t.zip_code = c.postal_
code
    LEFT JOIN sales s ON s.customer_id = c.customer_id
    WHERE public_transportation_pct >= 0
    GROUP BY 1
);
\copy (SELECT * FROM public_transport_statistics) TO 'public_transport_
distribution.csv' CSV HEADER;
```

First, we want to wrap our query in a temporary view, **public_transport_statistics**, so that we easily write the result to a CSV file later.

Next is the tricky part: we want to aggregate the public transportation statistics somehow. What we can do is round this percentage to the nearest 10%, so 22% would become 20%, and 39% would become 40%. We can do this by dividing the percentage number (represented as 0.0-100.0) by 10, rounding off, and then multiplying back by 10: **10 * ROUND(public_transportation_pct/10)**.

The logic for the remainder of the query is explained in step 6.

10. Next, we open up the **public_transport_distribution.csv** file in Excel:

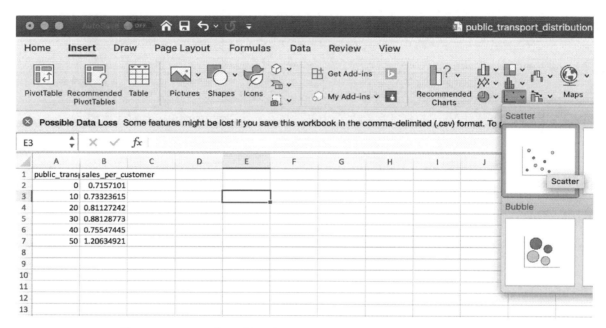

Figure 6.30: Excel workbook containing the data from our query

After creating the scatterplot, we get the following result, which shows a clear positive relationship between public transportation and sales in the geographical area:

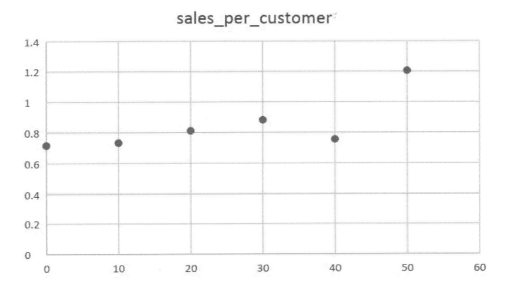

Figure 6.31: Sales per customer versus public transportation percentage

Based on all this analysis, we can say that there is a positive relationship between geographies with public transportation and demand for electric vehicles. Intuitively, this makes sense, because electric vehicles could provide an alternative transportation option to public transport for getting around cities. As a result of this analysis, we would recommend that ZoomZoom management should consider expanding in regions with high public transportation and urban areas.

Chapter 7: Analytics Using Complex Data Types

Activity 9: Sales Search and Analysis

Solution

1. First, create the materialized view on the **customer_sales** table:

```
CREATE MATERIALIZED VIEW customer_search AS (
    SELECT
        customer_json -> 'customer_id' AS customer_id,
        customer_json,
        to_tsvector('english', customer_json) AS search_vector
    FROM customer_sales
);
```

2. Create the GIN index on the view:

```
CREATE INDEX customer_search_gin_idx ON customer_search USING GIN(search_vector);
```

3. We can solve the request by using our new searchable database:

```
SELECT
    customer_id,
    customer_json
FROM customer_search
WHERE search_vector @@ plainto_tsquery('english', 'Danny Bat');
```

This results in eight matching rows:

```
{"email": "darundale87e@nytimes.com", "phone": null, "sales": [{"product_id": 8, "product_name": "Bat Limited Edition", "sale
s_amount": 699.99, "sales_transaction_date": "2017-05-16T08:41:03"}], "last_name": "Arundale", "date_added": "2016-10-15T00:00
:00", "first_name": "Danni", "customer_id": 10635}
{"email": "dsinkins8vv@theatlantic.com", "phone": null, "sales": [{"product_id": 7, "product_name": "Bat", "sales_amount": 59
9.99, "sales_transaction_date": "2018-01-10T14:25:09"}], "last_name": "Sinkins", "date_added": "2018-01-20T00:00:00", "first_n
ame": "Danny", "customer_id": 11516}
{"email": "dfalkusrnr@mysql.com", "phone": "360-138-1212", "sales": [{"product_id": 7, "product_name": "Bat", "sales_amount":
599.99, "sales_transaction_date": "2018-08-07T01:05:05"}, {"product_id": 3, "product_name": "Lemon", "sales_amount": 399.992,
"sales_transaction_date": "2018-07-05T09:51:51"}], "last_name": "Falkus", "date_added": "2018-06-16T00:00:00", "first_name":
"Dan
nie", "customer_id": 35848}
{"email": "dtyddwax@weebly.com", "phone": "626-781-3263", "sales": [{"product_id": 7, "product_name": "Bat", "sales_amount":
479.992, "sales_transaction_date": "2016-12-15T07:12:57"}], "last_name": "Tydd", "date_added": "2016-12-08T00:00:00", "first_n
ame": "Dannie", "customer_id": 41866}
{"email": "dberthelmotxt5@jigsy.com", "phone": "559-535-5099", "sales": [{"product_id": 8, "product_name": "Bat Limited Editi
on", "sales_amount": 699.99, "sales_transaction_date": "2019-01-30T12:58:20"}], "last_name": "Berthelmot", "date_added": "2018
-01-09T00:00:00", "first_name": "Danni", "customer_id": 43818}
{"email": "ddanev1b5@geocities.com", "phone": "415-491-7645", "sales": [{"product_id": 7, "product_name": "Bat", "sales_amoun
t": 479.992, "sales_transaction_date": "2017-07-12T01:07:30"}, {"product_id": 3, "product_name": "Lemon", "sales_amount": 499.
99, "sales_transaction_date": "2016-12-09T08:02:24"}, {"product_id": 3, "product_name": "Lemon", "sales_amount": 499.99, "sale
s_transaction_date": "2015-08-09T15:56:15"}], "last_name": "Danev", "date_added": "2015-08-21T00:00:00", "first_name": "Danni"
, "customer_id": 1698}
{"email": "dlamondpy0@soundcloud.com", "phone": "585-779-9709", "sales": [{"product_id": 7, "product_name": "Bat", "sales_amo
unt": 599.99, "sales_transaction_date": "2017-01-01T22:30:02"}, {"product_id": 3, "product_name": "Lemon", "sales_amount": 499
.99, "sales_transaction_date": "2016-12-19T03:55:45"}], "last_name": "Lamond", "date_added": "2016-12-17T00:00:00", "first_nam
e": "Danny", "customer_id": 33625}
{"email": "dmagister113r@canalblog.com", "phone": "860-336-0719", "sales": [{"product_id": 8, "product_name": "Bat Limited Ed
ition", "sales_amount": 699.99, "sales_transaction_date": "2017-03-14T02:25:39"}], "last_name": "Magister", "date_added": "201
7-02-27T00:00:00", "first_name": "Danni", "customer_id": 48088}
(8 rows)
```

Figure 7.29: Resulting matches for our "Danny Bat" query

In this complex task, we need to find customers who match with both a scooter and an automobile. That means we need to perform a query for each combination of scooter and automobile.

4. We need to produce the unique list of scooters and automobiles (and remove limited editions releases) using **DISTINCT**:

```
SELECT DISTINCT
    p1.model,
    p2.model
FROM products p1
LEFT JOIN products p2 ON TRUE
WHERE p1.product_type = 'scooter'
AND p2.product_type = 'automobile'
AND p1.model NOT ILIKE '%Limited Edition%';
```

This produces the following output:

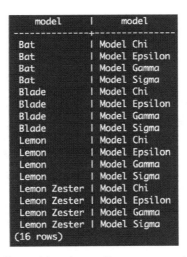

```
     model      |     model
----------------+----------------
 Bat            | Model Chi
 Bat            | Model Epsilon
 Bat            | Model Gamma
 Bat            | Model Sigma
 Blade          | Model Chi
 Blade          | Model Epsilon
 Blade          | Model Gamma
 Blade          | Model Sigma
 Lemon          | Model Chi
 Lemon          | Model Epsilon
 Lemon          | Model Gamma
 Lemon          | Model Sigma
 Lemon Zester   | Model Chi
 Lemon Zester   | Model Epsilon
 Lemon Zester   | Model Gamma
 Lemon Zester   | Model Sigma
(16 rows)
```

Figure 7.30: All combinations of scooters and automobiles

5. Next, we need to transform the output into the query:

```
SELECT DISTINCT
    plainto_tsquery('english', p1.model) &&
    plainto_tsquery('english', p2.model)
FROM products p1
LEFT JOIN products p2 ON TRUE
WHERE p1.product_type = 'scooter'
AND p2.product_type = 'automobile'
AND p1.model NOT ILIKE '%Limited Edition%';
```

This produces the following result:

```
'bat' & 'model' & 'chi'
'bat' & 'model' & 'sigma'
'blade' & 'model' & 'chi'
'lemon' & 'model' & 'chi'
'bat' & 'model' & 'gamma'
'blade' & 'model' & 'sigma'
'lemon' & 'model' & 'sigma'
'bat' & 'model' & 'epsilon'
'blade' & 'model' & 'gamma'
'lemon' & 'model' & 'gamma'
'blade' & 'model' & 'epsilon'
'lemon' & 'model' & 'epsilon'
'lemon' & 'zester' & 'model' & 'chi'
'lemon' & 'zester' & 'model' & 'sigma'
'lemon' & 'zester' & 'model' & 'gamma'
'lemon' & 'zester' & 'model' & 'epsilon'
(16 rows)
```

Figure 7.31: Queries for each scooter and automobile combination

6. Query our database using each of these **tsquery** objects, and count the occurrences for each object:

```
SELECT
    sub.query,
    (
        SELECT COUNT(1)
        FROM customer_search
        WHERE customer_search.search_vector @@ sub.query)
FROM (
    SELECT DISTINCT
        plainto_tsquery('english', p1.model) &&
        plainto_tsquery('english', p2.model) AS query
    FROM products p1
    LEFT JOIN products p2 ON TRUE
    WHERE p1.product_type = 'scooter'
    AND p2.product_type = 'automobile'
    AND p1.model NOT ILIKE '%Limited Edition%'
) sub
ORDER BY 2 DESC;
```

The following is the output of the preceding query:

```
                        query                 | count
----------------------------------------------+-------
 'lemon' & 'model' & 'sigma'                   |   340
 'lemon' & 'model' & 'chi'                     |   331
 'bat' & 'model' & 'epsilon'                   |   241
 'bat' & 'model' & 'sigma'                     |   226
 'bat' & 'model' & 'chi'                       |   221
 'lemon' & 'model' & 'epsilon'                 |   217
 'bat' & 'model' & 'gamma'                     |   153
 'lemon' & 'model' & 'gamma'                   |   133
 'lemon' & 'zester' & 'model' & 'chi'          |    28
 'lemon' & 'zester' & 'model' & 'epsilon'      |    22
 'blade' & 'model' & 'chi'                     |    21
 'lemon' & 'zester' & 'model' & 'sigma'        |    17
 'blade' & 'model' & 'sigma'                   |    12
 'lemon' & 'zester' & 'model' & 'gamma'        |    11
 'blade' & 'model' & 'epsilon'                 |     4
 'blade' & 'model' & 'gamma'                   |     4
(16 rows)
```

Figure 7.32: Customer counts for each scooter and automobile combination

While there could be a multitude of factors at play here, we see that the lemon scooter and the model sigma automobile is the combination most frequently purchased together, followed by the lemon and model chi. The bat is also fairly frequently purchased with both of those models, as well as the model epsilon. The other combinations are much less common, and it seems that customers rarely purchase the lemon zester, the blade, and the model gamma.

Chapter 8: Performant SQL

Activity 10: Query Planning

Solution:

1. Open PostgreSQL and connect to the **sqlda** database:

    ```
    C:\> psql sqlda
    ```

2. Use the **EXPLAIN** command to return the query plan for selecting all available records within the **customers** table:

    ```
    sqlda=# EXPLAIN SELECT * FROM customers;
    ```

    This query will produce the following output from the planner:

    ```
                                   QUERY PLAN
    ------------------------------------------------------------------
     Seq Scan on customers  (cost=0.00..1536.00 rows=50000 width=140)
    (1 row)
    ```

    Figure 8.75: Plan for all records within the customers table

    The setup cost is **0**, the total query cost is **1536**, the number of rows is **50000**, and the width of each row is **140**. The cost is actually in cost units, the number of rows is in rows, and the width is in bytes.

3. Repeat the query from *step 2* of this activity, this time limiting the number of returned records to **15**:

    ```
    sqlda=# EXPLAIN SELECT * FROM customers LIMIT 15;
    ```

    This query will produce the following output from the planner:

    ```
                                   QUERY PLAN
    -----------------------------------------------------------------------
     Limit  (cost=0.00..0.46 rows=15 width=140)
       ->  Seq Scan on customers  (cost=0.00..1536.00 rows=50000 width=140)
    (2 rows)
    ```

    Figure 8.76: Plan for all records within the customers table with the limit as 15

    Two steps are involved in the query, and the limiting step costs 0.46 units within the plan.

4. Generate the query plan, selecting all rows where customers live within a latitude of **30** and **40** degrees:

```
sqlda=# EXPLAIN SELECT * FROM customers WHERE latitude > 30 and latitude <
40;
```

This query will produce the following output from the planner:

```
                                    QUERY PLAN
--------------------------------------------------------------------------------
 Seq Scan on customers  (cost=0.00..1786.00 rows=26439 width=140)
   Filter: ((latitude > '30'::double precision) AND (latitude < '40'::double precision))
(2 rows)
```

Figure 8.77: Plan for customers living within a latitude of 30 and 40 degrees

The total plan cost is **1786** units, and it returns **26439** rows.

Activity 11: Implementing Index Scans

Solution:

1. Use the **EXPLAIN** and **ANALYZE** commands to profile the query plan to search for all records with an IP address of **18.131.58.65**:

```
EXPLAIN ANALYZE SELECT * FROM customers WHERE ip_address = '18.131.58.65';
```

The following output will be displayed:

```
                                    QUERY PLAN
--------------------------------------------------------------------------------
-
 Seq Scan on customers  (cost=0.00..1661.00 rows=1 width=140) (actual time=0.019..15.592 rows=1 loops=1)
   Filter: (ip_address = '18.131.58.65'::text)
   Rows Removed by Filter: 49999
 Planning Time: 0.191 ms
 Execution Time: 15.625 ms
(5 rows)
```

Figure 8.78: Sequential scan with a filter on ip_address

The query takes **0.191 ms** to plan and **15.625 ms** to execute.

2. Create a generic index based on the IP address column:

```
CREATE INDEX ON customers(ip_address);
```

3. Rerun the query of *step 1* and note the time it takes to execute:

```
EXPLAIN ANALYZE SELECT * FROM customers WHERE ip_address = '18.131.58.65';
```

The following is the output of the preceding code:

```
                                    QUERY PLAN
--------------------------------------------------------------------------------------------------------
 Index Scan using customers_ip_address_idx on customers  (cost=0.29..8.31 rows=1 width=140) (actual time=0.072..0.075 rows=1 loops=1)
   Index Cond: (ip_address = '18.131.58.65'::text)
 Planning Time: 0.467 ms
 Execution Time: 0.123 ms
(4 rows)
```

Figure 8.79: Index scan with a filter on ip_address

The query takes **0.467 ms** to plan and **0.123 ms** to execute.

4. Create a more detailed index based on the IP address column with the condition that the IP address is **18.131.58.65**:

   ```
   CREATE INDEX ix_ip_where ON customers(ip_address) WHERE ip_address =
   '18.131.58.65';
   ```

5. Rerun the query of *step 1* and note the time it takes to execute.

   ```
   EXPLAIN ANALYZE SELECT * FROM customers WHERE ip_address = '18.131.58.65';
   ```

   The following is the output of the preceding code:

```
                                    QUERY PLAN
--------------------------------------------------------------------------------------------------------
 Index Scan using ix_ip_where on customers  (cost=0.12..8.14 rows=1 width=140) (actual time=0.021..0.023 rows=1 loops=1)
 Planning Time: 0.458 ms
 Execution Time: 0.056 ms
(3 rows)
```

Figure 8.80: Query plan with reduced execution time due to a more specific index

The query takes **0.458 ms** to plan and **0.056 ms** to execute. We can see that both indices took around the same amount of time to plan, with the index that specifies the exact IP address being much faster to execute and slightly quicker to plan as well.

6. Use the **EXPLAIN** and **ANALYZE** commands to profile the query plan to search for all records with a suffix of **Jr**:

   ```
   EXPLAIN ANALYZE SELECT * FROM customers WHERE suffix = 'Jr';
   ```

   The following output will be displayed:

```
                                    QUERY PLAN
--------------------------------------------------------------------------------------------------------
 Seq Scan on customers  (cost=0.00..1661.00 rows=107 width=140) (actual time=0.023..14.191 rows=102 loops=1)
   Filter: (suffix = 'Jr'::text)
   Rows Removed by Filter: 49898
 Planning Time: 0.153 ms
 Execution Time: 14.238 ms
(5 rows)
```

Figure 8.81: Query plan of sequential scan filtering using a suffix

The query takes **0.153 ms** of planning and **14.238 ms** of execution.

7. Create a generic index based on the suffix address column:

    ```
    CREATE INDEX ix_jr ON customers(suffix);
    ```

8. Rerun the query of *step 6* and note the time it takes to execute:

    ```
    EXPLAIN ANALYZE SELECT * FROM customers WHERE suffix = 'Jr';
    ```

    The following output will be displayed:

```
                                    QUERY PLAN
-----------------------------------------------------------------------------------------
 Bitmap Heap Scan on customers  (cost=5.12..318.44 rows=107 width=140) (actual time=0.146..0.440 rows=102 loops=1)
   Recheck Cond: (suffix = 'Jr'::text)
   Heap Blocks: exact=100
   ->  Bitmap Index Scan on ix_jr  (cost=0.00..5.09 rows=107 width=0) (actual time=0.092..0.092 rows=102 loops=1)
         Index Cond: (suffix = 'Jr'::text)
 Planning Time: 0.411 ms
 Execution Time: 0.511 ms
(7 rows)
```

Figure 8.82: Query plan of the scan after creating an index on the suffix column

Again, the planning time is significantly elevated, but this cost is more than outweighed by the improvement in the execution time, which is reduced from **14.238 ms** to **0.511 ms**.

Activity 12: Implementing Hash Indexes

Solution

1. Use the **EXPLAIN** and **ANALYZE** commands to determine the planning time and cost, as well as the execution time and cost, of selecting all rows where the email subject is **Shocking Holiday Savings On Electric Scooters**:

    ```
    EXPLAIN ANALYZE SELECT * FROM emails where email_subject='Shocking Holiday
    Savings On Electric Scooters';
    ```

    The following output will be displayed:

```
                                    QUERY PLAN
-----------------------------------------------------------------------------------------
 Seq Scan on emails  (cost=0.00..10651.98 rows=19863 width=79) (actual time=7.843..117.840 rows=19873 loops=1)
   Filter: (email_subject = 'Shocking Holiday Savings On Electric Scooters'::text)
   Rows Removed by Filter: 398285
 Planning Time: 0.117 ms
 Execution Time: 119.801 ms
(5 rows)
```

Figure 8.83: Performance of sequential scan on the emails table

The planning time is **0.117 ms** and the execution time is **119.801ms**. There is no cost in setting up the query, but there is a cost of **10,652** in executing it.

2. Use the **EXPLAIN** and **ANALYZE** commands to determine the planning time and cost, as well as the execution time and cost, of selecting all rows where the email subject is **Black Friday. Green Cars.**:

```
EXPLAIN ANALYZE SELECT * FROM emails where email_subject='Black Friday.
Green Cars.';
```

The following output will be displayed:

```
                                    QUERY PLAN
---------------------------------------------------------------------------------------------
Seq Scan on emails  (cost=0.00..10651.98 rows=40645 width=79) (actual time=65.643..124.249 rows=41399 loops=1)
  Filter: (email_subject = 'Black Friday. Green Cars.'::text)
  Rows Removed by Filter: 376759
Planning Time: 0.097 ms
Execution Time: 127.736 ms
(5 rows)
```

Figure 8.84: Performance of a sequential scan looking for different email subject values

Approximately **0.097 ms** is spent on planning the query, with **127.736 ms** being spent on executing it. This elevated execution time can be partially attributed to an increase in the number of rows being returned. Again, there is no setup cost, but a similar execution cost of **10,652**.

3. Create a hash scan of the email subject field:

```
CREATE INDEX ix_email_subject ON emails USING HASH(email_subject);
```

4. Repeat *step* 1 from the solution and compare both the outputs:

```
EXPLAIN ANALYZE SELECT * FROM emails where email_subject='Shocking Holiday
Savings On Electric Scooters';
```

The following output will be displayed:

```
                                    QUERY PLAN
---------------------------------------------------------------------------------------------
Bitmap Heap Scan on emails  (cost=641.94..6315.23 rows=19863 width=79) (actual time=2.096..15.061 rows=19873 loops=1)
  Recheck Cond: (email_subject = 'Shocking Holiday Savings On Electric Scooters'::text)
  Heap Blocks: exact=289
  ->  Bitmap Index Scan on ix_email_subject  (cost=0.00..636.97 rows=19863 width=0) (actual time=1.936..1.936 rows=19873 loops=1)
        Index Cond: (email_subject = 'Shocking Holiday Savings On Electric Scooters'::text)
Planning Time: 0.130 ms
Execution Time: 17.028 ms
(7 rows)
```

Figure 8.85: Output of the query planner using a hash index

The query plan shows that our newly created hash index is being used and has significantly reduced the execution time by over 100 ms, as well as the cost. There is a minor increase in the planning time and planning cost, all of which is easily outweighed by the reduction in execution time.

5. Repeat *step* 2 from the solution and compare both the outputs:

```
EXPLAIN ANALYZE SELECT * FROM emails where email_subject='Black Friday.
Green Cars.';
```

The following is the output of the preceding code:

```
                                       QUERY PLAN
--------------------------------------------------------------------------------------------------
 Bitmap Heap Scan on emails  (cost=1311.00..7244.06 rows=40645 width=79) (actual time=4.085..29.296 rows=41399 loops=1)
   Recheck Cond: (email_subject = 'Black Friday. Green Cars.'::text)
   Heap Blocks: exact=531
   ->  Bitmap Index Scan on ix_email_subject  (cost=0.00..1300.84 rows=40645 width=0) (actual time=3.817..3.817 rows=41399 loops=1)
         Index Cond: (email_subject = 'Black Friday. Green Cars.'::text)
 Planning Time: 0.403 ms
 Execution Time: 33.216 ms
(7 rows)
```

Figure 8.86: Output of the query planner for a less-performant hash index

Again, we can see a reduction in both planning and execution expenses. However, the reductions in the "Black Friday..." search are not as good as those achieved in the "Shocking Holiday Savings..." search. If we look in more detail, we can see that the scan on the index is approximately two times longer, but there are also about twice as many records in the latter example. From this, we can conclude that the increase is simply due to the increase in the number of records being returned by the query.

6. Create a hash scan of the **customer_id** field:

```
CREATE INDEX ix_customer_id ON emails USING HASH(customer_id);
```

7. Use **EXPLAIN** and **ANALYZE** to estimate the time required to select all rows with a **customer_id** value greater than 100. What type of scan was used and why?

```
EXPLAIN ANALYZE SELECT * FROM emails WHERE customer_id > 100;
```

The following output will be displayed:

```
                                       QUERY PLAN
--------------------------------------------------------------------------------------------------
 Seq Scan on emails  (cost=0.00..10651.98 rows=417309 width=79) (actual time=0.024..121.483 rows=417315 loops=1)
   Filter: (customer_id > 100)
   Rows Removed by Filter: 843
 Planning Time: 0.199 ms
 Execution Time: 152.656 ms
(5 rows)
```

Figure 8.87: Query planner ignoring the hash index due to limitations

So, the final execution time comes to **152.656ms** and the planning time comes to **0.199ms**.

Activity 13: Implementing Joins

Solution

1. Open PostgreSQL and connect to the **sqlda** database:

```
$ psql sqlda
```

2. Determine a list of customers (**customer_id**, **first_name**, and **last_name**) who had been sent an email, including information for the subject of the email and whether they opened and clicked on the email. The resulting table should include the **customer_id**, **first_name**, **last_name**, **email_subject**, **opened**, and **clicked** columns.

```
sqlda=# SELECT customers.customer_id, customers.first_name, customers.
last_name, emails.opened, emails.clicked FROM customers INNER JOIN emails
ON customers.customer_id=emails.customer_id;
```

The following screenshot shows the output of the preceding code:

```
customer_id |  first_name   |    last_name    | opened | clicked
-------------+---------------+-----------------+--------+---------
         18 | Mareah        | Edgell          | f      | f
         30 | Kath          | Rivel           | f      | f
         41 | Rycca         | Oakwell         | t      | f
         52 | Giusto        | Backe           | f      | f
         59 | Laurene       | Lobbe           | f      | f
         78 | West          | Hampson         | f      | f
         82 | Claudie       | Cancott         | f      | f
         84 | Nels          | Beefon          | f      | f
        103 | Natalina      | Dell 'Orto      | f      | f
        119 | Hugibert      | Bullocke        | f      | f
        132 | Orrin         | Evennett        | f      | f
        134 | Emmalyn       | Hackney         | f      | f
        135 | Myrilla       | Starcks         | f      | f
        137 | Cindee        | Prandi          | f      | f
```

Figure 8.88: Customers and emails join

3. Save the resulting table to a new table, **customer_emails**:

```
sqlda=# SELECT customers.customer_id, customers.first_name, customers.last_
name, emails.opened, emails.clicked INTO customer_emails FROM customers
INNER JOIN emails ON customers.customer_id=emails.customer_id;
```

4. Find those customers who opened or clicked on an email:

```
SELECT * FROM customer_emails WHERE clicked='t' and opened='t';
```

The following figure shows the output of the preceding code:

```
customer_id |    first_name    |     last_name      | opened | clicked
------------+------------------+--------------------+--------+---------
        554 | Chet             | Melchior           | t      | t
        673 | Hirsch           | Kulver             | t      | t
       1255 | Randi            | Benzing            | t      | t
       1916 | Gabrielle        | Skeermer           | t      | t
       2109 | Augie            | Rhymer             | t      | t
       2308 | Natale           | Ruddiman           | t      | t
       2909 | Wilton           | Silversmid         | t      | t
       3367 | Aidan            | Hinzer             | t      | t
       3718 | Myrah            | Capstack           | t      | t
       4013 | Dalton           | Turrill            | t      | t
       4303 | Benson           | Pruvost            | t      | t
       4370 | Krystle          | Roiz               | t      | t
       6405 | Valaree          | Wedmore            | t      | t
```

Figure 8.89: Customers who had clicked on and opened emails

5. Find the customers who have a dealership in their city; customers who do not have a dealership in their city should have a blank value for the **city** column:

```
sqlda=# SELECT customers.customer_id, customers.first_name, customers.last_name, customers.city FROM customers LEFT JOIN dealerships on customers.city=dealerships.city;
```

This will display the following output:

```
customer_id |   first_name    |     last_name      |            city
------------+-----------------+--------------------+--------------------------
          1 | Arlena          | Riveles            |
          2 | Ode             | Stovin             | Saint Louis
          3 | Braden          | Jordan             | Pensacola
          4 | Jessika         | Nussen             | Nashville
          5 | Lonnie          | Rembaud            | Miami
          6 | Cortie          | Locksley           | Miami
          7 | Wood            | Kennham            | Orlando
          8 | Rutger          | Humblestone        | New Haven
          9 | Melantha        | Tibb               | Shawnee Mission
         10 | Barbara-anne    | Gowlett            | El Paso
         11 | Urbano          | Middlehurst        | Tulsa
```

Figure 8.90: Left join of customers and dealerships

6. Save these results to a table called **customer_dealers**:

```
sqlda=# SELECT customers.customer_id, customers.first_name, customers.
last_name, customers.city INTO customer_dealers FROM customers LEFT JOIN
dealerships on customers.city=dealerships.city;
```

7. List those customers who do not have dealers in their city (hint: a blank field is **NULL**):

```
sqlda=# SELECT * from customer_dealers WHERE city is NULL;
```

The following figure shows the output of the preceding code:

```
customer_id |   first_name   |   last_name   | city
------------+----------------+---------------+------
          1 | Arlena         | Riveles       |
         12 | Tyne           | Duggan        |
         21 | Pryce          | Geist         |
         24 | Barbi          | Lanegran      |
         30 | Kath           | Rivel         |
         38 | Carter         | Lagneaux      |
         44 | Waldemar       | Paroni        |
         49 | Hannah         | McGlew        |
         56 | Riva           | Cathesyed     |
         63 | Gweneth        | Maior         |
         70 | Caty           | Woolveridge   |
         72 | Jodi           | Fautly        |
```

Figure 8.91: Customers without city information

The output shows the final list of customers in the cities where we have no dealerships.

Activity 14: Defining a Maximum Sale Function

Solution:

1. Connect to the **sqlda** database:

```
$ psql sqlda
```

2. Create a function called **max_sale** that does not take any input arguments but returns a numeric value called **big_sale**:

```
sqlda=# CREATE FUNCTION max_sale() RETURNS integer AS $big_sale$
```

3. Declare the **big_sale** variable and begin the function:

```
sqlda$# DECLARE big_sale numeric;
sqlda$# BEGIN
```

4. Insert the maximum sale amount into the **big_sale** variable:

```
sqlda$# SELECT MAX(sales_amount) INTO big_sale FROM sales;
```

5. Return the value for **big_sale**:

```
sqlda$# RETURN big_sale;
```

6. Close out the function with the **LANGUAGE** statement:

```
sqlda$# END; $big_sale$
sqlda-# LANGUAGE PLPGSQL;
```

7. Call the function to find what the biggest sale amount in the database is:

```
sqlda=# SELECT MAX(sales_amount) FROM sales;
```

The following figure shows the output of the preceding code:

```
 max
--------
 115000
(1 row)
```

Figure 8.92: Output of the maximum sales function call

The output is created from a function that determines the highest sale amount, that is, **115000**, in the database.

Activity 15: Creating Functions with Arguments

Solution

1. Create the function definition for a function called **avg_sales_window** that returns a numeric value and takes a **DATE** value to specify the date in the form **YYYY-MM-DD**:

```
sqlda=# CREATE FUNCTION avg_sales_window(from_date DATE, to_date DATE)
RETURNS numeric AS $sales_avg$
```

2. Declare the return variable as a numeric data type and begin the function:

```
sqlda$# DECLARE sales_avg numeric;
sqlda$# BEGIN
```

3. Select the average sales amount into the return variable where the sales transaction date is greater than the specified date:

```
sqlda$# SELECT AVG(sales_amount) FROM sales INTO sales_avg WHERE sales_
transaction_date > from_date AND sales_transaction_date < to_date;
```

4. Return the function variable, end the function, and specify the **LANGUAGE** statement:

```
sqlda$# RETURN sales_avg;
sqlda$# END; $channel_avg$
sqlda-# LANGUAGE PLPGSQL;
```

5. Use the function to determine the average sales value since **2013-04-12**:

```
sqlda=# SELECT avg_sales_window('2013-04-12', '2014-04-12');
```

The following figure shows the output of the preceding code:

```
avg_sales_window
------------------
477.686246311006
(1 row)
```

Figure 8.93: Output of average sales since the function call

The final output shows the average sales within specific dates, which comes to around **477.687**.

Activity 16: Creating a Trigger to Track Average Purchases

Solution

1. Connect to the **smalljoins** database:

```
$ psql smalljoins
```

2. Create a new table called **avg_qty_log** that is composed of an **order_id integer** field and an **avg_qty numeric** field:

```
smalljoins=# CREATE TABLE avg_qty_log (order_id integer, avg_qty numeric);
```

3. Create a function called **avg_qty** that does not take any arguments but returns a trigger. The function computes the average value for all order quantities (**order_info.qty**) and inserts the average value along with the most recent **order_id** into **avg_qty**:

```
smalljoins=# CREATE FUNCTION avg_qty() RETURNS TRIGGER AS $_avg$
smalljoins$# DECLARE _avg numeric;
smalljoins$# BEGIN
smalljoins$# SELECT AVG(qty) INTO _avg FROM order_info;
smalljoins$# INSERT INTO avg_qty_log (order_id, avg_qty) VALUES (NEW.order_id, _avg);
```

```
smalljoins$# RETURN NEW;
smalljoins$# END; $_avg$
smalljoins-# LANGUAGE PLPGSQL;
```

4. Create a trigger called **avg_trigger** that calls the **avg_qty** function **AFTER** each row is inserted into the **order_info** table:

```
smalljoins=# CREATE TRIGGER avg_trigger
smalljoins-# AFTER INSERT ON order_info
smalljoins-# FOR EACH ROW
smalljoins-# EXECUTE PROCEDURE avg_qty();
```

5. Insert some new rows into the **order_info** table with quantities of **6**, **7**, and **8**:

```
smalljoins=# SELECT insert_order(3, 'GROG1', 6);
smalljoins=# SELECT insert_order(4, 'GROG1', 7);
smalljoins=# SELECT insert_order(1, 'GROG1', 8);
```

6. Look at the entries in **avg_qty_log** to see whether the average quantity of each order is increasing:

```
smalljoins=# SELECT * FROM avg_qty_log;
```

The following figure shows the output of the preceding code:

```
 order_id |       avg_qty
----------+--------------------
     1625 | 4.7500000000000000
     1626 | 5.0000000000000000
     1627 | 5.3000000000000000
(3 rows)
```

Figure 8.94: Average order quantity over time

With these orders and the entries in the log, we can see an increase in the average quantity of items per order.

Activity 17: Terminating a Long Query

Solution

1. Launch two separate SQL interpreters:

    ```
    C:\> psql sqlda
    ```

2. In the first terminal, execute the **sleep** command with a parameter of **1000** seconds:

    ```
    sqlda=# SELECT pg_sleep(1000);
    ```

3. In the second terminal, identify the process ID of the sleep query:

    ```
    pid   |                               query
    -------+-------------------------------------------------------------------
    14117 | SELECT pid, query FROM pg_stat_activity WHERE state = 'active';
    14131 | SELECT pg_sleep(1000);
    (2 rows)
    ```

    Figure 8.95: Finding the pid value of pg_sleep

4. Using the **pid** value, force the **sleep** command to terminate using the **pg_terminate_background** command:

    ```
    Sqlda=# SELECT pg_terminate_backend(14131);
    ```

    The following figure shows the output of the preceding code:

    ```
    pg_terminate_backend
    ----------------------
    t
    (1 row)
    ```

    Figure 8.96: Forcefully terminating pg_sleep

5. Verify in the first terminal that the **sleep** command has been terminated. Notice the message returned by the interpreter:

```
Sqlda=# SELECT pg_sleep(1000);
```

This will display the following output:

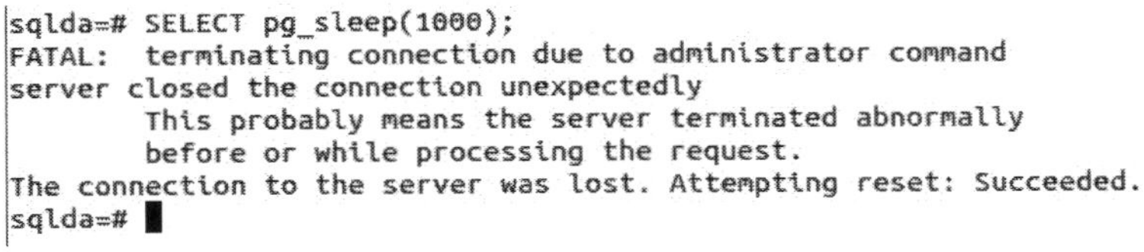

```
sqlda=# SELECT pg_sleep(1000);
FATAL:  terminating connection due to administrator command
server closed the connection unexpectedly
        This probably means the server terminated abnormally
        before or while processing the request.
The connection to the server was lost. Attempting reset: Succeeded.
sqlda=# █
```

Figure 8.97: Terminated pg_sleep process

We can see that the query is now terminated from the screenshot after using the **pg_sleep** command.

Chapter 9: Using SQL to Uncover the Truth – a Case Study

Activity 18: Quantifying the Sales Drop

Solution

1. Load the **sqlda** database:

    ```
    $ psql sqlda
    ```

2. Compute the daily cumulative sum of sales using the **OVER** and **ORDER BY** statements. Insert the results into a new table called **bat_sales_growth**:

    ```
    sqlda=# SELECT *, sum(count) OVER (ORDER BY sales_transaction_date) INTO
    bat_sales_growth FROM bat_sales_daily;
    ```

    The following table shows the daily cumulative sum of sales:

    ```
    sales_transaction_date | count | sum
    -----------------------+-------+------
     2016-10-10 00:00:00   |    9  |    9
     2016-10-11 00:00:00   |    6  |   15
     2016-10-12 00:00:00   |   10  |   25
     2016-10-13 00:00:00   |   10  |   35
     2016-10-14 00:00:00   |    5  |   40
     2016-10-15 00:00:00   |   10  |   50
     2016-10-16 00:00:00   |   14  |   64
     2016-10-17 00:00:00   |    9  |   73
     2016-10-18 00:00:00   |   11  |   84
     2016-10-19 00:00:00   |   12  |   96
     2016-10-20 00:00:00   |   10  |  106
     2016-10-21 00:00:00   |    6  |  112
     2016-10-22 00:00:00   |    2  |  114
     2016-10-23 00:00:00   |    5  |  119
     2016-10-24 00:00:00   |    6  |  125
     2016-10-25 00:00:00   |    9  |  134
     2016-10-26 00:00:00   |    2  |  136
     2016-10-27 00:00:00   |    4  |  140
     2016-10-28 00:00:00   |    7  |  147
     2016-10-29 00:00:00   |    5  |  152
     2016-10-30 00:00:00   |    5  |  157
     2016-10-31 00:00:00   |    3  |  160
    ```

    Figure 9.48: Daily sales count

3. Compute a 7-day **lag** function of the **sum** column and insert all the columns of **bat_sales_daily** and the new **lag** column into a new table, **bat_sales_daily_delay**. This **lag** column indicates what the sales were like 1 week before the given record:

    ```
    sqlda=# SELECT *, lag(sum, 7) OVER (ORDER BY sales_transaction_date) INTO
    bat_sales_daily_delay FROM bat_sales_growth;
    ```

4. Inspect the first 15 rows of **bat_sales_growth**:

```
sqlda=# SELECT * FROM bat_sales_daily_delay LIMIT 15;
```

The following is the output of the preceding code:

```
sales_transaction_date | count | sum | lag
-----------------------+-------+-----+-----
2016-10-10 00:00:00    |     9 |   9 |
2016-10-11 00:00:00    |     6 |  15 |
2016-10-12 00:00:00    |    10 |  25 |
2016-10-13 00:00:00    |    10 |  35 |
2016-10-14 00:00:00    |     5 |  40 |
2016-10-15 00:00:00    |    10 |  50 |
2016-10-16 00:00:00    |    14 |  64 |
2016-10-17 00:00:00    |     9 |  73 |    9
2016-10-18 00:00:00    |    11 |  84 |   15
2016-10-19 00:00:00    |    12 |  96 |   25
2016-10-20 00:00:00    |    10 | 106 |   35
2016-10-21 00:00:00    |     6 | 112 |   40
2016-10-22 00:00:00    |     2 | 114 |   50
2016-10-23 00:00:00    |     5 | 119 |   64
2016-10-24 00:00:00    |     6 | 125 |   73
(15 rows)
```

Figure 9.49: Daily sales delay with lag

5. Compute the sales growth as a percentage, comparing the current sales volume to that of 1 week prior. Insert the resulting table into a new table called **bat_sales_delay_vol**:

```
sqlda=# SELECT *, (sum-lag)/lag AS volume INTO bat_sales_delay_vol FROM
bat_sales_daily_delay ;
```

> **Note**
>
> The percentage sales volume can be calculated via the following equation:
>
> *(new_volume – old_volume) / old_volume*

6. Compare the first **22** values of the **bat_sales_delay_vol** table:

```
sqlda=# SELECT * FROM bat_sales_daily_delay_vol LIMIT 22;
```

The delay volume for the first 22 entries can be seen in the following:

```
 sales_transaction_date | count | sum | lag |          volume
------------------------+-------+-----+-----+------------------------------
 2016-10-10 00:00:00    |     9 |   9 |     |
 2016-10-11 00:00:00    |     6 |  15 |     |
 2016-10-12 00:00:00    |    10 |  25 |     |
 2016-10-13 00:00:00    |    10 |  35 |     |
 2016-10-14 00:00:00    |     5 |  40 |     |
 2016-10-15 00:00:00    |    10 |  50 |     |
 2016-10-16 00:00:00    |    14 |  64 |     |
 2016-10-17 00:00:00    |     9 |  73 |   9 |       7.1111111111111111
 2016-10-18 00:00:00    |    11 |  84 |  15 |       4.6000000000000000
 2016-10-19 00:00:00    |    12 |  96 |  25 |       2.8400000000000000
 2016-10-20 00:00:00    |    10 | 106 |  35 |       2.0285714285714286
 2016-10-21 00:00:00    |     6 | 112 |  40 |       1.8000000000000000
 2016-10-22 00:00:00    |     2 | 114 |  50 |       1.2800000000000000
 2016-10-23 00:00:00    |     5 | 119 |  64 | 0.8593750000000000000000
 2016-10-24 00:00:00    |     6 | 125 |  73 | 0.71232876712328767123
 2016-10-25 00:00:00    |     9 | 134 |  84 | 0.59523809523809523810
 2016-10-26 00:00:00    |     2 | 136 |  96 | 0.41666666666666666667
 2016-10-27 00:00:00    |     4 | 140 | 106 | 0.32075471698113207547
 2016-10-28 00:00:00    |     7 | 147 | 112 | 0.31250000000000000000
 2016-10-29 00:00:00    |     5 | 152 | 114 | 0.33333333333333333333
 2016-10-30 00:00:00    |     5 | 157 | 119 | 0.31932773109243697479
 2016-10-31 00:00:00    |     3 | 160 | 125 | 0.28000000000000000000
(22 rows)
```

Figure 9.50: Relative sales volume of the scooter over 3 weeks

Looking at the output table, we can see four sets of information: the daily sales count, the cumulative sum of the daily sales count, the cumulative sum offset by 1 week (the lag), and the relative daily sales volume.

Activity 19: Analyzing the Difference in the Sales Price Hypothesis

Solution

1. Load the **sqlda** database:

   ```
   $ psql sqlda
   ```

2. Select the **sales_transaction_date** column from the 2013 **Lemon** sales and insert the column into a table called **lemon_sales**:

   ```
   sqlda=# SELECT sales_transaction_date INTO lemon_sales FROM sales WHERE product_id=3;
   ```

3. Count the sales records available for the 2013 **Lemon** by running the following query:

   ```
   sqlda=# SELECT count(sales_transaction_date) FROM lemon_sales;
   ```

We can see that **16558** records are available:

```
count
-------
16558
(1 row)
```

Figure 9.51: Sales records for the 2013 Lemon Scooter

4. Use the **max** function to check the latest **sales_transaction_date** column:

```
sqlda=# SELECT max(sales_transaction_date) FROM lemon_sales;
```

The following figure displays the **sales_transaction_date** column:

```
max
---------------------
2018-12-27 19:12:10
(1 row)
```

Figure 9.52: Production between May 2013 and December 2018

5. Convert the **sales_transaction_date** column to a date type using the following query:

```
sqlda=# ALTER TABLE lemon_sales ALTER COLUMN sales_transaction_date TYPE DATE;
```

We are converting the datatype from **DATE_TIME** to **DATE** so as to remove the time information from the field. We are only interested in accumulating numbers, but just the date and not the time. Hence, it is easier just to remove the time information from the field.

6. Count the number of sales per day within the **lemon_sales** table and insert this figure into a table called **lemon_sales_count**:

```
sqlda=# SELECT *, COUNT(sales_transaction_date) INTO lemon_sales_count FROM lemon_sales GROUP BY sales_transaction_date,lemon_sales.customer_id ORDER BY sales_transaction_date;
```

7. Calculate the cumulative sum of sales and insert the corresponding table into a new table labeled **lemon_sales_sum**:

```
sqlda=# SELECT *, sum(count) OVER (ORDER BY sales_transaction_date) INTO lemon_sales_sum FROM lemon_sales_count;
```

8. Compute the 7-day **lag** function on the **sum** column and save the result to **lemon_sales_delay**:

```
sqlda=# SELECT *, lag(sum, 7) OVER (ORDER BY sales_transaction_date) INTO
lemon_sales_delay FROM lemon_sales_sum;
```

9. Calculate the growth rate using the data from **lemon_sales_delay** and store the resulting table in **lemon_sales_growth**. Label the growth rate column as **volume**:

```
sqlda=# SELECT *, (sum-lag)/lag AS volume INTO lemon_sales_growth FROM
lemon_sales_delay;
```

10. Inspect the first 22 records of the **lemon_sales_growth** table by examining the **volume** data:

```
sqlda=# SELECT * FROM lemon_sales_growth LIMIT 22;
```

The following table shows the sales growth:

```
sales_transaction_date | count | sum | lag |          volume
------------------------+-------+-----+-----+-------------------------
 2013-05-01             |     6 |   6 |     |
 2013-05-02             |     8 |  14 |     |
 2013-05-03             |     4 |  18 |     |
 2013-05-04             |     9 |  27 |     |
 2013-05-05             |     9 |  36 |     |
 2013-05-06             |     6 |  42 |     |
 2013-05-07             |     8 |  50 |     |
 2013-05-08             |     6 |  56 |   6 |       8.3333333333333333
 2013-05-09             |     6 |  62 |  14 |       3.4285714285714286
 2013-05-10             |     9 |  71 |  18 |       2.9444444444444444
 2013-05-11             |     3 |  74 |  27 |       1.7407407407407407
 2013-05-12             |     4 |  78 |  36 |       1.1666666666666667
 2013-05-13             |     7 |  85 |  42 |       1.0238095238095238
 2013-05-14             |     3 |  88 |  50 | 0.7600000000000000000000
 2013-05-15             |     3 |  91 |  56 | 0.6250000000000000000000
 2013-05-16             |     4 |  95 |  62 | 0.5322580645161290326
 2013-05-17             |     6 | 101 |  71 | 0.42253521126760563380
 2013-05-18             |     9 | 110 |  74 | 0.48648648648648648649
 2013-05-19             |     6 | 116 |  78 | 0.48717948717948717949
 2013-05-20             |     6 | 122 |  85 | 0.43529411764705882353
 2013-05-21             |    11 | 133 |  88 | 0.51136363636363636364
 2013-05-22             |     8 | 141 |  91 | 0.54945054945054945055
(22 rows)
```

Figure 9.53: Sales growth of the Lemon Scooter

Similar to the previous exercise, we have calculated the cumulative sum, lag, and relative sales growth of the Lemon Scooter. We can see that the initial sales volume is much larger than the other scooters, at over 800%, and again finishes higher at 55%

Index

About

All major keywords used in this book are captured alphabetically in this section. Each one is accompanied by the page number of where they appear.

Made in the USA
Columbia, SC
09 August 2021